PERCEPTION AND

Perception and Reason

BILL BREWER

CLARENDON PRESS · OXFORD

OXFORD

UNIVERSITY PRESS

Great Clarendon Street, Oxford OX2 6DP

Oxford University Press is a department of the University of Oxford.
It furthers the University's objective of excellence in research, scholarship,
and education by publishing worldwide in

Oxford New York

Auckland Bangkok Buenos Aires Cape Town Chennai
Dar es Salaam Delhi Hong Kong Istanbul Karachi Kolkata
Kuala Lumpur Madrid Melbourne Mexico City Mumbai Nairobi
São Paulo Shanghai Singapore Taipei Tokyo Toronto
and an associated company in Berlin

Oxford is a registered trade mark of Oxford University Press
in the UK and in certain other countries

Published in the United States
by Oxford University Press Inc., New York

© Bill Brewer 1999

The moral rights of the author have been asserted
Database right Oxford University Press (maker)

First published 1999
First published in paperback 2002

British Library Cataloguing in Publication Data

Data available

Library of Congress Cataloging in Publication Data
Brewer, Bill.
Perception and reason / Bill Brewer.
p. cm.
Includes bibliographical references (p.).
1. Knowledge, Theory of. 2. Perception (Philosophy)
3. Experience. I. Title.
BD181.B815 1999 121'.34—dc21 98–45925

ISBN 0–19–823567–4 (hbk)
ISBN 0–19–925045–6 (pbk)

1 3 5 7 9 10 8 6 4 2

Typeset by Invisible Ink
Printed in Great Britain
on acid-free paper by
Biddles Ltd, Guildford and King's Lynn

To Cathy, Ellie, and Daniel

Acknowledgements

John Campbell and Naomi Eilan have been a constant source of inspiration to me throughout the long period during which my ideas for this book have been taking shape. Their philosophical depth and direction have given me a model to emulate; their constructive criticism is evident—to me at least—in every chapter; and their friendship, encouragement, and support have been vital. I would like to take this opportunity to thank them both very much indeed for all that they have done.

Through discussions and comments in various contexts over the years, many other people have made a very significant and much appreciated contribution to this work. I would like to thank Michael Ayers, José Bermúdez, Justin Broackes, Quassim Cassam, David Charles, Bill Child, Martin Davies, Bob Frazier, Lizzie Fricker, Marcus Giaquinto, Bob Hargrave, Christopher Hookway, Jennifer Hornsby, Susan Hurley, Wolfgang Künne, Mike Martin, Peter Milne, Adrian Moore, Paul O'Grady, Manuel Perez Otero, David Owens, Christopher Peacocke, Carolyn Price, Daniel Quesada, Johannes Roessler, Ernest Sosa, Helen Steward, Tom Stoneham, Rowland Stout, Peter Sullivan, Mark Textor, Charles Travis, James Van Cleve, Ralph Walker, Asa Wikforss, and Tim Williamson. Special thanks are due to John Campbell, Naomi Eilan, Lizzie Fricker, Christopher Peacocke, Helen Steward, and Rowland Stout, who also gave me extended written comments on a previous version of the complete manuscript. Many graduate students have heard or read earlier versions of this material and provided extremely helpful feedback. I would like to acknowledge in particular the contributions of Christian Beyer, Alan Brown, Lisa Busch, Imogen Dickie, Brie Gertler, Greville Healey, Jason Kawall, Michael Oliva Cordoba, Kirsten Petzold, Hannah Pickard, Baron Reed, Angus Ritchie, Mark Siebel, and Christian Stein. I would also like to record my deep intellectual debt here to the formative writings of Peter Strawson, Michael Dummett, Michael Ayers, Gareth Evans, John McDowell, and Christopher Peacocke.

I am grateful to my colleges, St Catherine's and Magdalen, and also to Oxford University, for granting me sabbatical leave for two terms in 1997, during which a first draft of this book was written, and especially to the British Academy's Humanities Research Board for funding one of these terms of leave, without which this would certainly not have been possible. I made my final revisions, read proofs, and prepared the index during a very enjoyable semester visiting the University of California at Berkeley. I appreciate all the support and hospitality I received there. Although it was late in the day for the book, I had extremely productive discussions of the issues it addresses in Berkeley with Cheryl Chen, Alan Code, Eddie Cushman, Donald Davidson, Hannah Ginsborg, Peter Hanks, Sean Kelly, Jonathan Lebowitsch, Josh Sheptow, and Richard Wollheim.

Peter Momtchiloff of Oxford University Press has been a wonderfully supportive and flexible editor, from the moment he first approached me about this project until its final completion. I thank him very much for his enthusiasm, encouragement, advice and patience. Maura High was a first class copy editor, whose experience, wisdom, and keen eye are much appreciated. I am also very grateful to Angela Blackburn, my excellent production editor and typesetter.

I would also like to thank the following:

Cambridge University Press for permission to use material from my paper 'Experience and Reason in Perception', in A. O'Hear (ed.), *Current Issues in the Philosophy of Mind*, in Chapters 2, 3, and 6.

Blackwell Publishers Ltd. for permission to use material from my paper 'Internalism and Perceptual Knowledge', *European Journal of Philosophy*, 4 (1996), 259–75, in Chapter 4.

The editor and publishers of the *American Philosophical Quarterly* for permission to use material from my paper 'Foundations of Perceptual knowledge', *American Philosophical Quarterly*, 34 (1997), 41–55, in Chapter 7.

I should offer a word of explanation about the photograph on the cover. An unfolded origami figure in a sense displays what *would* be seen from different points of view upon the same object, in this case a sampan boat; but it does not integrate these elements so as to constitute a unified presentation of a single three-dimensional thing. Our capacity to integrate such different points of view, over different circumstances of perception, is a key element in my account of how perception presents the mind-independent world around us in such a way as to constitute a basic source of knowledge about it.

Finally, my wife, Cathy Gough, and my two children, Ellie and Daniel, have contributed more to this book than they will probably ever know, or I can easily say. They provide joy and depth to my life, and give me all the support and space for my work that I could possibly want. I dedicate this book to them with all my love.

Contents

xii   *Contents*

Introduction

This book is about the role of conscious perceptual experiences in the acquisition of empirical knowledge. I take it for granted that a person's beliefs about the way things are in the world around him causally depend to a large extent upon the course of his perceptual experiences. My central concern here is with the epistemological dimension of this relation, its provision of a peculiarly fundamental source of knowledge: *perceptual knowledge*. How is such knowledge, that particular mind-independent things are objectively thus and so, even possible? What is the nature of the conscious experiences upon which it is based? How should we conceive of the epistemic contribution which such experiences make to it? These are the questions which drive my enquiry.

Most of the answers which are offered to these questions in the standard epistemological tradition within analytic philosophy broadly conceived take a person's possession of beliefs about the mind-independent world, and especially his understanding of the contents of these beliefs, entirely for granted, and go on to propose an account of the further conditions which such beliefs must meet if they are to be cases of knowledge. A major theme of the book is that this approach is completely mistaken. Perceptual experiences must provide reasons for empirical beliefs if there are to be any determinate beliefs about particular objects in the world at all. So there are *epistemic* requirements upon the very possibility of empirical belief. The crucial epistemological role of experiences, in my view, lies in their essential contribution to the subject's understanding of certain perceptual demonstrative contents, simply grasping which provides him with a reason to endorse them in belief. I explain in detail how this is so; defend my position against a wide range of objections; compare and contrast it with a number of influential alternative views in the area; and bring out its connection with Russell's Principle of Acquaintance, and its consequences for the compatibility of content externalism with an adequate account of self-knowledge.

The structure of my overall argument is this.

In Chapter 1, I set out the epistemological context for my enquiry, by outlining the key moves in a formative phase of its historical development: the writings of Descartes, Locke, Hume, Reid, and Kant. My purpose here is not to engage in the detailed exegesis and interpretation of these philosophers' views, but to delineate the space of live options in the area, and to point out some dead ends.

Chapter 2 opens with a preliminary clarification of the thesis which is my central focus throughout Part 1.

(R) Perceptual experiences provide reasons for empirical beliefs.

I set out the following argument for (R).

(1) The most basic beliefs about the spatial world have their contents only in virtue of their standing in certain relations with perceptual experiences.

(2) Only reason-giving relations between perceptual experiences and beliefs could possibly serve the content-determining role required by (1).

∴ (3) The hypothesis that perceptual experiences do not provide reasons for empirical beliefs rules out the possibility of beliefs about a mind-independent spatial world.

(4) We have beliefs about a mind-independent spatial world.

∴ (R) Perceptual experiences provide reasons for empirical beliefs.

With a brief elucidation, I simply assume the obvious truth of (4). Thus, the burden of my argument for (R) rests upon the premises (1) and (2). The remainder of Chapter 2 and Chapter 3 contain extended arguments for these two premises in turn: the *Strawson Argument* and the *Switching Argument* respectively.

The Strawson Argument is derived from Strawson's discussion of the possibility of massive reduplication in the first chapter of his *Individuals* (1959). Only an experiential presentation of the particular mind-independent thing in question suffices to tie down knowledgeable reference to spatial particulars in the face of the permanent epistemic possibility of massive qualitative reduplication of any sector of the physical world elsewhere in the universe. So the possibility of beliefs about mind-independent particulars depends upon the most basic such beliefs' standing in certain content-fixing relations with perceptual experiences of the objects in question. I present this argument in detail, and refine it in the face of various possible sources of objection.

The Switching Argument establishes that non-reason-giving relations between perceptual experiences and such basic empirical beliefs could not possibly serve this content-determining role. For such relations would necessarily leave the subject quite ignorant of which mind-independent object her belief is supposed to be about, in a way which is incompatible with her having the understanding required for this to be a belief *of hers*, about just that thing, at all. I go on to consider three failed attempts by the proponent of non-reason-giving content-determining relations between perceptual experiences and empirical beliefs to avoid this argument. The first two aim to reinstate the subject's knowledge of the relevant worldly semantic values within this framework; and the third aims to illustrate the way in which no such knowledge is necessary for the understanding required for possession of perfectly determinate empirical beliefs.

Chapter 4 draws out the fatal consequences of thesis (R) for any reliabilist account of perceptual knowledge; it also contains extended critical discussions of the *classical foundationalist* and *classical coherentist* attempts to elucidate the truth of (R). Both of these are attempts to give what I call a *second-order* account, on which perceptual experiences provide reasons for empirical beliefs only in virtue of the subject's second-order reflection upon the reliability of the first-order process by which such experiences produce such beliefs, where the first and second orders are independent of each other in the sense that she might equally have acquired the same beliefs by just the same first-order method yet not have had the second-order knowledge in question. In order to give a satisfying elucidation of the truth of (R), then, as I believe we must, we should look to a *first-order* account, on which the truth of (R) emerges directly out of a correct account of a person's possession of certain beliefs about the mind-independent world around her, out of an elaboration of what is involved in her grasping their determinate empirical contents, rather than from any independent requirement upon her second-order reflection upon the process by which she acquires such beliefs.

Part II contains my articulation of, and further argument for, a specific such first-order account of (R). This, I hope, is compelling on its own terms, and therefore provides strong corroboration for (R) independently of my own argument for this thesis in Part I. The key idea is that a person's most basic empirical beliefs have essentially experiential contents, as I argued in Part I, of a kind such that her mere grasp of these contents provides her with a prima facie reason to endorse them in belief. Before presenting this account in detail, in Chapter 6, I argue, as an essential preliminary, in Chapter 5, that reasons require conceptual contents. That is to say, a person has a reason for believing something only if she is in some mental state or other with a representational content which is characterizable only in terms of concepts which the subject herself must possess and which is of a form which enables it to serve as a premise or the conclusion of a deductive argument, or of an inference of some other kind (e.g. inductive or abductive). Having given the *Basic Argument* for this claim, I consider a number of kinds of putative counterexample. I discuss at most length the various considerations, all of which I argue are ultimately inadequate, which might be advanced for supposing that perceptual experiences have *non-conceptual* representational contents, in virtue of which they nevertheless provide reasons of the required kind for the subject's empirical beliefs to which they give rise.

My question in Chapter 6 is this: how exactly do perceptual experiences provide reasons for empirical beliefs? My answer is that they furnish the subject with certain essentially experiential demonstrative contents—'That is thus' (fully conceptual, as they must be)—his grasp of which (defeasibly—see 7.3) provides him with a reason to endorse them in belief. For a person's grasp of such contents, as referring to the mind-independent objects which they do, and predicating the mind-independent properties which they do, essentially involves his appreciation of them as the joint upshot of the way things are anyway, in the mind-independent world around him, and his current point of view upon them and other relevant circumstances of perception. That is to say, he necessarily understands that his current apprehension that things are thus and so is in part due to the very fact that they are. He therefore recognizes the relevant content *as* his apprehension of the facts, his *epistemic openness* to the way things mind-independently are out there. I develop this account in some detail and set it in relief by a brief comparison with the views of Evans (1982, ch. 6) and Peacocke (1983, ch. 3), which are both similar to my own account in certain (different) respects and also crucially different from my account in certain (different) respects too. I end the chapter with a discussion of the cross-modality of these basic perceptual demonstrative contents.

Chapter 7 aims to clarify the epistemological outlook which arises from my positive elucidation of the truth of (R), and also to offer further defence against a number of key objections. First, I explain the location of my own views in the context of the standard opposition between foundationalist and coherentist theories of perceptual knowledge. This brings out precisely the sense in which I succeed in capturing the 'undeniable datum' with which I begin Chapter 2, that perception is a *basic* source of knowledge about the mind-independent spatial world. Second, I go on to consider two broadly sceptical objections, first, from the possibility of perceptual imagination, and second, from the possibility of perceptual error. Third, I consider whether my own position is in any way susceptible to objections parallel to those which I myself direct at its classical foundationalist opponents. Fourth, and finally, I discuss the way in which I am able to capture the intuitive phenomenon of a foreground and background in perceptual consciousness: surely far more is, in some sense 'experienced' by a person in perception that is the subject matter of any (conceptual) perceptual demonstrative content which is poised to be endorsed by him in belief.

In Chapter 8 I discuss a number of developments and consequences of my position. First, there is the very important issue of the relation between the basic, essentially experiential, perceptual demonstrative contents which I have been considering up to this point, and the more detached, linguistically articulated and categorized judgements which a person more standardly makes on the basis of perception, and which constitute the normal expression of his perceptual knowledge about the world around him. Second, I argue that my account entails a version of Russell's Principle of Acquaintance (1917, p. 159), which I elucidate, on which singular reference is possible only to objects about which the subject is in a position to acquire, or to express, non-inferential knowledge. This enables me to place my position in the context of Russell's own position, and what is probably the orthodox reaction to it. Finally, I exploit this version of the Principle of Acquaintance to provide what seems to me to be a fully satisfying response to an important objection to the possibility of combining a so-called 'externalist' theory of empirical content, of the kind which I myself favour and draw on in my account of perceptual knowledge, with a plausible account of a person's knowledge of the contents of his own beliefs. The difficulty is supposed to be that this combination entails the possibility of a kind of non-empirical knowledge about the mind-independent physical world which is intuitively intolerable. My response is that, in so far as such a possibility would indeed be intolerable, this difficulty is merely apparent. On the other hand, as I bring out in 6.2, there is nevertheless a parallel between my own first-order account of (R) and certain traditional conceptions of a priori reasons; but this is not, in my view, remotely problematic.

An overall message of the book is that the key to understanding perceptual knowledge lies in exploring the interconnections between the philosophical logic and epistemology of perceptual demonstrative thought. Much recent work, both on the nature of empirical concepts and on empirical knowledge, has in my view suffered, both by ignoring the central importance of demonstratives, and by focusing either upon epistemological issues to the exclusion of questions in philosophical logic (broadly construed), or vice versa. I hope here to illustrate the benefits to both areas of adopting a far more integrated approach, united by its focus upon the crucial level of perceptual demonstrative thought.

I

Perceptual Experiences Provide Reasons

Historical-Epistemological Context

The problem of perception has been a central focus in philosophy throughout its history. Its continual transformation during what I regard as a crucial phase of its historical development shapes the topics and orientation of this book. My own central concern with the role of perceptual experiences in the acquisition of empirical knowledge is therefore best introduced by a brief, and inevitably rather dogmatic, presentation of this historical-epistemological context. I offer this, not as a contribution to the detailed exegesis and interpretation of a series of historical texts, but as an outline of the key moves in an evolving dialectic out of which I believe my own position grows quite naturally: it serves as a delineation of the space of live options, and as a warning about some of the dead ends to be avoided.

Recall, to begin with, Descartes's account of our knowledge of the external world in his *Meditations* (1986). This proceeds through the discussion in the Second and Fifth Meditations concerning the precise nature of our clear and distinct ideas of material things, and culminates in the Sixth Meditation with an appeal to the existence of a non-deceiving God to establish that physical objects actually exist outside our minds conforming to such ideas. In crude outline, the overall argument goes as follows.

We have a rich variety of perceptual experiences, in response to which we are naturally and pretheoretically inclined to believe in the existence of a world of objects-as-they-appear-to-us: mind-independent, coloured, textured, shaped and sized, sonorous, fragrant, and flavoured macroscopic things. The Method of Doubt, though, dictates at the outset that we should suspend judgement upon all of this except for the (mind-dependent) existence of the various experiences themselves. For, with the aid of Descartes's sceptical scenarios, everything else is dubitable in the relevant sense.

Now, in so far as we have any genuine conception of what persisting material things might be like, never mind yet whether there actually are any such things, these experiences cannot be its source. For although we think that a single piece of wax, for example, remains throughout the various changes in its perceptible qualities when it is plucked fresh from the hive and left by the fire, 'everything that falls under the senses' has changed. Thus, any conception of it simply in terms of its fleeting sensible qualities is an inadequate basis for our idea of a single persisting material substance surviving as the subject of all of these changes. On reflection, it appears that we do indeed have a further idea of the wax as a variably extended, flexible, and changeable space-filling thing, independent of any particular sensible presentation of it, either in actual perception or from any store of possible sensory experiences. Hence, our clear and distinct ideas of persisting material things are neither sensory nor derived from the imagination, but purely intellectual: innate archetypes which we discover in our minds by thought alone.

These ideas of matter as pure extension, and of the properties of material objects as exclusively modes of extension—simply different ways of being extended in space—are precisely those involved in pure, abstract geometrical reasoning. They are ideas of particular shapes and sizes, for example, like triangularity, of the essences of which we have a clear and distinct conception, and of the relations between which we have a priori demonstrative certainty, regardless of whether any such things really exist in the world outside our minds in any way conforming to these ideas. Nevertheless, it follows from all of this, that *if* there are any external mind-independent objects, then these are simply variably extended space-fillers, whose properties consist exclusively of the ways in which they fill space, in the modes of their extension. For this is the only nature for such things which is even coherent.

The crucial question for our purposes then remains, to be dealt with in the final Meditation: are there *in fact* any such things? Descartes approaches this via the question of what explains the occurrence in our minds of those experiences which we are naturally inclined to take to be perceptions of external objects. By his famous causal principle, these experiences must have causes with at least as much reality as the experiences themselves have, both formally and objectively.[1] In particular, since such experiences have the objective reality of material substances—that is to say, this is the level of reality of their intentional objects—their causes must be either such things, mind-independent physical objects, or else things which are higher up the order of being, that is, either finite or infinite immaterial substances.

Now, we have a practically unstoppable natural inclination to believe that these experiences are explained by the real existence of material objects of some kind in the external world. Regardless of the rational criticism and doubt to which this common-sense view is subjected, our inclination to subscribe to and act upon it cannot be removed. This is precisely Hume's point (1975, p. 150), that the Cartesian Doubt is hardly even momentarily attainable, certainly no one could actually live the extreme scepticism into which the First Meditation apparently leads us. Far from being a criticism of Descartes's overall strategy, though, this is an essential premise in realizing it. For given this irresistibility of our belief in the existence of material bodies of some kind as the causes of our perceptual experiences, its falsity would make God a deceiver, which he is not and could not be. Paraphrasing from Bernard Williams (1978, p. 233), God has created and conserves us as rational minds capable of reaching the truth by a proper use of our faculties, and if the best possible use

---

[1] The correct interpretation of Descartes's notions of formal and objective reality is a controversial matter. In my view, his position is this. First there is an a priori hierarchy of levels of being, which obtains regardless of whether or not there really exist things at any such level. This proceeds downwards from the level of infinite mental substance in the following order: finite mental substance, material substance, mode or property of these substances. The *formal reality* of any entity whatsoever is its level on this hierarchy, considered as it is in itself. Any item which represents something also has *objective reality*, which is the level on the hierarchy of being of the thing which it represents. This objective reality may be different from the formal reality of the representing item. Thus, although the formal reality of all ideas and experiences is simply that of modes—for these are properties of mental substances—their objective reality may be higher, if they are ideas of material objects, finite minds, or an infinite mind (God). The crucial causal principle states that the cause of any item is at least as high up the order of being as that item's formal reality, and at least as high up as its objective reality too, if it has objective reality.

of these faculties left us with an inevitable tendency to error, then God would be deceiving us. This contradicts God's essential benevolence. Therefore there is a mind-independent material world of variably extended pure space-fillers and their determinate modes of extension, which causally explain our perceptual experiences.

Of course, this line of argument is full of difficulties; but it is the general strategy which I want to bring out. In so far as we have genuine knowledge, rather than mere prejudice, concerning the existence and nature of the external world on the basis of perception, this is ultimately *inferential* in nature, according to Descartes. It proceeds from our rationally indubitable possession of various perceptual experiences, modifications of our immaterial minds whose essence is our awareness of them, by *deductive argument*, via the proofs of God's existence and our intellectual clarification and distinction of the idea of a material substance, to the (mind-independent) existence of persisting physical objects as the causes of such experiences. In so far as they are a source of genuine knowledge, then, the senses provide mere data for the productive operation of reason in delivering the truth, which thereby has the certainty of pure geometry or logic. Our mind is a kind of instrument, like an ammeter or a speedometer, in the sense in which we infer from the deliverances of such instruments the truth about some causally connected but logically independent state of affairs. We read the relevant instrument itself in our infallible knowledge of the existence and nature of our perceptual experiences, and reason from there— by an elaborate and highly dubious inference—to the existence and nature of the material world around us. Although the classification is in many ways problematic, I take this type of strategy to be a definitive strand in the *rationalist* approach to perceptual knowledge.

Strangely, many philosophers interpret Locke (1975, esp. iv.xi) as applying a somewhat similar strategy, although one which of course makes use of different intermediary premises and a quite different mode of argument. A standard view along these lines (e.g. J. Gibson, 1960, pp. 172–6) is that Locke, like Descartes, assumes that we begin with certain knowledge of the existence and nature of our perceptual experiences. We then *argue* that certain related features of these experiences can only be, or more likely are best, explained by the realist hypothesis that they are the conscious mental effects of the impact upon our sensory surfaces from without of a physical world of something like the corpuscular nature at that time proposed by the natural sciences. The relevant features of *perceptual* experiences are their vivacity, their passivity and lack of voluntary control on our part, the irresistibility of the beliefs to which they give rise, and their peculiarly direct connection with pleasure, pain, and immediate action: precisely those features which distinguish such experiences from those involved in imagination, memory, and thought. Since the realist hypothesis best explains these data, we are justified in our inference to its truth. Hence perception is a source of knowledge about the existence and nature of the material world around us.

The fundamental difference between the two philosophers, *on this view*, is that Locke's mode of argument from indubitable awareness of mind-dependent sensations to the existence and nature of the mind-independent external world is abductive rather than deductive as it is in Descartes. Perceptual knowledge, on both accounts, is ultimately justified by rational argument of some kind: it is essentially *inferential* in nature.

I want to present a quite different interpretation of Locke's discussion of perceptual knowledge. I am confident that this is much closer to the historical truth, although I give no real evidence for this claim here (see Ayers, 1991, pts. II and esp. III). My concern is rather to offer a far more illuminating contrast with Descartes's account for my own purposes in this book.

Locke certainly thinks that only intuition and demonstration afford knowledge of *general* truths; but he regards perception as a further natural mode of belief acquisition whose proper operation constitutes an autonomous source of knowledge of *particular* matters of fact. This in no way depends upon any endorsement by combining intuition and demonstration in some process of inferential reasoning. As we have seen, Descartes insists that the epistemological credentials of the process by which perception yields empirical belief stand or fall with the possibility of giving this process a sceptic-proof rational reconstruction. Locke's view, on the other hand, is that in the domain in which perception is a reliable source of truth of a special kind (which inclines us not only to believe truths about the way particular things are in the physical world around us, but also truly to believe that the experiences which produce such beliefs are brought about things' being that way out there), this on its own—the reliable production of true beliefs about the world and true beliefs about how it is that we are right about the world in holding such beliefs—is sufficient to make perception a self-standing cognitive faculty, a quite independent source of knowledge.

On this view, it is misguided both to demand a rational justification for perceptual knowledge, as the traditional sceptic does, and equally to respond by attempting to give one, as Descartes does: these are analogous to demanding and attempting to give a perceptual justification for rational argument. Perception is simply an autonomous mode of acquisition for knowledge of particular matters of fact, in virtue of its de facto status as a special kind of reliable source of true beliefs about such things. In this respect it is quite on a par with reason, and in no need of any justificatory support from it. Perhaps, as Locke admits, the truths which perception generates are in some sense less certain than those delivered by intuition or demonstration, although our use of these is of course fallible; but this fact is of little epistemological significance. Perception is an independent route to knowledge of particular matters of fact, whose epistemological standing consists in its being the special kind of cognitive faculty which it is for informing us about the way things are around us, and how we are thereby right about them, rather than in the availability of any endorsement of its deliverances by rational argument. In contrast with the rationalism of Descartes, I think of this emphasis upon the epistemological autonomy of perception from reason as a characteristic of the *empiricist* approach to perceptual knowledge.

Interestingly, on this interpretation, Locke's accounts of intuitive and demonstrative knowledge of general truths can be seen, if anything, ultimately to draw upon certain parallels with the case of perceptual knowledge, rather than vice versa.[2] For he makes an essential appeal to conscious intellectual apprehen-

---

[2] See Ayers, 1991, pt. IV, for an extended discussion of Locke's account of a priori knowledge. My interpretation of Locke is greatly influenced by Ayers throughout.

sions in direct intuition, and so also at each stage of a demonstration, of the truth thereby known. These play a role parallel to that of sensory experiences in perceptual knowledge. Indeed, Locke appropriately speaks of our *perception* of the agreement and disagreement of, in this case abstract, ideas. For example, in geometrical reasoning, we *see* that the longest side of a triangle could not but be opposite its largest angle, when we reflect upon the abstract idea of a triangle, that is to say, when we entertain an image of a particular triangle and ignore in thought all but its definitively triangular features. Abstract imagistic reflection of this kind is essential to Locke's account of intuitive and demonstrative knowledge, and makes essential appeal to this conscious, quasi-perceptual, apprehension of the truth. This modelling of pure reason upon perception highlights Locke's empiricism.

What should we say, then, about the points in Locke's discussion at which he appears to be giving an argument to the best explanation as a rational justification for our belief in the existence and nature of the external world, along the lines of the standard interpretation above (e.g. iv.xi.4–7)? These passages play two roles in my view. First, they can be understood as Locke's articulation of the particular features of *perceptual* experiences—those which distinguish these from cases of imagination, imagistic thought, and memory—which *causally explain*, rather than in any sense rationally justify, the strength and immediacy of their influence upon our beliefs. It is because perceptual sensations are peculiarly vivid, in a certain sense out of our control, and immediately linked with pleasure and pain, that they tend irresistibly to take hold of our current beliefs and directly influence our actions in the way in which they do. This is not because these features of perceptual experiences ground any rational argument to the likely truth of such beliefs, but is, rather, a brute matter of fact about the way human perceptual faculties operate. Furthermore, it is precisely these features which also incline us to believe (truly, in most cases, according to Locke) that the relevant experiences are caused from without, by the mind-independent world's being just as we thereby believe it to be; and this second-order belief in turn helps to sustain the empirical beliefs to which such experiences give rise. Thus, the epistemic warrant for particular beliefs about the world consists in the fact that beliefs naturally formed in this way in perception are both normally true and normally accompanied by a true belief about their causal origin in the facts thereby known.

The second role for these passages in which Locke explicitly articulates the features of perceptual experiences which distinguish them from cases of imagination, imagistic thought, and memory, is to provide what he calls 'concurrent Reasons' for our empirical beliefs, which confirm the epistemic status of such beliefs should we enter into any kind of local sceptical reflection about this. This is absolutely not to say that any inference to the best explanation of these peculiar features of perceptual experiences constitutes the *source* of the status of certain empirical beliefs as cases of knowledge. It is rather that reflecting in this way about the likely reliability of perception is a way of confirming that such beliefs do indeed have that status, which they receive from a more basic source, as I outline above.[3] Relatedly, the characteristic features of perceptual experiences might become the subject of second-order reflection in various abnormal circumstances for the purpose of alleviating some kind of specific doubt. Thus, upon waking, and unsure of whether my experience is dream-inspired imaginative meandering or hazy perception, I might resolve the issue by attending to its vivacity or stability in the face of my attempt to modify it at will, for example. Similarly, I might appeal to these features of my experience when challenged to back up my claim to *hear* a child crying in bed, as opposed merely to imagining someone doing so, worrying that my daughter might do so, or remembering a previous night on which she did. Aside from such unusual circumstances, though, these phenomenal peculiarities of actual perception operate unreflectively in modulating the effect of conscious experiences of various kinds upon belief and action, rather than playing any indispensable role in the rational defence of perceptual knowledge on the basis of some kind of inference to the best explanation. Locke is offering an epistemologically explanatory description of how the mechanisms of

---

[3] See 7.3 for the importance to my own positive account of perceptual knowledge of the distinction which is implicit here in Locke's position between having a fully adequate reason to believe that *p* and having something conclusive to say to the sceptic who challenges one's right to believe that *p*.

perceptual belief formation operate, rather than any rational-inferential justification for their products.

Hume's (1978) reaction to this is, like Locke's position itself, best elucidated by contrast with a standard, but in my view mistaken, interpretation of his treatment of external-world scepticism (i.iv.2). According to this interpretation (e.g. Bennett, 1971, ch. 13), he argues as follows.

(H1) Rational argument from the nature of our ideas is incapable of establishing the existence of a mind-independent external world.

(H2) Rational argument from the nature of our ideas is our sole source of knowledge.

∴ (H3) We have no knowledge of the existence of a mind-independent external world.

Yet Hume frequently insists that we cannot possibly doubt the existence of a mind-independent external world. Indeed, its existence, and our knowledge of this, is a fundamental premise of his whole enterprise, which is to gain a proper understanding of the natural processes by which, given the way things are in the world out there, and the nature of our own minds, we come to believe what we do about it. In other words, he regards our knowledge of the existence of the external world as just about as secure as anything could be. This is precisely the datum which his philosophical science of the mind is intended to explain in this area. Thus, the direction of his argument is surely quite different (see e.g. J. P. Wright, 1983, ch. 2).

(H1) Rational argument from the nature of our ideas is incapable of establishing the existence of a mind-independent external world.

(H3') We have knowledge of the existence of a mind-independent external world.

∴ (H2') Rational argument from the nature of our ideas is not our sole source of knowledge.

Notice here that (H3') is the negation of (H3), above, and (H2') is the negation of (H2).

On this view, Hume is endorsing Locke's contention that

sense perception is an autonomous source of knowledge of particular matters of fact, from which our knowledge of the existence of a mind-independent external world is derived. This is in no need of any ratification by reason. Indeed, no such rational defence could possibly be given. So the faculty of pure reason alone is quite inadequate to account for the nature and extent our knowledge; it therefore loses a good deal of the divine status which Descartes strives to invest in it.[4]

It is natural at this point to reply to Hume's argument above along the lines suggested by Kant (1929, esp. A50–5/B74–9, and B141–2). His starting point is the insistence that a correct account of the nature of our perceptual experiences essentially draws upon the concepts involved in characterizing the objective spatial world around us. Furthermore, he contends, acknowledging this fact is crucial to understanding the way in which these experiences provide us with genuine reasons for the empirical beliefs to which they gives rise about the way things are out there. On this view, Hume's failure to discern any rational justification for our beliefs in the existence and nature of the external world is due in a large part to his failure to appreciate the nature and content of the perceptual experiences themselves which are involved in the production of such beliefs. His conception of the raw material is simply too crude. So it is no won-

---

[4] See Craig, 1987, esp. ch. 2, for an illuminating discussion of the basis for this disagreement between Descartes, on the one hand, and Locke and especially Hume, on the other. Roughly, Craig sees it as a disagreement about where the major qualitative distinction lies on the great chain of being leading from inanimate matter up through the brutes and man to God. Descartes is keen to see us as mini-Gods, each with the stamp of our maker upon us, in the form of our intellect, or faculty of reason, the proper use of which constitutes an adequate source of all knowledge. Below us lies a great divide, followed by a continuum of more or less intricate, blind, unknowing physical machines. Hume, on the other hand, conceives of us as highly sophisticated animals, at the top of a continuum of increasing complexity encompassing the whole of the natural world, whose habitual modes of belief acquisition put us in perfectly adequate contact with the practically relevant facts about how things are around us. Although there may be a regulative role for reason in keeping these habits in check, we should not, indeed, we simply cannot, confine ourselves in belief to what is rationally beyond doubt. This is a very good thing. For otherwise we would be condemned to a life of almost universal non-belief and inaction, and would rapidly perish as a result. There may or may not be a perfect, superhuman intellect on the other side of the chasm above this natural continuum. Hume's view on this matter is controversial.

der that this appears inadequate rationally to ground perceptual knowledge. In other words, the suggestion is that we should deny premise (H1) above, the premise which is common to both interpretations of Hume. Let me explain briefly how this line of thought might go.

On Hume's view, the direct objects of perception are mind-dependent 'impressions', the essence of which is simply their being perceived, and the nature of which is exhausted by the way they appear to us. As Strawson puts it, Hume assumes that the immediate objects of perception are 'of the same species as perceptions of them' (1974a, p. 49). He presents an argument for this assumption, a version of the argument from illusion; but this is an argument which is in my view undermined by Reid's (1983, pp. 175 ff.) straightforward response, and is subject to numerous other serious objections too. Hume's argument goes like this.[5]

Stage 1

Suppose that I am subject to an illusion, of a table shrinking as I move away from it, for example.

(1) What I directly perceive shrinks.

(2) The mind-independent table does not shrink (nor does any other plausible candidate external object of perception).

∴ (3) What I directly perceive is not the mind-independent table (or any other external thing), but a mind-dependent entity whose nature corresponds entirely with the way things appear to me: call this an *impression*.

Stage 2

Suppose that I am subject to a veridical perception, *P*.

(1) There is a possible illusion, *I*, subjectively indistinguishable from *P*.

(2) What I directly perceive in *I* is an impression. (Stage 1)

---

[5] In my presentation of Hume's argument below, I adopt Snowdon's (1992) decomposition of it into two separate stages.

(3) Since I and P are subjectively indistinguishable, then what I directly perceive in each is the same.

∴ (4) What I directly perceive in P is an impression.

So, putting Stages 1 and 2 together, we have Hume's assumption that the only direct objects of perception are mind-dependent impressions, 'of the same species as perceptions of them' (Strawson, 1974*a*, p. 49).

Reid responds by challenging Stage 1, and hence undermining Stage 2 altogether. He insists that the right way to characterize the kind of illusion to which Hume appeals is as a case in which a single external object has two perfectly compatible properties, that of actually being one way and that of (illusorily) appearing to be another. The mind-independent table actually remains constant in size, although, at least in a certain sense, it appears to shrink. Furthermore, on precisely the natural hypothesis denied by Hume, namely that the external object itself is the direct object of perception, we often have an adequate explanation of the illusory appearance. In Hume's case, for example, a little visual geometry immediately explains the rate and extent by which the table appears to shrink as I move away from it. Indeed, I am inclined to think that the context of some such simple geometrical story may be required to articulate the sense in which the table even *appears* to shrink. For this is not a mistake which even the most naive perceivers normally make in their perceptual judgements about the things around them or in their basic perceptually guided behaviour. Your friend does not *really* look as though she is actually shrinking to half her height as she moves away, doubling the distance between you: she just looks to recede into the distance, remaining of constant height. Three-month old babies (Bower, 1966), and even newborns (Slater and Morrison, 1985; Slater, 1989), seem to have this kind of visual grasp of constancy of size, and also of shape, over moderate variation in distance and angle of presentation. The sense of an apparent change in size in the supposedly illusory cases which Hume's argument exploits *can* be extracted, but only by exercising a mode of attention designed to bring the relevant geometric considerations to light. This, rather than any reflective strategy to avoid being taken in by illusions of objects' continually changing size and shape, is what has to be learnt, as an artist learns to hold up a pencil to enable her correctly to capture fore-shortening and perspective.

Thus, Stage 1 of the argument for Hume's assumption that impressions are the only direct objects of perception is unconvincing. The reading required for its first premise, if the conclusion is to follow, is quite indefensible. Stage 2 is also independently controversial, in the use it makes of the complex and elusive notion of subjective indistinguishability. I shall return to a far more detailed discussion of this notion later (7.3). For now it is sufficient to point out that the first premise of Stage 2 is uncontentiously true only on a reading of 'subjectively indistinguishable' on which any pair of experiential conditions meeting the following condition are subjectively indistinguishable: the subject is not infallible about which of the two conditions he is in. Yet it is far from clear that the third premise is true on this reading. For why should we accept that the subjective indistinguishability of two experiential conditions *in this sense* guarantees the identity of their direct objects? Depending upon how exactly the notion of a direct object is elucidated in this context, there may be *a* reading of 'subjectively indistinguishable' on which the third premise is true; but then it is at best debatable whether the first premise is true on this reading. Put as a challenge rather than a purported refutation, Stage 2 of Hume's argument requires interpretations of 'subjective indistinguishability' and 'direct perception' on which both its first and third premises are defensible without begging any questions about the mind-dependent status of the direct objects of perception. I myself do not see how this challenge is supposed to be met.[6]

Hume's assumption that the only direct objects of perception are impressions is therefore on extremely weak ground. Yet this is crucial to his argument for premise (H1) of the overall antirationalist strategy outlined above: (H1), (H3′), therefore (H2′). For the reasoning behind this premise goes as follows. Since the direct objects of all perceptions are mind-dependent impressions, the senses alone do not present us with persisting mind-independent things. Furthermore, any rational argument from the existence and nature of these impressions to the existence

---

[6] See Snowdon, 1980–1, 1990, and 1992, for further detailed argument against this possibility.

and nature of a mind-independent world would, *pace* Descartes, have to be inductive. For this is the only means by which we can possibly reason from the existence of one thing to that of another which is distinct from and logically independent of it. Inductive reasoning of this kind, though, is driven only by past experience of a constant conjunction between tokens of the two types in question. Yet since the only direct objects of perception are mind-dependent impressions, no such experience of a constant conjunction between impressions *and mind-independent objects* is possible. So rational argument from the nature of our ideas is incapable of establishing the existence of a mind-independent external world.

Thus, Hume's extreme antirationalism is indeed an overreaction to Descartes's theory of perceptual knowledge, and the possibility of a neo-Kantian account is still very much alive. As I said above, this approach starts with the insistence that we cannot even begin to characterize perceptual experiences other than as the presentation of an objective spatial world to the subject. As Strawson puts it, normal people 'distinguish, naturally and unreflectively, between their seeings and hearings (perceivings) of objects and the objects they see and hear. Indeed these distinctions are built into the very vocabulary of their perception-reports, into the concepts they employ, the meanings of the things they say, in giving (unsophisticated) accounts of their hearings and seeings of things' (1974*a*, p. 49). Nor is this just an optional extravagance: 'Of a fleeting perception, a subjective event, I give a description involving the mention of something not fleeting at all, but lasting [that tree, dog, desk, or book, for example], not a subjective event at all, but a distinct [mind-independent] object. It is clear, *contra* Hume, not only that I *do* do this, but that I *must* do it in order to give a natural and unforced account of my perceptions' (p. 51).

The point here is that our perceptions are *essentially* perceptions *as of* enduring things being thus and so in the objective world around us. Concepts appropriate to the characterization of persisting mind-independent external objects are ineliminable from a correct account of the nature of the conscious experiences involved. Furthermore, the neo-Kantian continues, it follows from this that we cannot give a satisfactory account of perceptual experiences other than as providing *reasons*, albeit defeasibly, for beliefs about the way things actually are in the mind-independent world out there. The crucial questions to address, then, in developing such a neo-Kantian account, are these. First, what does the ineliminability claim consist in? Second, what is the relation between this claim and the way in which particular experiences provide reasons for particular beliefs about the way things are in the external world around us? Much of what follows is directed towards answering these questions. To anticipate the outcome right away, though, the answers for which I shall be arguing are, absurdly briefly, as follows. First, any account of the nature of conscious perceptual experiences must capture their *objective demonstrative content*. In other words, the nature of perceptual experiences can only be elucidated through the use of demonstrative contents of the form 'That is thus', in which the singular demonstrative paradigmatically refers to a persisting mind-independent thing and the predicative demonstrative identifies the mind-independent way that that thing is experientially presented as being. Second, a correct account of the way in which these perceptions refer in this way to mind-independent spatial particulars and their properties itself yields an account of precisely how they provide non-inferential reasons for certain of our beliefs about the world around us, and therefore of how perception is fit to serve as a peculiarly direct source of knowledge about the way things are out there. Indeed, I believe that this is an instance of a more general epistemic condition upon determinate reference.[7]

---

[7] See 8.2 and 8.3 for further development of this point.

2

Belief and Experience

I regard it as an undeniable datum that perception is a basic source of knowledge about the mind-independent, spatial world. My overall project is to solve simultaneously for the nature of the conscious experiences involved in perception, the relation such experiences bear to perceptually based empirical beliefs, and the relevant sense of 'basic', in such a way that these solutions are both independently plausible in each case, and conjoin to illuminate and explicate this datum.

The first claim which I aim to establish is this:

> (R) Perceptual experiences provide reasons for empirical beliefs.[1]

This is the sense in which I contend that there are genuinely *epistemic* requirements upon the very possibility of empirical belief, and therefore the sense in which I accuse the dominant historical-epistemological tradition within philosophy of being seriously misguided. For that tradition takes a person's possession of beliefs about the mind-independent world, and especially his understanding of the contents of these beliefs, entirely for granted, as prior to, and independent of, any specifically epistemological relation which may or may not obtain between perceiving subjects and the constituents of the world in which they live. It then goes on to ask which further conditions such beliefs must meet if they are to be *reasonable for the subject*, in the sense in which this is crucial to their status as cases of knowledge. Yet I argue that unless perceptual experiences provide reasons for empirical beliefs in precisely this sense—in which the subject's

---

[1] This claim is a crucial component of McDowell's (1994*b*) position in this area. Indeed, the argument which I offer in support of it is my own extended development of his very suggestive comments on the matter (see especially Lecture 1).

possession of such reasons is central to the question of whether the beliefs in question are cases of knowledge—there can be no such beliefs at all about particular mind-independent objects that they are determinately thus and so. The epistemological relation between experiences and beliefs proposed by (R) is therefore a necessary condition upon the very possibility of empirical belief. So the traditional order of epistemological enquiry is quite mistaken.

2.1 *Preliminaries*

Thesis (R) is obviously in need of a certain amount of clarification. Which experiences are claimed to provide reasons for which empirical beliefs, for example; what exactly are reasons in this sense, and in precisely what way do perceptual experiences *provide* them? Roughly, the relevant empirical beliefs are those with contents which it is possible to come to know directly on the basis of perception; and the corresponding perceptual experiences are those which would be involved in the acquisition of such knowledge. Equally roughly, reasons for beliefs are features of the overall set of circumstances a person finds herself in—by which I mean to include both her mental condition and its wider context, perhaps over a significant amount of time—which make it reasonable *from her point of view* to come to have or retain the beliefs in question in those circumstances. Suppose that a person's coming to believe that *p* is reasonable from her point of view in certain circumstances; then the reasons in question are those features of her circumstances which make this so. Furthermore, as reasons *from her point of view*, they necessarily figure as such in the subject's reflective thinking about her situation. In some way or another, she recognizes these features of her circumstances as the reasons which they are. Only so can they actually succeed in moving her in such a way that it is appropriate to cite their status *as reasons* in an explanation of her coming to believe that *p*.[2] Finally, perceptual experiences provide such reasons, I believe, in the sense

---

[2] I discuss this crucial recognition requirement upon genuine reasons in some detail in 4.3 and especially 5.2.

that they involve the actual entertaining of certain empirical contents, simply grasping which defeasibly constitutes a reason of this kind for endorsing them in belief.

All of this is of course still rather loose; but a more precise characterization of the import of (R) will have to wait until the argument which I propose in support of it has been set out. My hope is that this argument will simultaneously establish the truth of (R), properly understood, and provide the further explication of its terms required to gain this understanding.

The basic form of the argument is that of a *reductio ad absurdum*, very broadly along the following lines. Suppose that (R) is false. Then all of a person's purportedly empirical beliefs are entirely rationally unconstrained by mind-independent reality through its impact upon her in experience. I shall argue that it follows from this that it is incorrect even to regard any of these as beliefs *about* such a reality, never mind as expressive of knowledge about it. This is absurd. So (R) must be true.

Staying at this level of abstraction and approximation, the following two things need to be shown if (R) is to be proved in this way.

(H) The hypothesis that perceptual experiences do not provide reasons for empirical beliefs rules out the possibility of beliefs about a mind-independent spatial world.

(W) We have beliefs about a mind-independent spatial world.

Clearly, (H) is the main substance of the proof; but (W) is at least worthy of comment. There is a weak and a strong reading of (W). Read weakly, it simply claims that some of our beliefs at least present themselves to us as being about particular things in a mind-independent spatial world, whether or not there are determinate such things to which they actually do refer. Read strongly, on the other hand, it claims that some of our beliefs actually succeed in making reference to mind-independent spatial particulars, and are determined as true or false by the way such things objectively are.[3] In line with the realism which

---

[3] There is a further issue here, as to whether, on the strong reading of (W), our understanding of the beliefs which actually succeed in referring to mind-independent things itself depends upon the existence of those things in the

I announced at the beginning of this chapter, I simply assume the truth of (W) on this strong reading.[4] We just do have numerous beliefs about particular mind-independent things to the effect that they are determinately thus and so. Taking (W) in this way, of course, correspondingly weakens the sense in which (H) must be established. What has to be shown is that it is a condition on beliefs actually succeeding in making reference to spatial particulars, rather than just presenting themselves to us as if they do so, that certain experiences should provide reasons for such beliefs. I should also note at this point that a further assumption, not just that (W) is true, but that we know that (W) is true on this strong reading, will play a role later on in the overall argument for (R), in the course of my argument for (H) above.[5]

Returning to this main substance of the overall case then, the basic idea is this. It is only in virtue of their relations with her perceptual experiences—the impact of mind-independent reality upon her conscious mental life—that a person's beliefs can be said to have genuine empirical content. These relations contribute essentially to fixing a given belief as a belief *about* a particular mind-independent thing *to the effect that* it is determinately thus and so. Yet if her experience gives her no more reason to judge that things are objectively one specific way rather than any other, then they cannot possibly fulfil this role. They cannot provide her beliefs with external worldly significance at all, that is to say, with genuine truth-conditions which are fulfilled, or not, depending upon how certain things

---

world. Those who think that it does (e.g. Evans, 1982, esp. ch. 6; and McDowell, 1984) may argue that the weak reading of (W) therefore entails the strong reading. My own view is that this 'existence-dependent', or 'object-dependent' view of singular reference is correct, for the reasons advanced in Ch. 3 and elaborated in 7.3; but it is not crucial at this stage.

[4] Both mind independence and spatiality are crucial to the claim. Arithmetical thought, for example, even though its subject matter may correctly be conceived as mind-independent, is clearly a different matter. Conversely, the sense in which I endorse (W) is intended to be incompatible with any attempted idealist understanding of spatial particulars as, ultimately, mind-dependent (see Foster, 1982, ch. 5). To avoid undue repetition in what follows, though, I shall often use just one of the two adjectives as shorthand for the pair.

[5] Having announced this as a *further* assumption, I do offer a brief argument in 2.3 below from the truth of (W) to our knowledge of it; and in 8.3 I explain in detail how this inference is possible, and why it does not create any unacceptable possibility of a non-empirical source of new empirical knowledge.

objectively are in the world around her. Her beliefs therefore fail altogether to *be* beliefs about mind-independent reality, to the effect that particular things are determinately thus and so. Thus, the hypothesis that perceptual experiences do not provide reasons for empirical beliefs rules out altogether the possibility of beliefs about a mind-independent spatial world.

Two premises can be distinguished in this argument for (H). The first insists that beliefs concern spatial particulars only in virtue of certain relations which they bear to perceptual experiences; the second claims that only *reason-giving* relations between experiences and beliefs will do here. More precisely:

(P1) There is a class of beliefs about the spatial world, E, whose members have the contents which they do—that a particular mind-independent thing is determinately thus and so—only in virtue of their standing in certain relations with various actual or possible perceptual experiences.

(P2) Only reason-giving relations between perceptual experiences and beliefs could possibly serve the content-determining role required by (P1).

Before I consider each of these two premises in detail, it is worth expanding a little more upon something which I flagged in my provisional clarification of (R) above. Strictly speaking, the argument for (R) requires a relativization of both (H) and (W) to the appropriate class of empirical beliefs, E, which in turn bounds the range of application of the thesis itself. That is to say, in so far as it is established by (P1) and (P2), (H) claims that it is the possibility of beliefs *in* E which is ruled out by the hypothesis that certain perceptual experiences do not provide reasons for them; similarly, if it is to entail (R) in conjunction with this, then (W) must be the claim that we actually have some of the beliefs *in* E; and then (R) itself is the thesis that the relevant perceptual experiences provide reasons for the empirical beliefs in E. Precisely what the elements of E are, and therefore exactly what is involved in my assumption of (W), and exactly how broad the application of (R) turns out to be, will emerge as the argument proceeds. Most importantly, though, it will emerge that E is a peculiarly basic class of empirical beliefs, in the sense that we could not have any beliefs about particular mind-independent objects in the world around us if we did not have some of the beliefs in E.

Turning now to the two premises themselves, I start, in the remainder of the present chapter, with a defence of (P1), the claim that certain beliefs about the mind-independent world have their contents only in virtue of their standing in certain relations with perceptual experiences.[6] Perceptual experiences, as I understand them, are the world's direct impact upon a person's mind. They are therefore the only immediate difference which is made to her mental life by her being the particular person which she is, tracing the particular spatio-temporal route which she does through the determinately constituted objective world. So unless her beliefs about the world are systematically related in some way to these experiences, they are utterly insensitive to her actual physical environment. Even if a person's 'world-view' somehow survives this 'confinement' (McDowell, 1994*b*, pp. 15 ff.), as a series of quasi-rational manipulations utterly isolated from any influence by the external world through perceptual experience—akin to the most abstract imaginable algebra perhaps—mind-independent reality drops out as quite irrelevant to whatever residual norms may govern it. It therefore fails to be a world-view, or set of beliefs *about* that reality, at all. Thus, beliefs concern mind-independent reality only in virtue of standing in certain relations with perceptual experiences.

I should stress that this requirement is more moderate than the quite general empiricist claim that every concept either has its source in experience, or is composed exclusively from simple concepts which do. It is certainly more moderate than the extreme verificationist idea that the significance of any empirical belief whatsoever is exhausted by its association with a set of experiences which conclusively verify it. Rather, it simply insists that without some anchoring to her particular worldly environment through some relations or other which they bear to her actual or possible perceptual experiences, certain of a person's purported beliefs about the way things are in the world around her collapse into an empirically empty game. All that this premise really amounts to is a denial of the extreme rationalist

---

[6] My defence of (P2) is given in Ch. 3.

suggestion that such beliefs simply sit there in a person's mind, with their infallibly recognizable, determinate yet genuinely *empirical*, contents engraved upon them, quite independently of any relations which they may or may not have with the actual things around her through the impact of such worldly affairs upon her conscious experiential life.

Further clarification and defence of this first premise can best be given by considering how it avoids the following dilemma. Either experiences themselves have empirical content or they do not. If they do, then there is some explanation of how this is so; and what is to prevent this same explanation being applied directly as an account of how beliefs acquire their empirical content without any relations to conscious experiences at all? Yet the possibility that the same explanation could be applied directly to empirical beliefs in this way would contradict the current premise, (P1), of my argument for (H).[7] If, on the other hand, experiences do not have empirical content, then it is at best unclear how they might be supposed to endow the beliefs with which they bear certain relations with any either, whatever these relations may be. The appearance of a dilemma here is illusory in my view. For I shall argue that the correct account of the empirical content of experiences is such that its application to contents of a given kind is sufficient for these to be *experiential* contents themselves, contents a person's grasp of which essentially depends upon her enjoying certain experiences. Thus, the second horn of the prima facie dilemma is indeed unacceptable: their role as the source of empirical content for certain beliefs requires that the relevant perceptual experiences themselves have empirical content. The first horn is perfectly compatible with my premise that the empirical content of beliefs depends upon their standing in these relations with experiences, though.

---

[7] A quick answer might be given to my question of the previous sentence along the following lines. The correct account of content determination for beliefs cannot simply be an application of the account appropriate to experiences. For (1) beliefs are held for reasons in a sense in which experiences are not had for reasons; and (2) these reasons for holding beliefs are crucial to the determination of their contents. I do not rest with this answer, though, for two reasons. First, both (1) and (2) require careful statement and extended defence, neither of which I give here. Second, the argument which follows in response to the dilemma objection is integral to the development of my overall position.

For the explanation of how it is that experiences themselves have empirical content is inapplicable directly to anything else. Either it applies, and what we are dealing with are necessarily experiential contents; or we are in the domain of non-experiential beliefs, in which case the explanation cannot apply, and their possession of genuine empirical content depends upon their standing in certain relations with perceptual experiences.

This reply to the dilemma objection would be completely justified by the following claim. A correct account of the content of perceptual experiences, in particular, of their reference to certain mind-independent spatial particulars, is both necessary and sufficient for explaining their status as *conscious experiences*.[8] Furthermore, I am confident that this claim is true. Unfortunately, though, I am not in a position to give a convincing demonstration of its truth here. Even so, it does suggest what I shall argue is the correct core of the set, E, of empirical beliefs whose contents are essentially determined by their relations with perceptual experiences; and this in turn points the way to a less ambitious justification for the form of my response to the present dilemma objection to premise (P1) above. The suggestion is that we should focus upon a person's perceptually based beliefs about particular mind-independent things in the spatial world around her; and the pointer is to an enquiry into the determinate singular reference of such beliefs.[9]

2.2 *The Strawson Argument*

To have a belief of the kind which I shall be interested in is to take a particular worldly object to be thus and so. Its content depends in part upon the subject's Idea (Evans, 1982, pp. 104 ff.; Geach, 1992, pp. 53 ff.) of the thing in question, where an *Idea* here is a singular Fregean sense (Frege, 1993). Evans characterizes the notion as follows: 'I shall speak of the Ideas a subject has, of this or that particular object, on the model of the way we

8 See Eilan, 1988, for a sustained discussion of this kind of claim.
9 The argument which I am about to give is my development of Strawson's famous discussion of these matters (1959, ch. 1, pt. 1). The discussion to follow draws heavily upon Eilan, 1988, ch. 5, in which she acknowledges the importance of conversations with Adrian Moore at crucial points.

speak of the concepts a subject has, of this or that property . . .
An Idea of an object, then, is something which makes it possible
for a subject to think of an object in a series of indefinitely many
thoughts, in each of which he will be thinking of the object in
the same way' (1982, p. 104).

Now, suppose that the Idea in question is constituted wholly
by a more or less complex general description. That is to say, the
belief comprises, as an Idea of its mind-independent object, a
description, 'the *F*', which is uniquely satisfied by the spatial particular in question. Although '*F*' may be quite complex, and will
no doubt identify the relevant object in part by its spatial relations with other things in the subject's environment, the Idea is
to be *purely* descriptive; so any further spatial particulars to
which it appeals in this way must also be picked out by description alone. So, 'the *F*' identifies a particular mind-independent
thing by its definitive properties and relations, spatial and otherwise, with a range of other such things of various kinds: 'The red
ball under the glass table between the chair and the sofa in front
of the round white window', as it might be. This Idea actually
succeeds in identifying a particular mind-independent thing only
if the definite description is uniquely satisfied. In other words, it
fails to do so either if there is no red ball in the whole universe
which is under a glass table between a chair and a sofa in front
of a round white window or, more importantly for our purposes,
if there is more than one such thing. The first possibility is
always a live one, in the sense that it can never be ruled out with
absolute certainty or infallibility. For the subject may have mis-
perceived the definitive location of the target object on the relevant descriptive map. Equally, though, it is always within his
power to recognize and rectify any *particular* such mistake, by
more careful perceptual investigation, or by wholesale revision
of the description intended to net the object in question. For
example, he might come to see that the table top which he previously took to be glass is actually a thin sheet of highly polished
wood caught in a misleading way by the light from the window;
or he might shift altogether to a description of the ball in question as 'the ball which was previously kept in the toy box under
the stairs', or whatever. The error, and its correction, are, in this
way, internal to his thinking, intrinsic features of the relevant
Ideas themselves.

Things are very different with the second possibility, of multiple satisfaction. Again, this is always a live possibility in a certain sense. For however detailed and extensive the description may be, there is always the possibility, in principle at least, of a reduplication elsewhere in the universe of the whole scene as described. The crucial difference with the first case of emptiness is that there is absolutely nothing which can be done within the subject's thinking, as it were, even to *attempt* to avoid the possibility of massive reduplication: nothing essential to any purely descriptive Idea rules out this possibility. As I say, no amount of additional context or further detail in the description itself can remove the possibility, in principle, of a massive reduplication of the *whole scene as described*, however large or specific this may be, elsewhere in the universe. Here, the Idea itself is *in principle* quite silent on whether or not this possibility of massive reduplication is actualized. If it is, then the Idea fails uniquely to identify any spatial particular as its object. So the belief fails altogether to be a belief that any particular mind-independent thing is determinately thus and so. Furthermore, it is difficult to see how anything upon which the Idea itself is in principle quite neutral, as it is about the actualization of the ineliminable possibility of massive reduplication, could make any immediate difference to its successful determination of a unique spatial particular as its object. Thus, its referential status is independent of whether the described scene is actually multiply realized in the universe or not. It follows that any such purely descriptive Idea fails directly to determine a unique mind-independent reference regardless of whether this possibility of massive reduplication is actualized or not.[10]

---

[10] Given a sufficiently strict interpretation of what is required for an Idea to be 'purely descriptive', where this rules out any appeal to essentially experiential demonstrative components figuring either in reference to particular objects or their general properties in the description in question, then I think that this claim is quite correct. For any such description is devoid altogether of empirical significance. The claim is not intended to rule out impure descriptive thoughts of various kinds about spatial particulars, though. For example, a person might use a demonstratively anchored description to think about a particular ball as 'the red ball under that table'; or, if the universe happens to contain one and only one such thing, exploiting his implicitly demonstrative grasp of which colour redness is, he might think of it simply as 'the red ball'. This stage of the Strawson Argument is elaborated in detail in 2.3 below.

Possession of genuine beliefs about particular mind-independent things therefore depends upon a person's exploiting a more fundamental form of reference to such spatial particulars than is possible with the use of purely descriptive Ideas alone. Indeed, the possibility of his having any descriptive empirical beliefs of the kind which we have just been considering at all depends upon his identification of at least some of the particulars exploited in the relevant descriptive maps by this more fundamental means. The Ideas involved at this level, I believe, are *essentially experiential* perceptual demonstratives. That is to say, the more fundamental mode of reference to spatial particulars, which is required to anchor a person's beliefs to a unique set of such things in the world around him, essentially involves a presentation of the particular thing in question *in his conscious experience*. The subject's Idea of which thing this is is not, and cannot be, exhausted by any more or less complex general description, which might equally be entertained in the absence of any experience of whatever happens uniquely to satisfy it. For reference determination at the most fundamental level essentially draws upon the actual identities of the things in the subject's environment about which he is currently acquiring information in experience. Unlike any putative purely descriptive reference to mind-independent particulars, then, this crucial foundation for empirical beliefs is essentially experiential.

Returning to the objection stated in the form of a dilemma above, the worry was this. In so far as certain relations between beliefs and experiences are supposed to be essential to the determinate empirical content of the beliefs in question, then the experiences involved must themselves have empirical content; but then what is to prevent beliefs from acquiring their content directly, by whatever method experiences are envisaged as doing so, independently of any relations which they may or may not bear to experiences of any kind? Very crudely, my response was this. The means by which experiences acquire their empirical content applies only to essentially experiential contents; so non-experiential beliefs do indeed acquire empirical content only on the basis of their relations with experiences. This response is supported by my recent contention that reference to spatial particulars rests fundamentally upon a level of perceptual demonstrative reference which is essentially experiential. For it follows from this that a complete account of perceptual reference to mind-independent particulars ineliminably involves an essentially experiential component. Hence no such account could be given as part of the account of the determination of empirical content for any non-experiential belief. Any non-experiential empirical beliefs therefore have their content determined in part by their relations with certain conscious perceptual experiences.

2.3 *Refinements*

Clearly this line of response to the dilemma objection is not yet entirely conclusive. I shall attempt to make it more so by considering in turn each of the following three issues. First, a significant amount hangs on a disanalogy between the two ways in which a definite description might fail to pick out any particular mind-independent thing—on the one hand, no object might satisfy the description; on the other hand it may be satisfied by more than one object. Is the disanalogy which I exploit here genuine? Second, I claim, on the basis of the supposed disanalogy between these two cases, that the referential standing of a purely descriptive Idea is in a certain sense independent of whether or not the possibility of massive reduplication is actualized. Is the justification which I offer for this crucial claim adequate? Third, I move straight from the inadequacy of purely descriptive Ideas of spatial particulars to the ineliminable role of essentially experiential perceptual demonstrative Ideas in a person's beliefs about particular things in the mind-independent world around him. Yet there are surely at least other candidate models for such reference. So is this final move in the argument really obligatory?

I said above that both types of descriptive reference failure are always live possibilities. In the first case, in which no object satisfies the description constitutive of the subject's putative Idea, this is because perceptual error can never *infallibly* be ruled out. Perception just is a fallible source of information about the world. So on any occasion on which it looks to a person that there is a red ball under a glass table between a chair and a sofa in front of a round white window, say, it is consistent with things looking just that way to him that there is no such thing.[11] Nevertheless, as I stressed at the outset, we can know, for example, that there is a red ball under a glass table between a chair and a sofa in front of a round white window, on the basis of perception. Hence perception may suffice *knowledgeably* to rule out the possibility of a reference failure of this first kind. Perception of a given sector of the universe, however detailed and extensive, on the other hand, cannot ever suffice on its own knowledgeably to rule out reference failure due to massive reduplication. The crucial disanalogy between the two possibilities of reference failure, then, is that the second—due to massive reduplication—is always an *epistemic possibility*, whereas the first—due to emptiness, as it were—is not.[12] To clarify this claim, what I mean here by an 'epistemic possibility' is this. It is an epistemic possibility for S that p if and only if it is logically possible that $[K_S \& p]$, where K_S is the conjunction of everything that S knows.[13] Thus, it is epistemically possible for S that p if and only if S is not in a position knowledgeably to rule out that p.[14] Put another way, then, the claim which distinguishes the two types of descriptive reference failure is that, although a per-

[11] The truth of this claim is independent of the choice between a disjunctive and a non-disjunctive account of visual experience (Hinton, 1973; Snowdon, 1980–1, 1990; McDowell, 1986; Child, 1994, ch. 5, esp. sect. 2). On a disjunctive account, when a person perceives a red ball under a glass table between a chair and a sofa in front of a round white window, he could not be in precisely that condition without the existence of such a thing. It might, nevertheless, have looked to him just as if there were such a thing when there was not, because he was in a distinct condition of being subject to a 'mere appearance' of a red ball under a glass table between a chair and a sofa in front of a round white window. The correctness of the characterization of his condition as one in which things look thus and so to him is neutral on the substantive question of which disjunct his condition actually instantiates. Hence the claim in the text holds.

[12] See the discussion later on in this section for a minor qualification to this claim, which I argue does not affect the force of the Strawson Argument.

[13] I mean this to be a stipulative definition of a technical notion of an epistemic possibility for my purposes. I believe that it captures what at least some others have intended in connection with contingent propositions. It will not do in connection with necessary falsehoods, though, for, intuitively, the negation of an as yet unproved theorem is still an epistemic possibility.

[14] This equivalence can be demonstrated as follows: it is epistemically possible for S that $p \Leftrightarrow$ it is logically possible that $[K_S \& p] \Leftrightarrow \{K_S, p\}$ is consistent $\Leftrightarrow$ 'K_S, therefore not-p' is invalid $\Leftrightarrow S$ cannot argue validly from what he actually knows to not-$p \Leftrightarrow S$ is not in a position knowledgeably to rule out that p.

son is often in a position knowledgeably to rule out the possibility that a purely descriptive Idea, like 'the red ball under the glass table between the chair and the sofa in front of the round white window', which he has in mind is empty, he is never, or at least not normally, in a position knowledgeably to rule out the possibility of a massive reduplication which leads to its multiple satisfaction.[15]

The second issue which I raised above can be put as the following objection. Of course definite descriptions succeed in identifying a particular mind-independent thing only if they are not multiply satisfied. Perhaps, furthermore, it is always an epistemic possibility for a subject entertaining such a description that this defeating condition of reduplication of the described scene obtains. Nevertheless, when it does not, and there is a unique object which satisfies the description, then this object is precisely what is thereby picked out by the description. Provided only that massive reduplication is not actualized (and assuming that there is no perceptual error, so at least one object satisfies the relevant description), then a purely descriptive Idea succeeds in identifying a unique spatial particular; and a belief comprising such an Idea succeeds in being a belief about that particular mind-independent thing. This must be so, on pain of obliterating altogether the possibility of any descriptive identification of spatial particulars, even in the surely uncontroversial *impure* cases, as I shall call them, in which certain of the particulars employed in the relevant descriptive map are uniquely pinned down by perceptual demonstrative identification, as in an Idea like 'the red ball under that table'. For here too, as I myself admit, there is always a possibility of perceptual error resulting in the description being empty. There may be no red ball under the relevant table, for example, just an unusually spherical red apple. Granting this possibility, though, all we insist on for

---

[15] Notice that I am assuming here, in my claim that the possibility of emptiness is not always an *epistemic* possibility, the datum with which I began Ch. 2, and which I aim to explicate in detail throughout this book, that people like us do have perceptual knowledge about the mind-independent world around them. This is how it is that a person is often in a position knowledgeably to rule out the possibility that a suitable description is empty: he can just see, say, that there is a red ball under the glass table between the chair and the sofa in front of the round white window in front of him.

successful descriptive identification (in these uncontroversial cases) is that it should not be actualized.[16] Thus, we must surely adopt the same attitude with respect to massive reduplication: provided only that this is not *actual*, then purely descriptive Ideas succeed perfectly well in identifying spatial particulars.

What this objection challenges is my apparent difference in standards with respect to the two admitted possibilities of descriptions failing to net a particular object. In the case of emptiness, in which no object satisfies the description, I claim that *actualization* of the possibility is required for failure, whereas, in the case of massive reduplication, in which more than one object satisfies the description, I claim that the mere *possibility* itself is sufficient for failure regardless of whether or not it is actualized. My defence of this asymmetry rests precisely upon the crucial distinction which I made above between the nature of the possibility in each case. Suppose that a person's putative Idea of a spatial particular is constituted by a definite description, 'the *F*', and that he has what he takes to be a belief comprising this Idea about a spatial particular. The possibility of emptiness consists in the fact that his perception that there is an *F* in his environment is not infallible, and hence in the fact that it is consistent with everything about which he is infallible, and with its looking to him that there is an *F* in front of him, that there is in fact no *F*, either nearby, or anywhere in the universe. Nevertheless, when there is, and he is looking at it, he may well know that there is one in his environment (and so at least one in the universe), in which case it is not consistent with all that he knows that there is not at least one *F*. That his description is empty is therefore not an epistemic possibility for him. The possibility of multiple satisfaction consists in the metaphysical possibility of massive reduplication of his environment as described by 'the *F*' elsewhere in the universe, a possibility which exists however detailed or extensive the description may be, provided it is pure, in the sense of not embedding any perceptual demonstrative reference to particular things in the world around him. That this defeating condition obtains is something which is not

---

[16] Indeed, some philosophers have wished to retain a notion of identificatory success even when there is limited descriptive error of this kind. See especially Donnellan, 1966.

only consistent with everything about which he is infallible—which may well be nothing at all—and with its looking to him that there is an F in front of him, but also with all that he actually does or is currently in a position to know about the world around him. That his description is multiply satisfied is therefore an epistemic possibility for him.

It is this last fact, precisely what distinguishes the possibility of multiple satisfaction from the possibility of emptiness, which justifies my claim that the referential standing of a purely descriptive Idea is independent of whether or not the possibility of massive reduplication is actualized. Since any such Idea fails genuinely to refer to a spatial particular when this possibility is actualized, every such Idea fails to do so always. The crucial question, then, is this: how does the fact that we are dealing with an epistemic possibility here lead to the invariance of referential standing with respect to the actualization of the possibility of massive reduplication? At this point, the further assumption to which I alluded to above (2.1) is essential. I assume not just that (W) is true—that we have beliefs about a mind-independent spatial world, in the stronger of the two senses which I distinguished earlier—but also that we know that (W) is true in this sense. More precisely, I take it for granted that in most, if not all, of the cases in which a person forms a belief about the world around him on the basis of perception, a belief which actually succeeds in making reference to a particular mind-independent thing, and is determined as true or false by the way that thing objectively is, he also knows that he is referring to that thing in this sense (although this is of course not something about which he is infallible, since perceptual illusions and hallucinations can never infallibly be ruled out). In other words, he knows that he is successfully identifying a spatial particular. Now, suppose that his Idea of the thing in question is purely descriptive, constituted wholly by a more or less complex general description, 'the F'. We have seen that massive reduplication leading to multiple satisfaction of this description is bound to be epistemically possible for him. That is to say, it is consistent with all that he knows that 'the F' is multiply satisfied. Thus, it is consistent with all that he knows that he fails to refer to anything on the basis of his purely descriptive Idea. But I have stipulated that the fact that he *does* refer to a unique particular in the world around him is one of the things that he knows. This is a contradiction. So we must reject the assumption that his Idea is purely descriptive. Putting this in a way which relates it more directly to the objection under consideration, the point is this. Since massive reduplication is always an epistemic possibility for a person entertaining a purely descriptive Idea, and perceptual reference to mind-independent particulars is epistemically transparent, in the sense that a person normally knows, or is at least in a position to know, that he is succeeding in achieving it when he is, then purely descriptive Ideas fail to refer to spatial particulars—at least, those which are even in principle perceptible—regardless of whether the possibility of massive reduplication is actualized or not.[17] Any parallel argument in connection with the possibility of descriptive reference failure due to emptiness cannot even get started. For emptiness is not normally an epistemic possibility when it is not in fact actualized; yet the claim that it is would be a crucial premise in any such parallel argument.

Since this phase of the Strawson Argument, from the possibility of massive reduplication to the inadequacy of purely descriptive reference to spatial particulars is an important core of my case for premise (P1) above—that certain empirical beliefs have their contents only in virtue of their standing in certain relations with various actual or possible perceptual experiences—I want briefly to consider a final line of objection to it, before turning to the third issue which I identified above, concerning the final move of my argument, from this inadequacy of purely descriptive Ideas to the fundamental role of essentially experiential perceptual demonstrative reference.

The argument turns on the fact that a person sometimes succeeds in making identifying reference to a particular mind-independent thing in the world around him in such a way that the following two conditions are both met. First, he knows that he is referring to a spatial particular. Second, massive reduplication is an epistemic possibility for him with respect to any purely descriptive Idea which he may have of the thing in question. But

---

[17] I return below to the highly abnormal case in which a person uses a purely descriptive Idea, 'the red ball', say, which fortuitously describes a unique particular, and therefore makes a kind of accidental or indirect 'reference' to it, totally unbeknownst to the subject.

why should we assume that this is ever the case? Indeed, it may be objected that in so far as a person ever knows that his beliefs actually succeed in referring to particular mind-independent things, this knowledge is necessarily derived from his prior and independent knowledge that the appropriate possibilities of massive reduplication are not actualized. The thought behind this objection is that simply referring to something is insufficient on its own, either for knowledge that any description which may be involved is not multiply satisfied throughout the whole universe, or for knowledge that one succeeds in referring to the thing in question; whereas, with independent knowledge of the former, and a little reflection about the descriptive nature of the belief in question, one might infer the latter, that one is indeed successful in one's purported reference. Furthermore, the objector continues, this is the only way of acquiring such knowledge of successful reference to mind-independent things. Thus, there are no cases in which the two conditions required by my argument are both met. So my claim that purely descriptive Ideas are inadequate is quite unsubstantiated.

I have three replies, of increasing strength, to this line of objection. (I myself am inclined to endorse all three.) Two preliminary points should be made first, though. First, all that my argument requires is that there have to be *some* cases in which the two conditions given above are both met, if there are to be beliefs about mind-independent things at all. Provided that reference to spatial particulars depends upon some such cases, then it follows that any kind of descriptive identification depends upon perceptual demonstrative reference to spatial particulars. For in such cases, in which the two conditions are met, no purely descriptive Idea is adequate, and, given the final move of the Strawson Argument, the successful reference involves at least a component of essentially experiential perceptual demonstration. Second, it is no good objecting that the epistemic possibility of multiple satisfaction can always be ruled out if S's descriptive Idea is of the form 'the unique-G', with 'unique-G' in place of 'F' in the original formulation. This may be correct, as far as it goes; but, in that case, reference failure due to the emptiness of this description is an epistemic possibility. For, again, S cannot knowledgeably rule out the possibility of massive reduplication with respect to G. So an appropriately adjusted version of my argument goes through. Note, also, to repeat, that the argument does nothing to undermine the possibility of thought about spatial particulars by what I have been calling *impure description*, in which reference is secured, in part, by an embedded demonstrative, as in, for example, 'the red ball under that table'.

That all said, my first, and weakest, reply to the present objection is this. In the most basic cases of successful perceptual belief about a particular thing in the subject's immediate environment, there are very strong pretheoretic intuitions that both conditions just are met. In the normal, and most basic case, a person knows that she is referring to a spatial particular, yet she is not in a position knowledgeably to rule out the possibility of massive reduplication with respect to any description she may have of the referent in question. So the argument goes through. This cannot be a case of purely descriptive reference, and experience has an ineliminable role.

Second, massive reduplication is *always* an epistemic possibility with respect to *any* pure description alone. More precisely, for any wholly general description which a person may have of a particular mind-independent thing in her environment, it is always an epistemic possibility for her that that description is multiply satisfied by spatial reality taken as a whole. Combined with the very weak claim that people sometimes know that they are referring to spatial particulars, indeed, that this is the normal case, this is sufficient to refute the objection. Strictly speaking, a slightly more moderate claim is correct here, and sufficient for this reply. Suppose, that is to say, that there are certain descriptions of spatial particulars for which certain thinkers are in a position knowledgeably to rule out the possibility of multiple satisfaction, on the basis of extraneous knowledge. For example, suppose that a certain astrophysicist knows that there is at most one F in the universe, for some wholly general predicate 'F', or that 'the F' is a very large-scale description entertained in the context of knowledge that the universe is less than a certain upper bound in size. Thus, massive reduplication is not an epistemic possibility for the subject in question. Her capacity to entertain the purely descriptive Idea, 'the F', is nevertheless quite independent of this knowledge in the following sense. Another person is equally capable, or equally incapable, of thinking of the thing in question, in exactly the same purely descriptive way, without knowing that there is at most one *F* in the universe or that the universe is less than such-and-such a size. Massive reduplication *is* an epistemic possibility for her. Conjoining this with the claim that people sometimes know that they are referring to spatial particulars other than by inference from their reflective knowledge of the descriptive nature of the Idea involved along with some independent knowledge that the relevant description is in fact uniquely satisfied, it follows that the two conditions required for my argument can be, and frequently are, jointly met. Hence the present objection fails.

Third, successful perceptual reference is sufficient for knowledge of success, or at least for the subject to be in a position to acquire such knowledge. Along with the claim that such reference is normally, or, given the second point above, always, achieved in cases in which massive reduplication is an epistemic possibility for the subject with respect to any description which she may have of the object in question, this is again sufficient to undermine the present line of objection. This last reply rests upon the following claim. Any person who has a perceptually based belief about a particular thing in the mind-independent world around her is thereby in a position to know that she is indeed referring to that spatial particular. All that I can offer here is a sketch of how this claim might be established, and a brief discussion of a couple of putative counterexamples.

It might be argued, to begin with, that successful perceptual reference requires that the subject has *some* beliefs about the object to which she refers, which she at least takes to be justified by her experience.[18] Suppose, then, that *S*, who is making successful perceptual reference to a particular object *a* in her environment, believes on the basis of perception in this way that *a* is *F*. That is to say, asking herself how things stand in the world around her, she arrives at the judgement that *a* is *F*. Then, given the concept of belief, she is in a position to exploit the so-called 'ascent routine' (Evans, 1982, ch. 7; Gordon, 1995, p. 60; Roessler,

---

[18] I shall suggest an argument much later (8.2) for a slightly stronger thesis, which is a descendent of Russell's Principle of Acquaintance (1917, p. 159), that perceptual reference to a spatial particular requires that the subject actually has *genuine* reasons for certain beliefs about the thing in question, not just experience which she takes to justify such beliefs.

1996, ch. 2), by prefixing this judgement with the operator 'I believe that', to arrive at the further *knowledge* that she believes that *a* is *F*. From here, she can *knowledgeably* infer that she is referring to *a*. It therefore follows, as required, that a person's successful perceptual reference to a mind-independent particular puts her in a position to acquire the knowledge that she is indeed referring to that thing.[19]

Two types of counterexample to this claim come to mind.[20] Suppose, first, that a person is prone to hallucinations of household objects, a problem which he is well aware of, and that he is currently suffering a bout of them. Suppose also that he sees a (real) telephone in front of him, and thinks, 'That phone is of the same kind as the one in my office'. Surely, he succeeds in referring to the phone, but does not know that he is doing so; for he might just as well be suffering a hallucination in a phoneless room. My own intuition is simply to deny that he does not know that he is referring to the phone in question, provided that he comes to the belief that he is by the ascent-routine-involving method which I outlined above. In this case, I think that his known proneness to hallucinations is irrelevant to the epistemic standing of his knowledge of successful reference, just as it is, I would say, to the epistemic standing of his belief about the telephone itself, provided that this is otherwise well grounded.[21] (Lack of confidence is not necessarily an obstacle to knowledge.) This may be denied. Even if it is, though, it must surely be conceded that such cases are essentially abnormal: successful perceptual reference and first-order perceptual knowledge about

---

[19] See Ch. 8 below, especially 8.2 and 8.3, for further discussion and generalization of this line of argument. Note also that the argument depends upon my commitment to the object-dependence of certain singular Ideas (see n. 3 above, Ch. 3, and 7.3). For only given object-dependence is the inference from 'I believe that *a* is *F*' to 'I am referring to *a*' (where '*a*' refers to an object and not simply an Idea) valid.

[20] The first of these was suggested to me by Christopher Peacocke; the second has been lurking throughout the discussion so far.

[21] These intuitions, I think, depend significantly upon the demonstrative content of the first-order belief in question, and might well be different with respect to non-demonstrative beliefs, like the belief that there is a real phone in the room, say. As with the second putative counterexample below, though, I would in this non-demonstrative case deny that there is genuine perceptual reference to the phone.

the mind-independent world depend upon the normality of cases in which there are no such (apparent) obstacles to a person's arrival at knowledge of his successful reference to spatial particulars by the above routine.

A second difficulty concerns cases in which a person uses a purely descriptive Idea, such as 'the red ball', which is, quite fortuitously and unbeknownst to him, not in fact multiply satisfied throughout the universe as a whole. The obvious thing to say about such a case is that it is one in which he succeeds in referring, or at least in arriving at a belief which is determined as true or false depending on the condition of the unique red ball, but is ignorant of his success in doing so. Thus, it appears to provide a counterexample to my argument that successful perceptual reference is sufficient for knowledge of success. Indeed, it might be urged further that cases like this one are really very common. For descriptive Ideas are normally used with an implicit restriction on the domain of quantification, say to objects in the same room as the subject, or whatever. Hence the risk of multiple satisfaction is dramatically reduced, and so the frequency of cases in which it is fortuitously not actualized in this way is likewise increased. Such cases, it might be claimed, are therefore the norm. Now, this final attempt to expand the significance of accidentally uniquely satisfied pure descriptions is unacceptable. For insisting upon an implicit restriction on the domain of quantification effectively embeds a demonstrative into the descriptive Idea in question, transforming it into something like 'the red ball *in this room*', say. In that case, it is no longer *purely* descriptive; and so it falls outside the scope of my argument. Nevertheless, the original possibility still stands, at least in principle. My response is that this is, in an important sense, *not* a case of genuine perceptual reference; and the sense in which this is so comes out when we work through my own argument with this example. All that the ascent routine allows the subject to conclude here is that he believes that the red ball is *F*, let us say. He is unable to infer from this that he is thereby referring to a particular ball, precisely because he does not know that the description 'the red ball' is in fact uniquely satisfied. Furthermore, the reason why this additional information is required is that any such general description fails to determine a particular object as its reference *as a matter of its sense*—that is, as a matter of what the subject knows about its reference in virtue of understanding the description in question. This is why he is unable to infer that he is referring to a particular thing simply in virtue of grasping any corresponding purely descriptive Idea. It is also precisely the sense in which I claim that these are therefore not cases of genuine perceptual reference. So the fortuitously uniquely satisfied case of 'the red ball' above is not, after all, a counterexample to the thesis that a person's successful perceptual reference to a mind-independent particular puts him in a position to acquire the knowledge that he is indeed referring to that thing.

This key phase of the Strawson Argument can therefore be summarized as follows. A person's knowledge of her reference to spatial particulars requires that her most basic referring terms determine a unique mind-independent thing as their reference simply as a matter of their sense.[22] Purely general definite descriptions fail this requirement. Therefore a person's reference to spatial particulars essentially rests upon a non-descriptive base.

Note, to conclude my discussion of this cluster of issues, that if, as I myself believe, both of the second and third replies above to the present line of objection are defensible, then it follows that my argument against purely descriptive reference to spatial particulars is quite general. No belief which makes genuine perceptual reference to a particular thing in the mind-independent world comprises a singular Idea constituted wholly by a purely general description.

Finally, I want to turn to the third issue which I raised above. Let us grant that purely descriptive reference to spatial particulars is impossible, and that there must be a more fundamental mode of such reference, upon which any genuine beliefs about the mind-independent world rest, and upon which any successful impure descriptive reference to spatial particulars depends. It might still be objected that I have simply asserted without argument that this crucial basis is provided by *essentially experiential perceptual demonstrative reference*. For it might well be thought that either proper names or certain descriptions embedding non-experiential indexicals provide an equally acceptable

---

[22] This is, of course, a version of what Gareth Evans calls 'Russell's Principle' (1982, esp. ch. 4).

alternative to pure descriptions, or that the demonstratives which are required are not essentially experiential. I take these three suggestions in turn, starting with proper names.

What is wrong with the proposal that the most basic reference to mind-independent things should be modelled upon the reference which I make to a particular person in my beliefs that *William Hague* is a nonentity, say, or that *Frege* was born in 1848? My answer is that reference to spatial particulars by the use of proper names along these lines is itself dependent upon essentially experiential demonstrative reference of some kind. This is of course a large issue; and I shall have to be rather dogmatic in my engagement with it. To begin with, I endorse Evans's (1982, ch. 11) distinction between *producers* and *consumers* in a proper-name-using practice. Consider 'an ordinary proper-name-using practice, in which the name "NN" is used to refer to the person *x*'. The *producers* are the members of the 'core group of speakers who have been introduced to the practice via their acquaintance with *x*', that is, on the basis of learning 'a truth which they could then express as "This is NN", where "This" makes a demonstrative reference to *x*', in the context of a certain capacity to recognize persons, or at least that particular person, over time. (p. 376). The *consumers*, on the other hand, 'who are not acquainted with *x*, can be introduced into the practice, either by helpful explanations of the form "NN is the φ" or just by hearing sentences in which the name is used' (p. 377). Producers' understanding of the name 'NN' clearly depends upon their perceptual demonstrative reference to *x*. Hence they do nothing to undermine my appeal to this as the essential and most fundamental mode of reference to spatial particulars. Two points can be made in opposition to the claim that consumers provide any more of a threat. First, their introduction to the practice is most likely, if not necessarily, to depend upon their essentially experiential demonstrative reference to the person in question, although the demonstratives involved will be what might be called *testimonial* rather than perceptual. For what brings a person into the proper-name-using practice involving 'NN', when she hears various things about *x* from people (either producers or already established consumers) discussing *x*, using 'NN' to refer to him, is her learning the truth that 'that is NN', where 'that' makes a perfectly good demonstrative reference to *x*, which draws, in its determination of *x* as its reference, upon the information conveyed about him by the discussants' testimony. This is precisely parallel to the way in which perceptual demonstratives draw, in their reference determination, upon the information about the object in question which is available in perception. Similarly, the subject's grasp of such testimonial demonstratives depends upon her actually receiving this information—that is to say, upon her *hearing* what is being said about the person in question. Thus, testimonial demonstratives are likewise essentially experiential; and so the consumers in proper-name-using practices constitute no threat to my argument. Second, such name-using consumers in any case provide an extremely implausible model for perceptual reference to mind-independent things. Recall that the ultimate purpose of the Strawson Argument is to establish that the correct account of how perceptual experiences refer to mind-independent objects is applicable only to experience-involving contents, and therefore cannot be applied directly to beliefs in a way which finesses the content-determining role of experiences. The present suggestion is that consumers in proper-name-using practices yield a counterexample to this claim by providing a model for perceptual reference which is not essentially experiential. Yet the most significant distinction between producers and consumers in this context is surely that it is only the former who are capable of employing the name in question *directly* on the basis of perception, in a judgement like 'NN is *F*', without appeal to some identity statement involving a demonstrative identification of the person in question: 'That person is *F*', and 'That person is NN'. So the consumer model of perceptual reference is untenable, and the counterexample fails.

What about the proposal that the most basic reference to mind-independent particulars is achieved by impure descriptions embedding non-experiential indexicals: Ideas such as 'the red ball a little to the right in front of me now'? Again this is a vast topic, and dogmatism is inevitable. My answer is that a person's grasp of such Ideas also depends upon his capacity for certain essentially experiential demonstrative identifications of things in the world. Indeed, I would claim that this dependence is multiply overdetermined. First, the subject's grasp of the egocentric spatial concepts by means of which the target object is identified on the basis of such indexical-embedding descriptions arguably depends upon his prior perceptual demonstrative reference to particular objects around him which stand in the relevant spatial relations with him. If not, the obvious alternative—and the only one which I can think of—is that this depends instead upon his tactual-kinaesthetic demonstrative identification of the spatial relations in question through performing various actions canonically characterized in terms of these spatial concepts: '*That* is my right', and so on. Thus, again, it depends upon essentially experiential demonstrative reference. Second, a similar dependence upon perceptual demonstrative reference very likely also obtains with respect to the predicative concepts involved in such descriptions. For example, a person's knowledge of which colour red is in my view ultimately depends upon his perceptual demonstrative identification of it, as 'that colour'. Third, a person's reference to himself, as a spatial particular in the world, using the first-person pronoun, 'I', or, as it is in the indexical-embedding description above, 'me', also depends upon his perceptual demonstrative identification of such things. On one quite popular view (Evans, 1982, ch. 7; Cassam, 1997), this is because the first-person pronoun is itself effectively a perceptual demonstrative, drawing in its determination of the person using it as its reference upon his tactual-kinaesthetic experience of his bodily self. This view is not without difficulties. For example, it appears to have the implausible consequence that a person without tactual-kinaesthetic sensation is incapable of referring to himself using the first person. Its most promising alternative also supports the dependence which I require, though, of a person's grasp of the first person upon his perceptual demonstrative reference to spatial particulars. This would be a view on which grasp of the first person is dependent upon its use in a *Simple Theory of Perception* (Strawson, 1966, 2.ii; Evans, 1982, ch. 7; Peacocke, 1992, ch. 3; Brewer, 1992; Campbell, 1984–5, 1994, esp. ch. 6; Cassam, 1989, 1997) by appeal to which a person makes sense of the course of his experience, *and his capacity for perceptual demonstrative reference to particular things in the world around him*, as the joint upshot of the way things mind-independently are out there and his own continuous spatio-temporal route through them, as one object among many, whose capacity for perception and action is conditioned by his location amongst them.[23] Fourth, similar comments to those which I have just made about the first person might equally be made about the use of the present-tense indexical 'now' in the description above, although in this case the difficulties with the first, perceptual demonstrative, view about the nature of the temporal reference involved would, I think, be even more severe, and a view highlighting the role of explicitly present tense thinking in a Simple Theory of Perception correlatively even more attractive. Thus, as with the case of proper names, the possibility of impure indexical-embedding descriptive reference to mind-independent things is no threat to my argument. The indispensable and most basic mode of such reference is by means of essentially experiential demonstratives.

A third, and final, line of objection to this final phase of the Strawson Argument goes like this. Let us grant that reference to mind-independent spatial particulars depends upon a most basic level of *demonstrative* reference, which essentially exploits the subject's actual relations with the objects in question. Let us even grant that the paradigm exemplar of this basic mode of reference is the *perceptual* demonstrative. Nevertheless, it does not follow that this crucial and most basic mode of reference is *essentially* experiential. After all, a blindsighted patient, for example, apparently refers to a particular object in her blind field when encouraged to point to it. Yet she has no experience of it. 'I simply cannot see *that*,' she may say whilst pointing to a particular object, 'although I have a feeling that it is there.'[24] This appears to be a direct counterexample to my claim that the correct account of how perceptual experiences make reference to particular mind-independent things cannot be applied to any non-experiential reference to such things, even if I am right that the correct account of experiential reference gives a central place to perceptual demonstratives. In response, I simply insist that a blindsighted patient does not *understand* any demonstrative thought which she may appear to others to be expressing. For,

---

[23] See Ch. 6, especially 6.1, for a detailed development of this idea; 6.2 draws out its epistemological consequences.

[24] See Weiskrantz, 1986, for a comprehensive study of such cases.

even though she may point to an object and mouth the word 'that', and even though she may thereby be taken by others— especially those unaware of her blindsight condition—to be expressing a thought *about that object*, she has absolutely no idea *which* object is in question, and therefore has no Idea of that particular object. So she is incapable of genuinely understanding any content which refers to that thing rather than anything else. She is therefore incapable of making reference to it in genuine belief. The same goes, I would say, for any other case in which it appears that a person is making (quasi)-perceptual demonstrative reference to a spatial particular without a conscious presentation of it in experience. Hence the move from perceptual demonstrative reference to essentially experiential reference is valid.

Bringing the whole of this discussion together, here is a relatively formal presentation of my argument for premise (P1), above, that there is a class of beliefs about the spatial world, E, whose members have the contents which they do—that a particular mind-independent thing is determinately thus and so— only in virtue of their standing in certain relations with various actual or possible perceptual experiences. Premise (1) follows from my assumption (W) above (2.1), and licenses (2). Premise (3) follows from my argument above for the thesis that a person's successful perceptual reference to a mind-independent particular puts him in a position to acquire the knowledge that he is indeed referring to that thing. I argued above that (5) is normally, if not always, true. For, however detailed or extensive 'F' may be, S is not in a position, simply in virtue of referring to *a* as he does, knowledgeably to rule out the possibility of a massive qualitative reduplication elsewhere in the universe of the relevant sector of his environment. In the abnormal circumstances in which S has independent knowledge that there is at most one F in the universe, then the argument can be run for a related subject, S′, who thinks of *a* in just the same way as S does, yet lacks this knowledge. Premise (6) follows from (3) and (5), given my definition of epistemic possibility. Premise (7) is a consequence of Russell's (1905, 1993, ch. 15) Theory of Descriptions. Premise (8) follows from (4), (6), and (7), by *reductio ad absurdum*. I have recently defended the move from (2) and (8) to (9). Premise (10) follows from (9), to complete my response to the dilemma raised above (2.1) for my premise (P1); and the core of that premise, (11), follows directly from (10).

(1) Reference to spatial particulars is possible.

(2) Consider a person, S, with a perceptually based belief about a particular mind-independent thing, *a*.

(3) S knows that he is referring to *a*.

(4) Suppose for *reductio* that S's Idea of *a* is purely descriptive, constituted wholly by the general description, 'the F'.

(5) Multiple satisfaction with respect to 'F' is an epistemic possibility for S.

(6) There is a possible world in which 'F' is multiply satisfied and S refers in the way in which he does to *a*.

(7) 'The F' fails to 'refer' in any possible world in which 'F' is multiply satisfied.

(8) S's Idea of *a* is not purely descriptive.

(9) S's Idea of *a* involves some kind of demonstrative with respect to which his experience is essential to his grasp of which object is in question.

(10) Perceptual reference is essentially experiential: nothing non-experiential can refer to spatial particulars in the way in which experience does.

(11) Beliefs about spatial particulars have their contents only in virtue of their relations with perceptual experiences.

Put like this, an important final objection to the very heart of the Strawson Argument comes to mind.[25] For there is a striking similarity between my sub-argument (3)–(8) and a very familiar sceptical argument. Since almost everyone wants to resist the sceptical argument, though, this similarity generates an obvious problem: it may be possible to raise a parallel objection to my (3)–(8) to that offered in reply to the sceptic. The familiar sceptical argument is as follows, where *p* is anything which the subject, S, is supposed to know on the basis of perception, and *h* is some sceptical hypothesis, on which *p* is false, such as that the subject is being deceived by a malicious demon.

---

[25] A number of people have raised something along these lines with me in discussion. The present formulation is derived from correspondence with Manuel Pérez Otero.

(S1) *S* does not know that not-*h*.

(S2) If *S* does not know that not-*h*, then *S* does not know that *p*.

∴ (S3) *S* does not know that *p*.

My argument (3)–(8) can be re-ordered as follows, where *r* is the hypothesis that massive reduplication with respect to 'the *F*' is actual.

(B0) Assume for *reductio* that *S*'s reference to *a* is purely descriptive.

(B1) *S* does not know that not-*r*.

(B2) If *S* does not know that not-*r*, then *S* does not know that he is referring to *a*.

∴ (B3) *S* does not know that he is referring to *a*.

(B4) But *S* does know that he is referring to *a*.

∴ (B5) *S*'s reference to *a* is not purely descriptive.

This form of objection to the Strawson Argument clearly raises many difficult issues. I cannot possibly engage with all of these here. All that I can do is to make, very briefly, and without any of the argument required to defend them adequately, what seem to me to be the two most important points. First, it is extremely implausible, in my view, to reject the closure principle which underlies (S2) and (B2). This is the principle that if *S* knows that *p* and *S* knows that *p* implies *q*, then *S* is able on that basis to deduce the knowledge that *q*. Although rejecting this principle, and therefore denying premise (S2), is perhaps the standard response to the sceptical argument, I regard it as untenable, not least because this makes it extremely difficult to see how an adequate account might be given of the genuine possibility of a person's extending his knowledge by deductive argument. Second, the analogue of what I take to be the correct response to the sceptical argument is unacceptable as an objection to my own argument, (B0)–(B5). The right response to the sceptic is to deny (S1). *S* may well know that not-*h*. For he can infer this from many things which he knows directly on the basis of perception, like *p*, his knowing which does not require *prior* knowledge of the falsity of *h*. A person cannot similarly infer that massive reduplication is not actual, though, from what he knows directly on the basis of perception. This is precisely the point that massive reduplication is always an epistemic possibility. Thus, I contend, my argument for (P1) is perfectly compatible with a reasoned rejection of the sceptical argument given above.[26]

This Strawson Argument establishes premise (P1) of my argument for (H), then. The class of beliefs, E, whose contents have so far been shown to depend upon their standing in certain relations with various perceptual experiences contains all those which are about particular mind-independent things, those which are determined as true or false by the way such spatial particulars objectively are, and make reference to those particular things simply as a matter of what the subject knows about their reference in virtue of understanding their content. I think that it could plausibly be argued that E should be extended to include beliefs making reference in this way simply to certain perceptible properties of mind-independent objects whilst not actually referring to any particular such object, such as the belief that that colour (demonstratively identified) is scarlet. Again, the argument would turn upon the conditions required for a person to have a conception of a unique such property in mind. I shall not give any such argument here. For, first, the conclusion which I have already established is sufficient for me to proceed with the overall argument of Part I; and, second, I shall return to consider the predicative component of our worldly beliefs in Chapter 6 below.

---

[26] See Ch. 4, n. 2, for further discussion of this sceptical argument and one version of what I call here the standard response to it; and see 7.3 for a development of my own response to the argument.

3

Experience and Reason

The second premise of my argument for (H), (P2) above, claims that the crucial content-determining relations between beliefs and experiences, whose existence I established in the previous chapter, must be reason-giving relations. The role of perceptual experiences in furnishing empirical beliefs with determinate contents consists in their provision of reasons for such beliefs. By this, I mean that a person's experiences enable her to grasp various contents which are apt to figure in rationalizing explanations of her holding certain beliefs about the mind-independent world around her, to figure, that is, as *her reasons* for holding them. In other words, I do not just mean that perceptual experiences are such as to make it advisable relative to some externally prescribed goal for the subject to adopt such beliefs. Nor do I mean this along with the claim that they are in some way causally relevant to her actually acquiring the beliefs in question. It is rather that perceptual experiences put a person in a condition, the causal relevance of which to her acquisition of certain empirical beliefs is dependent upon its making such beliefs reasonable from her point of view.[1] Reasons, in this sense, present themselves as such from the subject's point of view. The question which I want to consider now is why we should believe that the content-determining role of perceptual experiences necessarily requires that they provide reasons of this kind for empirical beliefs.[2]

---

[1] See Brewer, 1995*b*, for further discussion of these issues.

[2] The fact that experiences provide reasons for beliefs may be thought to be intuitively obvious. For perceptual beliefs are rationally held, and it is hard to know what else, other than experiences, could provide the subject's reasons for them. Nevertheless, both the precise sense in which such beliefs *are* rationally held, and the considerations which rule out any account of their being so which does not make reference to the reason-giving role of experiences, require extended discussion. So I prefer here to give my own independent positive argument for (P2), by investigating the question how exactly perceptual experiences

3.1 *The Switching Argument*

In crude outline, the idea here is this. We have seen that the empirical significance of beliefs depends in some way upon their relations with perceptual experiences. These relations contribute essentially to the determination of objective truth-conditions for particular beliefs, which is what makes them genuinely beliefs *about* mind-independent reality. Now, suppose that these content-determining relations between experiences and beliefs are not reason-giving relations. It follows that for any pair of empirical contents, x and y, a person's perceptual experiences give her no more reason to believe that x than to believe that y, and vice versa. Consider, then, a person, S, who believes that p, where this is supposed to be an empirical belief, about how things are in the mind-independent world around her. Since their relations with certain perceptual experiences play an *essential* role in the determination of the contents of empirical beliefs, there is a range of alternative such beliefs—beliefs which she might have had instead—whose difference in content with her actual belief that p would have been due *entirely* to their standing in the relevant relations with different perceptual experiences. Suppose that the belief that q is one of these.

So, the situation is this. S actually believes that p, because her actual perceptual experiences determine this, as opposed to q, as the empirical content of her belief. She does not believe that q. Had her perceptual experiences been appropriately different, though, her position would have been precisely the reverse: she would have believed that q, and not believed that p. Yet the relevant content-determining relations between experiences and beliefs are not reason-giving relations. So S's actual perceptual experiences give her no more reason to believe that p than to believe that q. Thus, she has, and could have, no reason whatsoever to believe that p rather than that q, or vice versa. For, recall, nothing other than their relations with experiences decides between the two contents—this is how q was introduced. Which belief she actually has is due entirely to the course of her perceptual experience. Any supposed difference between

might make a genuine contribution to the determination of empirical belief content: the Switching Argument below.

believing that *p* and believing that *q* is therefore nothing to her; for there *could be* no reason *for her* to decide between them. So she does not really *understand* them *as alternatives*. Believing that *p* and believing that *q* are identical for her. Hence the supposedly content-determining role of *S*'s perceptual experiences is empty. For there is nothing more, or less, to the content of a belief than the way the subject takes the world to be. Thus, if the relevant relations between experiences and beliefs are not reason-giving relations, then they contribute *nothing* to the determination of specific worldly truth-conditions for empirical beliefs.

The argument can obviously be generalized in two ways. First, the content *q* might be replaced throughout with any other content from the relevant range of alternatives to *p*, whose differentiation from *p* is likewise supposed to be due *entirely* to its standing in the relevant content-determining relations with different possible, but non-actual, perceptual experiences. Second, *S*'s initial belief that *p* might be replaced by any other empirical belief, of any other person, whose content is supposed to be partially determined by its relations with that person's perceptual experiences. The result of these generalizations is this. However the putative content-determining relations between experiences and beliefs are conceived, in so far as these are supposed not to be reason-giving relations, they contribute nothing to the determination of specific worldly truth-conditions for the empirical beliefs in question. In other words, if perceptual experiences do not provide reasons for empirical beliefs, then the relations in which such beliefs stand to various actual or possible such experiences contribute nothing to the determination of specific empirical contents for the relevant beliefs. Put slightly differently again, only reason-giving relations between perceptual experiences and beliefs could possibly serve the content-determining role required by the first premise of my argument for (H), (P1) above. This is its second premise, (P2).

The form of my argument for (P2), henceforth the *Switching Argument*, is that of what Peacocke calls 'the *switching* tactic' (1988, pp. 475 ff.).[3] A more familiar historical paradigm is

---

[3] So called, I presume, because the tactic is to object to a theory on the grounds that it is in principle incapable of making sense of switches which are by the theory's own lights crucial.

provided by Strawson's (1959, ch. 3, 1966, pt. III, sect. 2, esp.
pp. 168 ff., and 1974*b*) reading of Kant's (1929, A341/B399 ff.)
argument against Descartes's (1986, pp. 107 ff.) substance dualism. According to this Kantian argument, substance dualism
entails the coherence of a distinction between qualitative and
numerical identity for immaterial minds; yet the dualist's own
conception of such things as exhaustively characterized by what
is infallibly given to their own subjective point of view denies her
the resources to give any genuine content to the idea of two qualitatively identical but numerically distinct minds. So, the substance dualist depends upon a distinction—between qualitative
and numerical identity for immaterial minds—which she is, by
her own lights, incapable of making. Thus, the position is internally inconsistent.

Similarly, here, we are to consider a theorist who insists that
non-reason-giving relations between perceptual experiences and
empirical beliefs are essential to the determination of specific
contents for the latter. Such a theorist is therefore committed to
the existence of pairs of beliefs with genuinely distinct contents,
the distinction between which is entirely due to their relations
with different possible courses of perceptual experience for their
subject. For he admits that their relations with experiences are
essential to the determination of the empirical contents of certain beliefs—that is to say, he endorses (P1). Given his own conception of the nature of these content-determining relations,
though, as non-reason-giving relations, this entails an overall
conception of belief content which countenances the following
situation. A person believes that p, and does not believe that q,
even though he has, and could have, no more reason to believe
that p than to believe that q and vice versa, that is, no reason to
believe that p as opposed to believing that q or vice versa. It follows from this that the theorist in question is committed to a
conception of belief content which is more discerning than the
subject's own understanding of the contents of his beliefs. For he
is obliged to distinguish p and q, even in the face of the fact that
they are absolutely on a par as far as the subject's reasons for, or
against, endorsing them in belief are concerned. In other words,
he is obliged to distinguish between them even though it is necessarily irrational for the subject, given full understanding of both
of them, ever to take different attitudes towards them, or, as

Evans puts it (1982, p. 19), to accept (reject) one while rejecting (accepting), or being agnostic about, the other. Thus, the purported distinction between p and q outstrips anything which is essential to the subject's understanding of these contents. This is surely unacceptable by anybody's standards. For the content of a belief is precisely, no more and no less than, the way the subject takes things to be. Hence the position under consideration is incoherent. It entails a distinction which, by its own lights, it is incapable of making. So, if their relations with perceptual experiences are to contribute essentially to the determination of the empirical contents of beliefs, then experiences must provide reasons for beliefs: premise (P2) of my argument for (H).

This all sounds a little abstract; but the crucial point is really quite simple. I think that it is best illustrated by the failure of a putative counterexample to my claim that any content-determining relations between experiences and beliefs are necessarily reason-giving relations. Of course, it might be admitted, the determination of empirical content draws essentially upon certain relations between perceptual experiences and the beliefs which have this content. The experiences which figure in these relations need not provide reasons for the beliefs to which they are related in this content-determining way, though. Instead, perhaps they 'indicate' certain worldly phenomena, in virtue of the various systematic causal relations in which they stand to these external items.[4] This empirical significance may then be transmitted to the beliefs to which these experiences in turn give rise, or with which they are otherwise associated by whatever relations are proposed as partially determinative of belief content. However exactly this position is to be developed, the crucial point is that it is supposed to secure empirical contents for beliefs on the basis of their explicitly *non*-reason-giving relations with experiences. For, although the relevant experiences stand in various relations with the worldly phenomena which they are thereby supposed to indicate, they do nothing to make beliefs about just those phenomena any more appropriate *from the*

---

[4] Fodor (1987, ch. 4) gives an illuminating discussion of the way in which such causal relations might be specified, although he presents his account as one of the direct determination of *belief* contents, bypassing any essential role for perceptual experiences. For the reasons given in the previous chapter, I reject any such account.

subject's point of view than beliefs about any alternative such phenomena, which might reliably have caused the relevant experiences instead.

A familiar, although in my view mistaken, account of our experiences of, and beliefs about, secondary qualities provides an illustrative example of the proposal. On this view, sensations of certain immediately recognizable types constitute our experiences of the secondary qualities of the things around us, in virtue of the systematic causal relations between the two. The sensations in question are specific modifications of conscious experience, the subject's recognition of which on any particular occasion, as tokens of the relevant type, is supposed to be unproblematic: subjectively evident, or 'given'.[5] The corresponding secondary qualities of mind-independent objects are those microphysical properties, or massive disjunctions of such, which causally explain the occurrence of sensations of the type in question in normal observers under normal circumstances.[6]

---

[5] I return to a critical discussion of any position which attempts to exploit the order of epistemological priority implicit in this view in an account of perceptual knowledge in Ch. 4, esp. 4.2, below.

[6] This is sometimes called the 'primary quality theory of secondary qualities' (e.g. Jackson, 1998). It shares with the dispositional theory the view that the individuation of secondary quality experiences is prior to the individuation of the corresponding secondary qualities themselves. It shares with Campbell's (1993*a*) 'Simple View' the claim that secondary qualities are the categorical grounds of objects' dispositions to appear in certain ways to us. Note that the microphysical features to which secondary quality predicates refer—at least in their normal, unprimed occurrences (see the next paragraph of the text for my elucidation of Peacocke's (1983, pp. 20 ff.) notion of 'primed predicates')—are mind-independent. So it is incorrect to assign the difficulties to which the current account gives rise to the peculiar status of *secondary* qualities in the world, in contrast to the mind-independence of the worldly phenomena in connection with which the idea of non-reason-giving content-determining relations between experiences and beliefs is explicitly proposed as a counterexample to premise (P2) of my argument for (H). My choice of this particular account of our experiences of, and beliefs about, secondary qualities as an illustration is intended to finesse the further confusions which I think are inevitable when a parallel, non-reason-giving account of *primary* quality experience is combined with an attempt to do justice to Locke's (1975, II.viii, esp. sects. 15 ff.) claim that, unlike our ideas of secondary qualities, our ideas of primary qualities *resemble* the primary qualities in objects which are their cause. Locke himself was deeply confused at just this point; and the confusion is well preserved in any such view—to my mind the current orthodoxy (see McGinn, 1983, for a paradigm case of this). I think that Michael Ayers (1991, pp. 68 ff.) correctly identifies its

Peacocke's (1983, pp. 20 ff.) introduction of 'primed predicates' helps to clarify the proposal. Red' experiences are those colour experiences which are normally produced by red objects. Correlatively, red objects are those which normally produce red' experiences. Although the former claim serves to introduce the notion of observational-predicate priming, it is the latter which captures the correct order of explanation. For token red' experiences are unproblematically identifiable as experiences of the same subjective type by their subject. Red objects are those which have the (perhaps massively disjunctive) microphysical property which normally produces red' experiences: this defines what redness in the world actually is. Red' experiences *indicate* the presence of red objects in virtue of the reliable relations between them. Beliefs that certain mind-independent things are red acquire their content, in turn, as beliefs that those things have just that colour—that is to say, that microphysical property—on the basis of their relations with red' experiences. They are precisely the beliefs which are normally formed in response to such experiences. This is what makes them beliefs that the things in question are *red*.

This position is an illustration of the kind of counterexample which I described above. It introduces a relation of *indication* holding between perceptual experiences and determinate mind-independent phenomena with the following two properties. First, this serves in turn to provide certain appropriately related beliefs with their empirical content, as beliefs about just those mind-independent phenomena. Second, it does so other than by appeal to the idea that having the experiences in question provides the subject with a *reason*, which he recognizes as such from his point of view, to endorse the relevant beliefs. Thus, the proposed content-determining relations between perceptual experiences, with their causally accomplished worldly indication, and empirical beliefs are *not* reason-giving relations. Having a red' experience in itself gives the subject no more reason to form beliefs about the microphysical structure constitutive of something's *being red* than beliefs about any other such structure. For

source in Locke's ambivalence between two radically different conceptions of *ideas*, 'one broadly Aristotelian or Scholastic, the other owing more to Epicurean and Stoic ideas' (p. 68).

it is simply the occurrence of a sensation of a particular identifiable type, which is intrinsically, and *from the subject's point of view*, no more appropriately, or intelligibly, associated with *that* structure than with any other. Nevertheless, it is supposed to indicate the presence of just that microphysical property, as opposed to any other, because that is the property which happens to be its normal cause. Hence it is that property which he believes is instantiated when he believes that there is something red in front of him. His beliefs about the redness of things therefore acquire their empirical significance—in the sense that they succeed in being beliefs to the effect that things in the world have a particular microphysical structure, that is, beliefs which are determined as true or false by whether or not the things in question have the microphysical structure which is the normal cause of red′ experiences—in virtue of the relations which they bear to red′-type experiences, even though these experiences give him no reason to take the world to contain just that property rather than any other. Indeed, had it been a quite different property in the world—a quite different microphysical structure, that is—which happened to be the normal cause of red′ experiences, then his beliefs about redness would, on this account, have been beliefs about that instead, in this sense of being determined as true or false by whether or not that property is appropriately instantiated, regardless of the fact that what is supposed to provide such beliefs with their determinate content—namely their relations with red′ experiences—is exactly the same in both cases.

The consequence of this proposal, then, is that the putative source of the empirical content of a person's beliefs about redness in the world is, *as far as the subject himself is concerned*, entirely neutral on which property of things their redness actually turns out to be. In believing that there is something red in front of him, a person is bound to be believing that there is something which is some way or other which things can be, and sometimes are out there. Furthermore, given that redness is defined as the *normal* cause of red′ experiences, he will normally be right that there is something that way in front of him. Yet he has not the slightest idea *which* way this is, in the sense that had it been a quite different way, he would have been none the wiser. Although it appears to succeed in assigning determinate worldly truth-conditions to a person's beliefs about the colours of things, the account on offer does so in a way which guarantees the thinker's ignorance about which of a range of alternative such truth-conditions these actually are, in this particular case, his ignorance about which of range of alternative microphysical structural properties redness actually is. Hence it must be wrong to claim that he nevertheless believes that the thing in question is just that way—red—rather than any other. So the account under consideration fails after all to provide a satisfactory explanation of the contents of a person's beliefs about the colours of things around him.[7]

The argument here can be put more explicitly as an instance of the switching tactic which I outlined in the abstract above. According to the present account of our experiences of, and beliefs about, secondary qualities, a person's beliefs about various things around him, to the effect that they are red, are beliefs to the effect that the things in question have a specific microphysical structure, call it M—this is what redness *is*, on the account in question.[8] They have these truth-conditions because

---

[7] It might be thought that I have made this argument too easy for myself by selecting a particularly implausible illustration of the proposed counterexample. Surely, a more plausible view would be one on which empirical beliefs have their contents determined in part by their relations with perceptual experiences which have some kind of non-conceptual representational content (e.g. Peacocke, 1992). (See 5.1 for my account of the distinction between conceptual and non-conceptual mental states and representational contents.) At this point in the dialectic, though, the proponent of this alternative faces a dilemma. If, on the one hand, he claims that these content-determining relations are not reason-giving, in my sense, then I claim that his position is on a par with that of the proponent of the familiar account of our experiences of, and beliefs about, secondary qualities, to which I am currently objecting in the main text. A minimally modified Switching Argument goes through against this first version of the alternative. If, on the other hand, he insists that these content-determining relations are reason-giving, then his account no longer constitutes a counterexample to my claim that only reason-giving relations between experiences and beliefs will do to provide the latter with determinate empirical contents. Furthermore, I argue in 5.3 below that reasons of the relevant kind can only be provided by fully conceptual mental states. Peacocke (1992) opts for the second horn of my dilemma, although not as a counterexample to (R), which he would, I think, accept; but he would resist my objection to the coherence of this proposal that *non-conceptual* perceptual experiences nevertheless provide reasons for empirical beliefs. See 5.3 for extended discussion of his account.

[8] When I talk of beliefs *to the effect that* things are M, say, I mean beliefs which are determined as true or false depending upon whether or not the things

they are his normal responses to red' experiences, whose normal
cause is things' being M. Such beliefs have quite different contents to any beliefs which he might have had to the effect that
the things in question have some quite different microphysical
structure, N, say. Had being N been the normal cause of his red'
experiences, though, his beliefs that various things around him
are red would have been the quite different beliefs to the effect
that the things in question are N. Yet, in that counterfactual
case, everything supposedly involved in the determination of
these alternative contents would be identical from the subject's
point of view to what is involved in the determination of the contents of his actual beliefs about red things around him, to the
effect that they are M. Thus, it is proposed that the subject actually has beliefs to the effect that things are M, as opposed to
beliefs to the effect that they are N, even though, had it been precisely the reverse, he would himself have been none the wiser. So
the contribution of his red' experiences to the determination of
the contents of his beliefs is to induce discriminations in their
truth-conditions of which he is himself entirely ignorant. The
upshot of such non-reason-giving content-determining relations
between experiences and beliefs, then, as I argued in the abstract
above, is an account of belief content which unacceptably transcends the subject's understanding of his own beliefs. It depends
upon distinctions in content which cannot be sustained.⁹

   If this is correct, then the present account faces a difficulty
which is equal and opposite to one of Descartes's (1986). On the
Cartesian account, a person's knowledge of the contents of his
own thoughts is absolutely guaranteed by the defining charac-

in question are M, beliefs, that is, for which M is a determinant of their truth-
conditions, at the level of Fregean *Bedeutung*, or semantic value. See Dummett,
1978, and Evans, 1982, pp. 8 ff., for extensive explication of the notion of *semantic value* which I am using here and throughout this book. Roughly, the semantic value of a singular term or predicate is that object or property whose
association with the term or predicate in question fixes the contribution which
that term or predicate makes to the determination of the truth-conditions of
sentences in which it occurs (in transparent position). I also write, slightly slop-
pily, of the semantic value of an Idea or concept, to refer to the semantic value
of a singular term or predicate which has that Idea or concept as its Fregean
sense.

   ⁹ See 3.4 below for an objection that my requirements upon understanding
here are untenably demanding.

teristic of the category to which they belong. For thoughts are essentially things whose nature is exhausted by their subject's infallible knowledge of them. The contents of a person's mind simply sit there entirely transparent to him in every respect. This is a feature of the extreme rationalism which I rejected in arguing that certain beliefs have the contents which they do only in virtue of their standing in certain relations with various actual or possible perceptual experiences above. In making a person's knowledge of his own thoughts so easy, though, Descartes renders knowledge of the mind-independent world unattainable. For the latter, on this account, depends upon a person's knowledge that there is some correspondence between the contents of his thoughts and the mind-independent facts. Yet it is notoriously difficult to give any satisfactory account of how this might be possible for him, given the Cartesian starting point.[10] Certainly, Descartes's own ingenious detour via his knowledge of the existence of a non-deceiving God is deeply problematic. So, a quick way with self-knowledge constitutes an obstacle to knowledge of the world. Conversely, the current proposal about the relationship between colour experiences and beliefs seems designed precisely to secure knowledge of mind-independent things. Yet it does so, if at all, only at the expense of forcing a person's knowledge of the truth-conditions of his own beliefs quite out of reach. The account of content-determination ensures that beliefs about the world are normally true. Yet I have argued that it also has the unacceptable consequence that a person has no real understanding of how he thereby believes the world to be. Thus, a quick way with knowledge of the world constitutes an obstacle to self-knowledge and understanding.[11]

Two strategies are possible in reply to my Switching Argument against the familiar account of our experiences of,

---

[10] See my critique of classical foundationalism in 4.2 below, for more discussion of the options and difficulties here.

[11] Note that this problem is a serious one for Locke's anti-Cartesian account of perceptual knowledge as I sketch it in Chapter 1. The account of experiential indication involved here is very like Locke's view of the way in which intuitively known variations in a person's ideas represent mind-independent variation in the external qualities which cause them in him. The present problem also lies at the heart of Ayers's objection to this Lockean conception of ideas as 'blank effects' (Ayers, 1991, pp. 62 ff. and pt. III).

and beliefs about, secondary qualities, which I have presented as an attempt to exploit non-reason-giving content-determining relations between perceptual experiences and empirical beliefs. First, it might be argued that the non-reason-giving account is not committed to a person's ignorance of the semantic values of certain of the concepts figuring in the contents of his empirical beliefs in the way in which I suggest. Second, it might be argued that, in so far as a non-reason-giving account is indeed committed to this ignorance, it is nevertheless perfectly compatible with the relevant beliefs having just those contents all the same. In 3.2 and 3.3 respectively, I consider two versions of the first strategy, the first of which attempts to supply the required knowledge, on the part of the subject, of the truth-conditions of his beliefs about the colours of things around him *by description*, the second of which insists that the present account already provides it, for a person can simply *reuse* the concepts given application to the world by their relations with experiences in beliefs about the truth-conditions of his own first-order beliefs. In 3.4, I discuss what seems to me to be the most natural version of the second strategy; and my response to this is completed in 3.5.

3.2 *Knowledge by Description*

The first response which I want to consider, then, is to deny that the present account necessarily consigns a person who believes that there is something red in front of him to ignorance of which property he thereby believes the thing to have. For he may know perfectly well what it is for something to be red, by thinking of redness in the world (correctly, according to the account in question) as, something like, 'the microphysical property which is causally explanatory of this type of experience (making an internal demonstrative reference to his present red' experience) in normal observers under normal circumstances'. There are at least four difficulties with this line of response.[12]

First, there is an obvious danger of circularity in the proposed

---

[12] Further, closely related difficulties with the embedded internal demonstrative reference to particular experience-types emerge below, in my critical discussion of the classical foundationalist approach to perceptual knowledge (4.2).

identification of redness as the cause of red' experiences in normal observers under normal circumstances. For the following two supplementary clauses have to be added in order to make sense of this descriptive identification as it stands: (1) normal observers are, *inter alia*, those in whom red things cause red' experiences in normal circumstances; (2) normal circumstances are, *inter alia*, those in which red things cause red' experiences in normal observers. Yet without an independent constraint upon normality, the resultant identification as a whole is clearly useless. It may be replied, though, that it is possible to specify normality in observers and circumstances quite independently along the following lines. Normal observers are people who perform in such and such a way on certain specific tests of eyesight and general intelligence, are awake, attentive, not wearing dark glasses, and so on; normal circumstances are those in which the subject is facing the relevant object, with nothing between it and him, with his eyes open, in good daylight, and so on.

Second, it is implausible to suggest that a person's beliefs about the perceived colours of things around him essentially require this conceptual sophistication. For example, it is surely possible for a person to believe that a certain item in his environment is red, and know perfectly well how he takes that thing to be, without any explicit understanding of the idea of a normal observer under normal circumstances, even if these notions could be given a non-circular characterization. It may be replied here that *implicit* understanding of such notions is all that is required. The onus is on such a respondent, though, to give some account both of what such implicit understanding consists in, and how it is supposed to provide a satisfactory descriptive source for a person's knowledge of the semantic values of his secondary-quality terms.[13]

This leads on to a third point. Even if the red things in the world are all and only those which produce red' experiences in normal observers under normal circumstances (or are disposed to do so), this is not the only, and certainly not the most basic, way in which a person thinks of their colour when he does so on the basis of such experiences. In other words, not only is it implausible to require the conceptual sophistication implied by

---

[13] See Peacocke, 1998*b*, for sympathetic discussion of these issues.

this descriptive account of colour beliefs, but it is also inappropriate to assign to all of a person's beliefs about the colours of things in the world around him the structural complexity which is currently being proposed. The most simple perceptually based beliefs about such matters are more naturally articulated by way of a demonstrative, 'that colour', than by any causal description. Indeed, the inappropriateness of the present suggestion can be brought out by the fact that a person who knows precisely what colour he believes something is when he sees it in front of him in ordinary viewing conditions can perfectly rationally doubt whether the object in question has the microphysical property causally explanatory of certain specific experiences—just those which he is currently enjoying—in normal observers under normal circumstances. In other words, any such description fails to capture *his* conception of which colour property is in question. So the way in which relations with colour experiences provide empirical significance for a person's beliefs about colours in the world is not by furnishing sensational-experiential effects by reference to which these colours can be identified as their normal causes.

It may be thought that there is still important work to be done by the descriptive identification of redness as 'the microphysical property which is causally explanatory of the occurrence of red' experiences in normal observers under normal circumstances', in a *theorist's* account of the conceptual role of the concept 'red' in connection with such experiences. Given this role, it may then be insisted that red' experiences therefore licence structurally simple demonstrative reference to whichever microphysical property this turns out to be. Thus, my objection that the descriptive theorist invokes excessive structural complexity in his account of reference to secondary qualities in the world is unfounded. In so far as the descriptive identification figures *only* in the theorist's account, though, and is quite unknown to the subject himself, which is to say, in so far as the supposedly content-determining relations between red' experiences and beliefs about redness in the world remain non-reason-giving *from the subject's point of view*, this purely theoretical identification fails to make any contribution to the subject's knowledge of what he is talking about when he describes something as red. The ignorance of semantic value which is fatal to his purported understanding of his beliefs about redness in the world is left untouched.

A fourth and final difficulty is that it is far from clear whether the descriptive view even succeeds in assigning genuinely *object-ive* truth-conditions to a person's beliefs about the colours of things at all. Much will depend here upon the account which is given of the embedded concept of causation. If this is supposed to be given empirical application by its relations with experi-ences in the same way as the colour concepts themselves, then a number of difficulties arise. To begin with, there is Hume's chal-lenge (1975, sect. 7; 1978, I.iii.14), to identify our sensory impres-sion of causation, that is, to identify causation' experiences, in the current terminology. Furthermore, even if this could be done, the likely outcome is some kind of idealist construction of the physical world. For, if causation is conceived of as the relation which is causally explanatory of causation' experiences in nor-mal observers under normal circumstances, in other words, as the relation, R, which normally bears R to causation' experi-ences, then it is far from clear whether 'the property which is *causally* explanatory of red' experiences in normal observers under normal circumstances' is genuinely a conception of a property of mind-independent things at all. If it is not, then the familiar account under consideration, of our experiences of, and beliefs about, secondary qualities, fails in its official task of pro-viding a model for the non-reason-giving determination, by their relations with experiences, of empirical contents for beliefs about *mind-independent* reality. Of course, it may be denied that the correct account of the empirical significance of the concept of causation, which is on this account embedded in a person's descriptive knowledge of which properties the secondary quali-ties of external things are, is to be given on the very same model. In that case, the account is incomplete without an alternative source of empirical content for beliefs about causation; and in any case the first three objections above remain.

3.3 *Conceptual Redeployment*

A second possible reply to the Switching Argument, which is also a version of the first strategy above, of denying ignorance

of semantic value on the non-reason-giving account, is to insist
that a person's knowledge of which property he believes that the
relevant object has, when he believes that there is something red
in front of him, has already been provided for on the familiar
account of secondary qualities under consideration, independently of any descriptive knowledge which the subject may have
about the relation between his red′ experiences and red things in
the world. Indeed, it may be argued, it has been provided for in
a way which has the advantage of *explaining* its notoriously
problematic first-person authority. Recall that the account under
consideration is supposed to explain how a person's belief that
there is something red in front of him is a belief to the effect that
a determinate property of mind-independent objects is instantiated: that microphysical structure which is the normal cause of
the red′ experiences which are suitably related to his beliefs
about redness, and thereby determine their empirical content.
The objection posed by my Switching Argument is then that this
account leaves the subject quite ignorant about which property
he thereby believes is instantiated, when he believes that there is
something red in front of him. So the familiar account fails as an
explanation of a person's beliefs about redness in the world, and
therefore also as a model for non-reason-giving empirical-
content-determining relations between experiences and beliefs
generally. The reply now is that the initial charge is incorrect. A
person is not rendered ignorant about exactly which way he
believes things to be out there, when he believes that they are
red, on this account. For he can simply redeploy the concept of
redness which figures in his first-order belief about the world in
the thought 'I am thinking that there is something *red* in front
of me' (see Burge, 1996, and Peacocke, 1996). Then, whichever
property it is that his first-order belief ascribes, which depends
upon which microphysical property happens to be the normal
cause of red′ sensations and thereby constitute mind-independent redness, his second-order belief will successfully self-ascribe
a belief to the effect that the object in question has just that property. So he does, after all, know exactly how he believes the
object to be, or at least he can authoritatively come to do so if
only he turns his mind to the matter. This routine, then, provides
an authoritative source of knowledge of the semantic values of
his secondary-quality concepts, which is consistent with the cur-

rent account, on which these are determined by the non-reason-giving relations between secondary quality experiences and the beliefs in whose contents such concepts occur. So the Switching Argument is invalid.

I find this response quite unconvincing. Unless he already knows what redness is, he cannot inform himself simply by reusing the *word* in an attempt to tell himself what it is. I am absolutely not insisting here that concept possession is in every case a matter of having some explicit, reductive definition of the concept in question in terms of more basic concepts. That would obviously be viciously regressive. It is just that a person does not grasp a concept unless he knows its semantic value, that is, the contribution which it makes to determining the truth-conditions of beliefs in whose contents it occurs. Only then is he in a position genuinely to understand such beliefs; for only then can he appreciate what their truth-conditions must be. If he does not know this semantic value, then he cannot hope to help matters simply by—apparently—taking on further beliefs, this time about his own beliefs, which invoke the very same concept, and which he therefore equally fails to understand. Although this charade guarantees that the subject's (pseudo-) self-ascription of a (pseudo-) belief about redness will be (pseudo-) true, it leaves him hopelessly ignorant about which truth this is supposed to be, which belief he has thereby self-ascribed. So the appearance that he thereby knows how he supposedly believes the world to be in the first place is just an illusion. Rather, the fatal ignorance at that first-order level is simply recycled at the level of the self-ascription itself. Once again, it is clear that we do not really have an account of genuine belief here at all, that is, belief with understanding, about the mind-independent world, about the subject's own beliefs, or about anything else.[14]

---

[14] I should stress that I mean this objection to apply only to the appeal to conceptual redeployment in response to the challenge raised by my Switching Argument, for a proponent of non-reason-giving content-determining relations between perceptual experiences and empirical beliefs to give an account of a person's knowledge of the semantic values of the concepts figuring in such beliefs. Given a satisfactory account of knowledge of semantic value at this level of first-order beliefs about the world, conceptual redeployment in second-order self-ascriptions does, I believe, have an important place in an account of the authority of a person's knowledge of the contents of his own beliefs.

My objection to this second line of response to the Switching Argument, based upon the conceptual redeployment routine, can itself be put as a switching objection. According to the present account, a person's beliefs that certain things around him are red are beliefs to the effect that the things in question have microphysical structure M. Furthermore, he knows which way he thereby believes such things to be, because he has, or can easily come by, corresponding second-order beliefs that he believes that they are red, which are, by the very same account, beliefs about his first-order beliefs to the effect that these ascribe M. These second-order beliefs have quite different contents to any beliefs which he might have had to the effect that his first-order beliefs ascribe a different microphysical structure, N, say. It is precisely the difference between his actual second-order beliefs and all such non-actual alternatives which constitutes his knowledge of the determinate truth-conditions of his first-order beliefs, in particular, his knowledge of which property redness is, the very knowledge which my original Switching Argument contends he lacks. Had being N been the normal cause of his red' experiences, though, his first-order beliefs that various things around him are red would have been the quite different beliefs to the effect that the things in question have N. Equally, his second order beliefs would have been the quite different beliefs about his first-order beliefs to the effect these do indeed ascribe N. Yet, in that counterfactual case, everything supposedly involved in the determination of these alternative contents for his second-order beliefs would be identical from the subject's own point of view to what is involved in the determination of the contents of his actual beliefs about his first-order beliefs, to the effect that they ascribe M. Thus, it is proposed that the subject actually believes that he has beliefs to the effect that certain things have M, as opposed to beliefs to the effect that they have N, even though, had it been precisely the reverse, he would himself have been none the wiser. So the suggested routine for knowledge of the semantic values of concepts figuring in first-order empirical belief contents induces discriminations in the truth-conditions of the second-order beliefs supposedly constituting such knowledge of which the subject is entirely ignorant. Hence the upshot of the conceptual redeployment response is an account of a person's knowledge of the semantic values of his empirical concepts which unacceptably transcends his own understanding of this knowledge. It depends upon distinctions in the content of this knowledge which cannot be sustained.

My point here is absolutely not that a person does not know which property redness is, in the required sense, unless he knows whether it is M or N, that is, unless he can give an explicit characterization of which microphysical structural property redness in the world is supposed to be. It is, rather, that it is a decisive objection to a proposed account of what a person's knowledge of which property redness is consists in that precisely the same account might equally be given as an account of what his knowledge of which property redness is consists in, in a counterfactual situation in which redness is a quite different property. Nothing can constitute knowledge of which property redness is which is neutral on which property redness actually turns out to be.[15] The moral, I think, is clear. Unless the basic account of content determination for first-order empirical beliefs itself constitutes an account of the subject's knowledge of their truth-conditions, no amount of higher-order conceptual redeployment can genuinely remedy his ignorance. The second possible reply to my initial Switching Argument against the familiar account of secondary-quality experiences and beliefs therefore fails.[16]

3.4 *Natural Kinds and Proper Names*

The third possible reply to the Switching Argument which I shall consider here develops the second strategy, which I distinguished above as follows. It does indeed follow from the proposed account of our colour experiences and beliefs that a person is in a sense ignorant of the semantic values of the secondary-quality

---

[15] See 3.4 below for extended discussion this crucial condition.

[16] The difficulties with this conceptual redeployment account of knowledge of semantic values and truth-conditions is closely related to issues discussed below, first, in connection with the use of antisceptical transcendental arguments in the context of classical foundationalism (4.2.6), and, second, in connection with the prima facie incompatibility of content externalism with a plausible account of a person's knowledge of the contents of his own beliefs (8.3).

concepts which she applies to the things around her; but this is perfectly compatible with these concepts figuring in the contents of her empirical beliefs all the same, which have precisely these contents in virtue of their non-reason-giving relations with her perceptual experiences according to just this account. Indeed, it might be insisted that ignorance of semantic value in this sense is a familiar phenomenon, perfectly compatible with grasp of a determinate empirical content. Consider, for example, beliefs about natural kinds. A person's beliefs about gold, or to the effect that something is gold, say, may be about just that chemical stuff—gold—and may be beliefs to the effect that the thing in question is sample of it, regardless of whether she knows which stuff this is, and regardless of whether she can distinguish it in any way whatsoever from the stuff which presents the same superficial appearance on Twin Earth, or from fools' gold around here. Thus, it cannot be right to reject non-reason-giving content-determining relations between perceptual experiences and empirical beliefs on the basis that these lead to this kind of ignorance of semantic value with respect to the relevant empirical concepts. Such ignorance is perfectly acceptable.

Note that this is a quite different response to my criticism of the familiar secondary-quality model from the first reply which I considered above (3.2), on which knowledge of semantic value is supposed to be provided by description in these cases. The present suggestion is not that natural-kind beliefs involve implicit descriptions of the form 'the microphysical structure of S_1, S_2, . . ., S_n' (where the S_i's are various samples of gold, say, with which the subject has had suitable contact—through perception, testimony, or whatever) and that all beliefs about particular mind-independent things to the effect that they are determinately thus and so are to be assimilated to these descriptive natural kind beliefs. It is rather that beliefs about natural kinds constitute a ubiquitous example of cases in which a person succeeds in having beliefs to the effect that certain things have a particular microphysical structure—that is, beliefs which are determined as true or false by whether or not the relevant things have that microphysical structure—and beliefs about that structure—in the sense of beliefs which are determined as true or false by whether or not things with just that microphysical structure have the relevant property, which gold things are believed to have—in the absence of any detailed knowledge of which structure this is. Indeed, the present respondent will continue, everything involved in the subject's conception of which property is in question might be shared by a Twin Earth counterpart, who equally succeeds in referring to a determinate property in the beliefs which she expresses using the word 'gold', whilst these are nevertheless beliefs to the effect that the relevant objects have a quite different chemical composition, or beliefs about things with a quite different chemical composition, in the sense given above. Thus, a person might believe that certain things are gold—Au—as opposed to believing that they are twin gold—ABC, say—even though, had it been precisely the reverse, she would herself have been none the wiser. Here, there is determinacy in content and truth-conditions which outstrips anything in the subject's knowledge of the appropriately determining semantic values. Yet these are clearly *her beliefs*, if anyone ever has beliefs about natural kinds, which I simply assume that they do. Hence this type of ignorance of semantic value is consistent with the understanding required of a person for her to be the subject of the beliefs in question. Similarly, it must therefore be a mistake for me to infer, in the *reductio* Switching Argument given above, from a structurally similar position in the envisaged case of the secondary qualities, that the subject has no real understanding of her own beliefs. Genuine understanding is, after all, perfectly compatible with wholly non-reason-giving content-determining relations between experiences and beliefs. So it has not yet been established that perceptual experiences must provide reasons for empirical beliefs.

One point should be granted right away to the proponent of this line of attack. It is not a necessary condition upon a person's grasping the concept 'gold' that she should know which stuff gold is in the sense of knowing *that gold is Au* as opposed to ABC, for example, that is, in the sense of being able to give an explicit characterization of its definitive chemical composition. This much, I take it, is uncontroversial. Nor is this a condition upon which my argument in any way depends, though. The accusation which I make against the familiar model of secondary-quality experiences and beliefs, as a representative of the attempt to exploit non-reason-giving content-determining relations between them, is, rather, that it leaves a person without any genuine conception of which property redness is in the following sense. A complete account of what a person knows about which property redness is, in virtue of grasping the concept 'red', with the semantic value M, might equally have constituted her grasp of the quite different concept 'red*', with quite different semantic value N, and have likewise been given as an account of her knowledge of which property this is. It is this, I claim, which is incompatible with her being in a position genuinely to have beliefs—with understanding—to the effect that things have one of these properties rather than the other, and hence with her having beliefs that things are red at all.

That said, I have a bold and a cautious reply back to this third line of response to the Switching Argument, which does indeed attempt to show that even this situation is perfectly compatible with possession of determinate empirical beliefs about natural kinds. The bold line is to stand by the original argument in complete generality, and to conclude, therefore, that the account offered above of beliefs about natural kinds must be mistaken for the very same reason: it assigns determinate truth-conditions in a way which goes beyond the subject's own knowledge of the semantic values which purportedly determine them, and hence unacceptably transcends her understanding of her own beliefs. A person's understanding of her own natural-kind beliefs requires that the word 'gold' has different semantic values on two speakers' lips *only if* they have different conceptions of what gold is, in some sense; where a person's conception or, as I shall often say, *subjective conception* of what gold—say—is, is what she knows about the semantic value of 'gold' on the basis of those experiences—both perceptual and testimonial—in virtue of her possession of which she associates with that word a concept with just that semantic value. Put slightly differently, a person's subjective conception of gold is constituted by all that she knows of the form 'gold is . . .' on the basis of the experiences in virtue of her possession of which she grasps that concept, where 'gold' does not appear, used, on the right-hand side, in what replaces '. . .', although ''gold'' may do so.[17] There are then a number of ways of developing the position, depending at

[17] I justify the claim in 8.2 below, that a genuine subjective conception of this form must comprise some *knowledge* about the semantic value in question.

least upon the answers which are given to the following two questions. (1) Do these subjective conceptions necessarily supervene upon the physical condition of a person from the skin in? (2) Are differences in subjective conception necessarily something about which the subject is infallible? I cannot possibly go into all the issues which are raised here (see Woodfield, 1982; and Pettit and McDowell, 1986, for a good start); but the way in which I would be inclined to develop this bold reply is, extremely briefly, as follows.[18]

First, familiar arguments, paradigmatically from the causal explanatory efficacy of the mental in connection with bodily action, for an affirmative answer to (1) are unconvincing. Second, familiar arguments, paradigmatically from the transparency of the subjective, for an affirmative answer to (2) are also unconvincing. Third, stories can be told on which Putnam's original insight (1975) that 'gold' (in his case 'water') has different semantic values on an earthling's lips and those of his Twin Earth counterpart is compelling, even when the two counterparts are physically identical from the skin in, and neither can infallibly distinguish his position from that of the other. Fourth, they nevertheless have, and, given the wholly general conclusion of the Switching Argument above, they must have, different subjective conceptions of what the stuff is which they call 'gold'; and these conceptions contribute to their respective knowledge of the (different) truth-conditions of the beliefs which they each express using that word. Of course, as I have repeatedly emphasized, this knowledge cannot require possession of the concepts of proton, neutron, and electron, or any grasp of the way in which they are employed in the systematic construction of the periodic table in which Au has its characteristic place. For the

---

[18] I take it that this is one way of filling out the suggestion in the introduction to Pettit and McDowell, 1986, of a more radical response to Putnam's original (1975) discussion of these matters than Putnam's own 'composite' account (see Pettit and McDowell, 1986, intro., sect. 3). My sketch of this development owes a great deal to this treatment, and to other work by McDowell too. A complete consideration of the current riposte to the Switching Argument would have to include an examination of the parallel possibility of social content determination, in the absence of any appeal to the underlying nature of the type or kind in question (see Pettit and McDowell, 1986, intro., sect. 7, for some helpful initial remarks here).

word 'gold' in English had its current semantic value before these theoretical advances were made by anyone; and presently has it on the lips of competent English speakers without this knowledge of basic chemistry. The conception itself is likely to be essentially demonstrative, 'Gold is *that stuff*', or 'Gold is *that metal*', say: a legitimate subjective conception of which stuff is correctly called 'gold', nevertheless, which differs, as required, between earthlings and their Twin Earth counterparts. This is a perfectly consistent position. Its key component is a strongly externalist account of the nature of thinkers' subjective conceptions of semantic values: these features of a person's mental life are themselves essentially world-involving demonstrative-recognitional capacities (Evans, 1982, ch. 8).[19] So the case of beliefs about natural kinds does not constitute one in which determinacy of belief content is really compatible with ignorance of the semantic values determining the associated truth-conditions. It is not one in which understanding transcends the subject's knowledge of these truth-conditions at all. Thus, it does not constitute a counterexample to the original Switching Argument.

It may well be objected at this point that a proponent of what I called above the 'familiar account' of our experiences of, and beliefs about, secondary qualities could equally appeal to this bold response, and therefore deny that his account of the non-reason-giving content-determining relations between experiences and beliefs leads to ignorance of semantic value in the damaging way in which the Switching Argument accuses it of doing so. On this view, then, we actually have a different, although essentially demonstrative, subjective conception of which colour redness is—redness is *that colour* of things—than we would have if red' experiences were normally caused by a different microphysical structure, N, say, instead of M, as they actually are. The problem with this move, though, given the overall dialectical position, is that this revised 'familiar account' is no longer one on which the crucial content-determining rela-

---

[19] Of course, the precise nature of such capacities is a very difficult matter. Their possession presumably requires some sensitivity to the fact that any putative reidentification of the kind in question is defeasible by scientific investigation; and, relatedly, the ability to keep track of samples over certain changes in appearance, along, perhaps, with a rough idea of what types of change are compatible with continued instantiation of the kind.

tions between secondary quality experiences and beliefs are *non-reason-giving*. Thus, it is no objection, from my point of view, that the position is immune to the Switching Argument. Put slightly differently, my point is that the revised position is no longer a version of the 'familiar account', in the sense in which this really is a counterexample to premise (P2) of my argument for (R)—the premise that the crucial content-determining relations between beliefs and experiences must be *reason-giving* relations. For the key feature of that account is that the relevant perceptual experiences, relations with which determine the contents of colour beliefs, are conceived as quite neutral, from the subject's point of view, between the cases in which their normal cause is M, as it actually is, or N, as it might have been. That is how red' experiences were defined, and it is to these experiences themselves, as opposed to any property of external objects, to which the demonstratives which are made available by having such experiences refer. Yet on the revised position, on which the present strongly externalist bold account of natural kinds is applied to secondary qualities, the subject's actual experiences are supposed to make available a demonstrative subjective conception of which colour redness is, which is *different* from the conception that is made available by colour experiences in the counterfactual case in which redness is a different property of things in the world. Red' experiences themselves have to be characterized derivatively, according to this revised position, by reference to the specific external property of redness which they reveal; they are not in themselves neutral on the question of which property this turns out to be. Colour experiences therefore provide reasons for beliefs to the effect that things are M rather than N, in the actual world.[20] Thus, a radical revision of the familiar account of secondary quality experiences and beliefs along these lines poses no difficulty for my use of the Switching Argument in defence of (R).

Note, also, returning to the case of natural kinds, that a proponent of the current bold response can quite consistently

[20] This move, from the fact that perceptual experiences make available demonstrative contents which refer directly to persisting mind-independent things and their properties, to the fact that such experiences therefore provide reasons for determinate empirical beliefs about such things, is the focus of extended discussion and defence in Part II. See especially Ch. 6.

appeal as follows to a distinction between what might be called *transparent* and *opaque* concepts in characterizing the peculiar status of concepts of more directly perceptible properties of things, such as the standard primary and secondary qualities of shape and colour, perhaps, as against natural-kind concepts. A concept is *transparent* if its associated subjective conception is sufficient for knowledge of everything which is necessarily true about the property which constitutes its semantic value.[21] Otherwise it is, to some degree, *opaque*. Then it is clear that natural-kind concepts are at the opaque end of this spectrum; and perhaps some concepts of perceptible properties, maybe colour concepts and those of certain other secondary qualities, and certain spatial concepts are fully transparent. Certainly these are far more transparent than natural-kind concepts, whose associated subjective conceptions, such as 'Water is *that liquid*', explicitly leave room for a scientific investigation of the essential underlying nature of the relevant semantic values. It does not follow from their opacity, though, on the bold theorist's account, that grasp of natural-kind concepts is compatible with ignorance of these semantic values in the sense in which the Switching Argument contends that this combination is unacceptable.

The cautious reply, on the other hand, admits the possibility of cases of beliefs about natural kinds which *are* as described in this third response to the Switching Argument. A person might have the understanding required for his having a belief with certain specific empirical truth-conditions, even if he is ignorant of the semantic values of the component concepts which determine these very truth-conditions, in the relevant sense that he would have been none the wiser had these semantic values been different in some way. The key claim here, though, is that ignorance of semantic value, in this sense, is compatible with determinacy of content in such cases, only when the following condition is met.

(O) Possession of the relevant natural-kind concepts (and of others which figure in beliefs, the determinacy of whose empirical contents is consistent with this kind of igno-

---

[21] See Campbell, 1993*a*, for a use of 'transparent' along these lines in connection with colour concepts; and Smith, 1993, for some critical discussion.

rance) depends upon possession of more basic *observational concepts*, grasp of which is *in*compatible with such
ignorance of their semantic values.

The thought here is this. Possession of natural-kind concepts
like *gold* requires *some* subjective conception of which stuff is
correctly called 'gold', or whatever—that is, some knowledge of
the form 'gold is . . .'.[22] This may be common, or at least, what
replaces '. . .' may be common, though, to two speakers—an
earthling and his Twin Earth counterpart, say—on whose lips
the word 'gold' has different semantic values. It must therefore
be supplemented by certain facts about the environment in
which any particular subject of this shared conception is embedded in order uniquely to determine the appropriate semantic
value. Nevertheless, the existence of some such conception, as
the 'narrow' component common to subjects with distinct
'broad' concepts in this way, is a presupposition of the present
argument that reflection on natural-kind concepts undermines
the Switching Argument against non-reason-giving content-
determining relations between experiences and beliefs. So, we
can ask what determines the content of this subjective conception itself: what determines the semantic values of the terms
replacing the '. . .' in the subject's knowledge that gold is . . ., in
virtue of his possession of which he grasps the concept 'gold'.
Crudely, this will be his appropriate cognitive transactions—
through perception, testimony, or whatever—with samples of
the kind in question—gold—on the basis of which he acquires
this concept. At this point, though, the original Switching
Argument can be offered again as a *reductio* of the suggestion
that the content-determining relations between the subject's
experiences during these transactions and his narrow subjective
conception of the stuff which is correctly called 'gold' are non-
reason-giving relations. Since the conception in question is, by
hypothesis, narrow, in the sense that it supervenes only upon the
properties which a given earthling subject and his Twin Earth
counterparts share, it follows that the concepts upon which it
draws *cannot* correctly be understood on the present model of
natural-kind concepts: they are directly *observational* in this

----

[22] See 8.2 for extended discussion of this requirement.

sense. Hence, given the present state of the dialectic, they must be concepts which figure only in beliefs, the determinacy of whose contents is *in*compatible with the subject's ignorance of their truth-conditions, and the semantic values which determine them. Thus, condition (O) is correct.

It follows directly from this that the model of beliefs about natural kinds exploited by this third line response to the Switching Argument cannot possibly be universally appropriate. Hence, again given the present dialectical situation, a non-reason-giving account of the content-determining role of perceptual experiences with respect to empirical beliefs cannot be correct in all cases either. There must be a basic class of concepts, which figured in the argument above as *observational concepts*, for which a reason-giving account of the determination of their semantic values is imperative. Now, let E be the set of beliefs whose contents contain these observational concepts. E is therefore a set of empirical beliefs whose members have the contents which they do only in virtue of the reason-giving relations in which various perceptual experiences stand to them. Which experiences are these? Those involved in the subject's perception of the instantiation of the properties figuring in his narrow conception of which stuff is correctly called 'gold', and similarly for all his other kind concepts, natural or otherwise.

So, let me summarize the position we have reached according to a proponent of this cautious reply to the third—natural-kind—response to the Switching Argument. Many of a person's empirical beliefs have determinate contents even though there is a sense in which the subject would have been none the wiser had these contents been different—had he been a Twin Earthling instead of an earthling, in being surrounded by natural kinds with different natures, say. Nevertheless, his possession of these beliefs depends upon his possession of the kind concepts figuring in their contents. This, in turn, depends upon his possession of some subjective conception of what falls under the kinds in question, which is shared between him and the relevant Twin Earth counterparts. This narrow conception, in its turn, draws upon certain concepts applicable to the things around him, whose application enables his recognition that such things, in his environment, fall under the kinds in question. *These* are concepts for which Twin Earth thought experiments *cannot* be given. (It is then, of course, the duty of the cautious theorist to give us a properly motivated account of which properties are *their* semantic values: colours, shapes, textures, pitches, egocentric directions perhaps, and so on). Furthermore, the experiences in which he perceives that these properties are instantiated necessarily provide reasons for his beliefs that they are. Hence a restricted version of (R) above is true: perceptual experiences must provide reasons for *certain kinds* of empirical beliefs.

The most striking difference between this, and the position envisaged by a proponent of the bold line of reply above, is in the extent of the set of empirical beliefs, E, for which perceptual experiences of certain kinds necessarily provide reasons, in the strong sense in which I am using this term, for a feature of a person's circumstances which evidently makes it rational *from his point of view* to hold the belief in question.[23] According to the bold view, beliefs about natural kinds, and most likely non-natural kinds too, must be included. For Twin Earth thought experiments of the relevant form cannot be set up for concepts of these either, as the cautious view acknowledges that they cannot with respect to observational concepts, in the sense that any difference in semantic value entails *a* difference in the subject's conception of which property is in question, although this neither requires a physical difference within his skin, nor is it infallibly detectable. Thus, letting E be the set of empirical beliefs whose contents contain concepts of any mind-independent properties, it follows that E is a set of empirical beliefs whose members have the contents which they do only in virtue of the reason-giving relations in which various perceptual experiences stand to them. Which experiences are these? Those involved in the subject's perception of the instantiation of the properties in question. Again, then, a precise version of (R) is true: perceptual experiences (of certain kinds) provide reasons for empirical beliefs (of certain kinds). The difference between the cautious and bold readings of (R) is in the range of perceptual experiences and empirical beliefs over which it is claimed to hold.

---

[23] This notion of a reason, the constraints it imposes on a theory of perceptual knowledge, and the way in which perceptual experiences might constitute reasons of this kind, are prominent topics of detailed discussion in what follows (see especially 5.2 and 6.2).

Another way of putting this difference between the cautious and bold positions is this. Both agree that (R) holds with respect to beliefs whose contents contain concepts with respect to which Twin Earth stories *cannot* be told, in which an alternative concept, with a *distinct semantic value*, plausibly corresponds with the *same subjective conception* on the part of the subject of what the appropriate semantic value is. In other words, they agree that (R) obtains in connection with concepts for which subjects' conception of their semantic value uniquely determines their semantic value. Call such concepts *unitary concepts*, as their semantic value is determined by the associated conception of a person who possesses them *alone*, rather than by any composite of this conception along with environmental and/or social features external to and quite independent of it.[24] (Note, though, to repeat once more, that the determination of a subjective conception itself may well involve considerations both outside the subject's skin, and beyond any realm there may be about the constitution of which he is infallible; and recall in this light that the bold theorist insists that natural-kind concepts are unitary in this sense, because, in the standard thought experiments, although different semantic values are involved, the associated subjective conceptions are different too.) Proponents of the two positions disagree, though, about the kinds of beliefs in which such unitary concepts occur, or more directly, about which empirical concepts are unitary concepts. The cautious view insists that these include only a small subset of the concepts applied to spatial particulars: those which I called the observational concepts above, whichever these may be. The bold view, on the other hand, contends that they include concepts of a far wider range of categories and kinds into which a person sorts the mind-independent things around him.[25] On either account, a version of (R) is true. So reflection on the case of beliefs about natural kinds and related matters is no threat to my overall argument.

To draw this discussion of natural kinds to a close, it is worth pointing out that a proponent of the cautious line of thought

---

[24] My terminology here, and the category of concepts expressed by it, is derived from Eilan, 1988, pp. 11–12 and ch. 5.

[25] I offer an account in Part II below (8.1) of how this position might be developed and defended.

might challenge this way of putting the difference between the two views as follows. Although there is a genuine disagreement over the number and variety of unitary concepts, this need not lead to a disagreement about the range of application of (R). For the following condition may in her view be a plausible additional requirement upon the compatibility of ignorance of semantic value with determinacy of belief content, in the cases we are considering.

(T) Natural-kind words have determinate semantic values, even in the face of people's ignorance of these in the relevant sense, only if subjects have some knowledge, however hazy, of the *theoretical* nature of the concepts which they express.

That is to say, a person who has non-unitary natural-kind concepts must have some grasp of the fact that their correct application is related to that of his more basic observational concepts in a theoretical manner of some kind. A parallel point might also be urged in connection with concepts for which linguistic practice plays a more autonomous role in the determination of semantic value—cases like 'arthritis', 'sofa', 'brisket', and so on, for example (see Pettit and McDowell, 1986, intro., sect. 7). If this is right, then it might be argued that beliefs involving natural-kind concepts, and possibly those involving other non-unitary concepts too, should be added to those involving the unitary observational concepts in E. For, although content determinacy is compatible with a certain ignorance on the subject's part of the nature of the kind in question, in these cases, and so the Switching Argument is powerless to include them in E directly—for the third line of response presently under consideration is therefore effective—his grasp of the theoretical structure of the concepts involved, or of the need to defer to social practice in the appropriate way, may, nevertheless, suffice for it normally to be the case that his experiences provide him with reasons for the relevant beliefs anyway.

Briefly, the thought here would be this. Certain of a person's perceptual experiences provide reasons for his empirical beliefs about the instantiation in the world around him of the various properties which constitute the semantic values of his observational concepts, whichever properties the cautious theorist takes these to be. Given the subject's rough grasp of the theoretical or sociological relations between these properties and various natural or other kinds, and assuming that the external context is suitably compliant in the particular case in question, then these beliefs may in turn give him reasons for certain beliefs about the instantiation of the kinds in question. His experiences therefore provide him with reasons for his beliefs about such kinds, even though the concepts involved are *composite*, by which I mean simply that they are not unitary, as defined above. These are what I shall call *instrumental reasons*, though, by analogy with the way in which a person's perception of the behaviour of appropriate instruments can give him reasons to believe that the current running through a circuit is 5 amps, say, or that the temperature around him is 30°C. For he might have had precisely the same experience, hence a reason to believe that there is something shiny yellow in front of him, say, yet have had no reason to believe that it is gold, because he had no idea of the relations between these properties, for example, that the former is, perhaps in certain circumstances, a good indicator of the latter, more theoretical property. Possession of the reason in question, to believe that the stuff is gold, goes beyond anything which is essential to having the experience which in certain circumstances contributes to it. Similarly, a person can only have a reason to believe that the current through a circuit is 5 amps, on the basis of his perception of the position of a needle on a dial, if he has, additionally, a reason to believe that the needle's position is a reliable indicator of current, perhaps because he knows that it is on the dial of an ammeter.

Now, this distinction between instrumental and non-instrumental reasons will eventually be crucial in spelling out the sense in which perception is a *basic* source of knowledge about the mind-independent spatial world.[26] For the moment, though, I shall conclude the present discussion by indicating an objection which the bold theorist is likely to raise for any cautious theorist advancing this argument. If the perceptual experiences in question are to provide a reason for the subject to believe that the stuff in front of him is gold, then they must obviously provide a reason for him to believe that it is gold *as opposed to any-*

---

[26] See 7.1 for a detailed discussion of this matter.

thing else. Put slightly differently, they cannot provide an equal reason, in the very same way, for him to believe that the stuff is non-gold of some specific kind. By hypothesis, though, the subject's conception of which stuff is correctly called 'gold', which draws both upon his experiences of the observational properties indicative of gold—Au—in his environment, and his rough grasp of the theoretical nature of the concept itself, are *common* to him and his Twin Earth counterpart. Hence, applying the cautious theorist's argument to the latter, the very same experiences do provide an equal reason, in the very same way, for a person to believe that the stuff in front of him is twin gold—ABC. Thus, the argument must be fallacious, and our initial subject has no reason after all to believe that the stuff in front of him is gold— Au. I can see three replies to this objection, none of which seems to me to be very promising. What is required, clearly, is some way of distinguishing between the earthling subject and his Twin Earth counterpart, so that the former's experiences provide him with a reason to believe that the stuff in front of him is gold and not twin gold, and vice versa for the latter. Each of the three replies which I envisage to the bold theorist's objection attempts to do this; they differ in how, exactly, the distinction is supposed to be drawn.

First, it might be claimed that the relevant perceptual experiences themselves differ between the two subjects. This goes directly against the caution of the cautious view though. For, recall that these are a person's experiences of the observational properties of the stuff in front of him—that it is shiny yellow, say—where these are supposed to be precisely the experiences which contribute to his subjective conception of the stuff which is correctly called 'gold', which is shared by both of them. Second, it might be argued that the theoretical background, with which these shared experiences are supplemented in the two cases differs, because in each case this essentially involves the concept expressed by the word 'gold' itself, which is, of course, a different concept, with a different semantic value, for the earthling and his Twin Earth counterpart. Again, this compromises the caution of the position. For it denies that there is a shared subjective conception of the stuff which is correctly called 'gold' between the two thinkers, involving both experientially based concepts of associated observational properties *and a rough grasp of the kind concept's responsiveness to some unifying theoretical nature underlying these*, which determines the appropriate semantic value only along with the actual environment in the two cases. So it makes a distinction between them in a respect which was originally envisaged as belonging to the shared subjective conception. Furthermore, this second reply therefore requires a *prior* and independent account of a person's possession of the appropriate kind concept to feed into the relevant theoretical understanding which contributes to the provision by certain perceptual experiences of instrumental reasons for its application. This must be an alternative to the earlier suggestion that natural-kind concept possession consists in having a subjective conception of the kind in question, composed of its characteristic appearances and some grasp of its theoretical relation with them, *which is common to earthling subjects and their Twin Earth counterparts*, in the context of the actual existence in the particular subject's environment of an appropriate kind appropriately answering to this conception. It is far from clear, though, how such an account might be given, which is both genuinely cautious, in retaining a composite approach to these kind concepts, and yet is also immune to the present line of objection from the bold theorist. Third, it might be claimed that a person can have a reason to believe that something is gold, as opposed to twin gold, even though his thinking is in all respects identical to that of a Twin Earth counterpart who equally has reason to believe that something is twin gold, as opposed to gold. For a person's possession of a reason to believe that *p*, as opposed to *q*, can be affected significantly by the world external to all that is involved in his thought and experience. Hence the only difference which is required between an earthling and his Twin Earth counterpart, if the former's experiences are to provide him with a reason to believe that there is gold, as opposed to twin gold, in front of him, and vice versa for the latter, is the uncontroversial difference that the former's experiences are normally caused by gold, and the latter's by twin gold. This may be compatible with *a* way of using the word 'reason'; but it goes directly against my explicit stipulation to use it only for features of a person's situation whose reason-giving status is evident *from the subject's point of view*. So this reply is simply not available here.

Perhaps one of these three suggestions can be revised satisfactorily, or there may be other, more successful, ways of blocking the bold theorist's worry about this way of extending the application of (R) beyond beliefs involving unitary concepts on the cautious view. If so, then it may be possible for the cautious theorist to expand the crucial set, E, of empirical beliefs which have their contents only in virtue of their standing in reason-giving relations with perceptual experiences, to coincide with that which arises directly on the bold position. I am myself very doubtful about the prospects for this move, though. In any case, the most important point is to repeat my contention that reflection upon the case of beliefs about natural kinds does nothing to undermine my Switching Argument for the claim that *reason-giving* content-determining relations with perceptual experiences are essential for certain empirical beliefs.

The Switching Argument presents an objection by *reductio ad absurdum* to the possibility of non-reason-giving content-determining relations between experiences and beliefs. These give rise to a degree of discrimination in belief contents which unacceptably transcends the subject's understanding of his own beliefs. My discussion of natural kinds was prompted by the reply that this situation is not at all unacceptable. Indeed, it is quite common. The bold response denies that determinacy of content is ever compatible with ignorance of semantic value, in the case of beliefs about natural kinds or anything else, as this line of reply to the Switching Argument suggests. The cautious response, on the other hand, accepts that it is; but it insists that this situation cannot be universal, and depends upon the subject's possession of more basic observational beliefs for which the Switching Argument is successful. A complete treatment of the issues here would have to consider parallel replies to the Switching Argument based upon alternative models drawn from other cases in which the combination of determinacy of content with ignorance of the semantic values of component concepts in the relevant sense appears to be the norm. An obvious possibility would be to appeal to the case of proper names. The structure of the situation here is, I believe, just the same as that in the case of natural kinds.

There is a prima facie plausible description of certain cases in which a person has a belief about a particular person express-

ible by a sentence including a proper name, on which it appears
that this determinacy of singular reference is perfectly compatible with the fact that her Idea of which person this is might
equally have been involved in a belief about a different person.
Consider the following example. A person believes that Perlman
is giving a concert in London on such and such a date. Kripke
(1980) and Evans (1980) have, I think, established respectively
that her reference to Perlman is achieved neither by her having
a specific definite description in mind which is uniquely satisfied
by Perlman, nor by her use of the name on this occasion simply
standing in an appropriate causal relation with Perlman's originally being given his name. It may appear, then, that she has
some subjective conception associated with the name 'Perlman',
consisting of all that she knows of the form 'Perlman is . . .' on
the basis of the perceptual and testimonial experiences in virtue
of her possession of which she has the Idea she has of Perlman,
which is nevertheless insufficient on its own uniquely to determine *Perlman* as the reference of the name, and in conjunction
with which various contextual features—causal, social, and so
on—somehow fix that particular man as the appropriate semantic value for the name. In other words, there is a possible world
in which her associated Idea is the same, yet in which, due to
suitable differences in context she believes that a different man
is performing in London on the date in question: perhaps it was
Zuckerman who had polio as a child, looked as Perlman actually does, was performing on the relevant CDs, and so on. Thus,
the person actually has a belief about Perlman, even though she
would have been none the wiser had she had a belief about
Zuckerman instead. So this is a case in which determinacy of
belief content is compatible with ignorance of semantic value, in
the relevant sense. Furthermore, if this situation is acceptable
here, then might it not obtain in every case of a person's believing something about a particular thing in the mind-independent
world around her? If so, the Switching Argument fails, and a
non-reason-giving account of the content-determining relations
between experiences and beliefs may be satisfactory after all.

   As with my discussion of natural kinds, there is a bold and a
cautious line of reply to this argument. On the bold view, the fact
that different semantic values are involved—Perlman in the
actual case and Zuckerman in the counterfactual case—*entails*

that the two subjects' Ideas are different too. Although these do not supervene upon the subjects' physical properties from the skin in, nor are they something about differences in which the subjects are necessarily infallible, the two subjective conceptions of which person 'Perlman' names are in fact distinct: in the actual world the subject knows that 'Perlman' names *that man* (Perlman), whereas, in the counterfactual world, she knows that 'Perlman' names *that man* (Zuckerman), say. Hence there is no ignorance of semantic values in the relevant sense: the two Ideas are unitary in the sense that the semantic value of the name is uniquely determined by the subjective conception associated with it. Therefore the case does not constitute a counterexample to the Switching Argument. According to the cautious response, on the other hand, the case of beliefs expressed using proper names is indeed one in which determinacy of content is compatible with a certain ignorance of semantic value on the subject's part. Nevertheless, it does not provide a universal model for beliefs about mind-independent things to the effect that they are determinately thus and so. For it cannot apply to the beliefs constitutive of the *narrow* subjective conception shared by the subject in both the actual and counterfactual circumstances under consideration, which employs only unitary Ideas and concepts, for precisely the reasons given above in the discussion of the cautious response to the natural-kinds model.

So, the upshot of reflection upon the case of proper names is the same as that of my discussion of natural kinds. Regardless of whether one opts for the bold or the cautious reply, and again my sympathies are on the bold side, the Switching Argument is successful in certain central cases: beliefs involving unitary concepts or Ideas, with respect to which the associated subjective conception uniquely determines the appropriate semantic value. This will be a larger set of cases, according to the bold theorist, of course, than according to the narrow theorist. Nevertheless, the latter may attempt to extend the application of (R) beyond these central cases by appeal to the idea that perceptual experiences provide instrumental as well as non-instrumental reasons for empirical beliefs. But this argument faces a difficult task steering a middle course between contradiction and collapse into a version of the bold position, as with the parallel move in the case of natural kinds above. Again, though, whatever the outcome of this debate, the attempt entirely to discredit the Switching Argument fails.

Before considering an important final objection to my whole discussion of both of these cases in 3.5 below, I want to end this section by clarifying in turn the views of both the bold and the cautious theorist about the relations among three distinctions which have played a key role in this discussion so far: (1) the distinction between transparent and opaque concepts; (2) the distinction between observational and theoretical (i.e. non-observational) concepts; and (3) the distinction between unitary and composite concepts. According to the bold account, most, if not all empirical concepts are unitary. Some of these are more transparent than others, perhaps some are even fully transparent. There is no obvious independent use for the observational/theoretical distinction, unless this is simply mapped onto the transparent/opaque spectrum. On the cautious position, not all empirical concepts are unitary; indeed, many are composite. Nevertheless, possession of any of these composite concepts depends upon possession of some unitary, observational concepts. Indeed, the observational concepts are those unitary concepts whose possession is essential for possession of various theoretical concepts. Although necessarily unitary, it is not essential to the position that all observational concepts are transparent; some may be more so than others.

3.5 *Are There Unitary Concepts of Mind-Independent Things?*

All of this raises an obvious final objection to the Switching Argument. What if there are *no* unitary Ideas or concepts whose semantic values are *mind-independent* objects and their properties? In that case, my claim that the argument applies at least to beliefs comprising unitary Ideas or concepts is of no value in my overall case for (R). For this is the thesis that perceptual experiences provide reasons for empirical beliefs, where these are assumed to be beliefs about particular mind-independent things to the effect that they are determinately and objectively thus and so. Yet the present objector's suggestion is that the Switching Argument applies, at best, only to beliefs about *mind-*

dependent appearances and experiences. For, it is alleged, only concepts and Ideas of such mind-dependent things are capable of playing the acknowledged crucial role of the observational concepts in the cautious position above. Thus, the natural-kind and proper-name models are fatal to (R) after all.

I want to make two points in response to this final challenge. First, its own motivation is extremely weak. Second, the positive account it recommends faces serious difficulties of its own. I shall take these briefly in turn.[27]

I take it for granted that demonstrative Ideas and concepts are unitary (see Evans, 1982, ch. 6, 1985c). If a person is thinking of a particular object, *a*, as *that F*, then her conception of *a*, '*a* is that *F*', uniquely determines *a* as the object whose condition determines whether her thought is true or false. Nothing else could possibly have been the thing she is thinking about when she thinks of *a* in this way. (This, I believe, is an assumption shared by my opponent at this stage.) Thus, the proponent of the present line of objection is committed to denying that genuine demonstrative reference is ever possible to mind-independent things: all demonstrative reference is to mind-dependent experiences and their properties. This is clearly an extremely counter-intuitive commitment. So the strength of the challenge to my position depends very heavily upon the strength of the arguments which can be mounted in favour of this highly restricted conception of demonstrative reference. The only way which I can see to establish this result, though, rests upon the assumption of a person's *infallibility* about the contents of her subjective conceptions, which, although implicit in a lot of thinking in this area, is in my view quite mistaken.

The argument goes like this. A person who is thinking about a certain thing, *a*, has some subjective conception of which thing this is, about the contents of which she cannot possibly be mistaken. Demonstrative subjective conceptions depend for their existence and nature upon the existence and nature of their objects. (This is the assumption acknowledged above, which I

[27] Further related discussion is given in Ch. 6, in which I give my own positive account of perceptual demonstrative reference to mind-independent things as involving unitary Ideas and concepts, and in 8.1, in which I suggest a way in which further, non-demonstrative unitary Ideas and concepts can be built upon these.

share with these opponents, that demonstrative Ideas and concepts are unitary). Hence demonstrative subjective conceptions can only possibly be conceptions of things about the existence and nature of which a person is infallible. Therefore all demonstrative reference is to mind-dependent experiences and their properties.

As I say, I simply reject its first premise. There is a related claim which is, I believe, true, and which correctly captures the subjectivity of subjective conceptions.

(S) A person is normally in a position to know the contents of her subjective conceptions.[28]

Recall that a subjective conception is what a person knows about the thing that she is thinking about, on the basis of the perceptual and testimonial experiences in virtue of her possession of which she is able to think about that thing in that way. Hence, her knowledge of the contents of a subjective conception is a special case of her knowledge of the contents of her own beliefs which are formed on the basis of perception and testimony. Suppose, then, that S believes that p on the basis of perception (the argument would go through equally on the assumption that the source of this belief was testimony). That is to say, asking herself how things stand in the world which she perceives around her, she arrives at the judgement that p. Then, given the concept of belief, she is in a position to exploit the so-called 'ascent routine' (Evans, 1982, ch. 7; Gordon, 1995, p. 60; Roessler, 1996, ch. 2), by prefixing this judgement with the operator 'I believe that', to arrive at the further belief that she believes that p, which normally constitutes knowledge.[29] Hence condition (S) above.

The second point which I want to make against the present

---

[28] The distinction between this claim and the mistaken assumption of infallibility here is crucial to my response to a sceptical objection to my own positive position, which I discuss in 7.3 below.

[29] See Roessler, 1996, ch. 2, for a detailed discussion of the epistemology of this ascent routine. The qualification 'normally' is required to take account of what Williamson (1994, ch. 8) calls *margin for error principles* governing inexact knowledge: 'A is true in all cases similar to cases in which "It is known that A" is true' (1994, p. 227). For these allow the construction, in certain cases, of a situation in which, although it is true that S believes that p, it cannot be true that S knows that S believes that p.

final challenge to my Switching Argument is that its proponents face serious difficulties in giving their own account of belief and knowledge about a mind-independent spatial world. If all demonstrative reference is supposed to be reference to mind-dependent things, then, given the crucial role of experiential demonstratives in determinate reference to particular mind-independent things, it is difficult to see how the latter is to be achieved. How, on this position, does a person ever succeed in thinking about persisting mind-independent things and their properties? I have already argued that grasp of proper names and non-experiential indexicals referring to mind-independent things depends upon the capacity for demonstrative reference to such things. So neither of these is any help at this point. Furthermore, I argued above (3.2) that the only remaining possibility which I can envisage, on which reference to mind-independent things is supposed to be achieved by descriptions embedding demonstrative reference to perceptual experiences in an attempt to identify worldly things as their causes, very likely fails in securing reference to such things at all.[30]

Even if some conception of belief about a mind-independent world can be constructed on the basis of demonstrative reference only to mind-dependent things, which I very strongly doubt, the prospects for a satisfactory non-sceptical epistemology are, perhaps, even less promising. I argue in the following chapter against both the reliabilist approach to this task, and any classical foundationalist or coherentist account which shares its starting point in the assumption that knowledge about the mind-independent world is to be derived somehow from epistemologically more basic and more secure knowledge about mind-dependent experiences. It should be no surprise that difficulties with both reference and knowledge come together for the proponent of this final challenge. For it is a key message running through this book, and brought out more explicitly in Part II below, that issues in the philosophical logic of reference to mind-independent things, and issues in the epistemology of our knowledge about the spatial world around us are far more

---

[30] A view along these lines is presented by Searle (1983, esp. ch. 2), and is a development of one plausible way to interpret Russell (see 8.2). For effective criticism, see Burge, 1991, and McDowell, 1991.

closely related and interconnected than is standardly recognized. In any case, I conclude that this final challenge to my Switching Argument is unsuccessful: unmotivated and indefensible.

So, to return, finally, to the overall argument which I have been advancing so far. I gave the Switching Argument against a very natural model for the possibility of non-reason-giving content-determining relations between perceptual experiences and empirical beliefs. The objection raised by this argument is that appeal to such relations generates a degree of content determinacy which unacceptably transcends the subject's knowledge of the determinate truth-conditions of his own beliefs. I then considered three lines of reply to this objection. The first two deny that it is a consequence of this familiar secondary-quality model that a person is ignorant of the truth-conditions of his beliefs at all, by giving a descriptive account, on the one hand, of his knowledge of the appropriate semantic values determining these truth-conditions, and by exploiting the possibility of conceptual redeployment in second-order self-ascriptions, on the other, to provide an explanation of the possibility of the knowledge of such semantic values required by genuine understanding. The third reply to the Switching Argument claims that although the non-reason-giving nature of the proposed relations between secondary-quality experiences and beliefs about secondary qualities in the world does indeed yield a degree of ignorance on the subject's part of the semantic values of certain concepts figuring in these beliefs, this is perfectly compatible with his grasp of concepts determinately possessing just those semantic values rather than any others. I have argued that none of these three attempts to save the familiar account of our experiences of, and beliefs about, secondary qualities succeeds. Furthermore, although this account was originally proposed simply as a putative counter-example to the second premise, (P2), of my argument for (H), I believe that, having accepted its first premise, (P1)—that there is a class of beliefs about the spatial world, E, whose members have the contents which they do only in virtue of their standing in certain relations with perceptual experiences—the account models the only possible way of denying its second premise—that only reason-giving relations between perceptual experiences and beliefs could possibly serve this content-determining role. I established (P1) in Chapter 2 above. Hence, I conclude that (P2) must be true too. Thus, I derive (H), the conclusion that the hypothesis that perceptual experiences do not provide reasons for empirical beliefs rules out the possibility of the beliefs in E, about a mind-independent spatial world. Given my commitment to (W) above, the claim that we do indeed have these beliefs about a mind-independent spatial world, I therefore conclude that (R) is true. Perceptual experiences provide reasons for the empirical beliefs in E.

Furthermore, I am now in a position to give the clarification and explication of this claim which I promised at the outset (2.1). E is at least the set of beliefs about the mind-independent spatial world whose contents involve unitary Ideas and concepts of its constituent objects and their properties. Note, in this light, that my commitment to (W) is therefore equivalent to the claim that we have beliefs about mind-independent things comprising unitary Ideas and concepts, which I defended explicitly against the final objection which I have just considered. I shall eventually argue that these unitary Ideas and concepts all figure in contents which it is possible for a person to come to know directly on the basis of perception. The corresponding perceptual experiences, which I have established provide reasons for these beliefs, on pain of the subject's failing genuinely to understand the contents in question, are precisely those which would be involved in the acquisition of such knowledge.

4

Epistemological Consequences and Criticisms

To recapitulate once more, the argument so far consists of an extended clarification and defence of the following claim.

(R) Perceptual experiences provide reasons for empirical beliefs.

In what follows in this final chapter of Part I, I shall first trace out a number of important consequences of this claim; then I shall go on critically to assess the two standard attempts to explain how something like (R) might indeed be true. This will pave the way for my own account of the nature of perceptual experiences, and the precise details of their reason-giving role in connection with empirical beliefs, which I develop throughout the remainder of the book as a correct explication of the truth of (R).

4.1 *Reliabilism*

The most significant immediate consequence of (R) is the failure of any pure reliabilist account of perceptual knowledge. *Pure reliabilism* is the view that the epistemic standing of the beliefs a person forms about the world around him on the basis of perception rests entirely upon the *reliability* of this process of belief acquisition about such matters. A true belief acquired in this way constitutes knowledge because perception (in the relevant modality, and in suitably similar circumstances, perhaps) is reliable: such beliefs 'track the truth' (Nozick, 1981, ch. 3).

The intuitive motivation for this view is clear enough. The truth of a belief is insufficient for its status as knowledge. For the subject may have acquired it fortuitously in any number of ways, as the result of a lucky accident of some kind. The literature abounds with examples of this phenomenon, in which a true belief is clearly not a case of knowledge: Gettier's original (1963) counterexamples to the tripartite definition of knowledge as justified true belief; cases in which there are an unusually large number of counterfeits or fakes in the vicinity, like Goldman's (1976) case of the papier-mâché facsimiles of barns; cases of erratic perceptual functioning (Ayers, 1991, p. 130); and so on. To rule out such cases, the reliabilist supplements actual truth with a further counterfactual condition upon knowledge. Had things been different in certain specific ways, the subject would also have had certain appropriately related true beliefs. In this sense, the truth of a piece of knowledge is to be *no accident*. One way of putting the reliabilist suggestion, then, is that the status of a person's belief as a case of knowledge depends upon the truth, in the possible worlds (including the actual world) in which he has them, of a specific subset of all his beliefs in every possible world in which he exists.

This way of putting the position immediately raises a familiar difficulty. How, precisely, is the appropriate subset of the subject's beliefs-in-possible-worlds to be specified? All that is uncontroversial here is that this must include the belief whose status as a piece of knowledge is in question in the actual world. For truth is a universally acknowledged necessary condition upon knowledge. What remains is the *Specification Problem*, which can usefully be set out along three dimensions. Reverting to the intuitive formulation of reliabilism as the thesis that a true belief that p is a case of knowledge if and only if it is acquired or sustained by a method which is reliable on such matters, the difficulty arises in connection with each of the following: the notion of a 'method', the property of 'reliability', and the range of 'such matters'. I shall outline each of these dimensions of the Specification Problem in turn.

First, how is the relevant process or *method* of belief acquisition to be identified? This must be circumscribed; for the falsity of beliefs which might have been acquired by quite different methods in different circumstances is irrelevant to the assessment of the actual belief in question, as Nozick brings out with the following example (1981, p. 179): 'A grandmother sees her grandson is well when he comes to visit; but if he were sick or dead, others would tell her he was well to spare her upset. Yet this does not mean she doesn't know he is well (or at least ambulatory) when she sees him.' Only the reliability of the method which is actually involved in acquiring or sustaining it is relevant to the epistemic assessment of the belief in question. So, we need to know *which* of the subject's beliefs, in alternative possible worlds, are acquired *by the same method* as his actual belief which is up for assessment.

The serious threat here is that our intuitions about the correctness of any putative characterization of the method involved, for the purpose of answering this question in any particular case, are guided entirely by reflection upon the likely outcome of this choice with respect to adjudicating the epistemic credentials of the belief in question, of which we have a prior and more direct grip, quite independently of any such considerations. Yet if the analysis is to be in any way illuminating, then there must be a way of individuating methods to yield the right answers, and ideally also of providing a rationale for this individuation, which can be specified quite generally, prior to and independently of any piecemeal appeal to our intuitions in each specific case.[1]

The second dimension of the Specification Problem concerns the core notion of reliability itself. Given a particular method of acquiring beliefs, what does its reliability consist in? This is again extremely important. For the reliabilist is very likely to hold that there are logically possible, non-actual circumstances sufficiently outlandish and unlikely that the method's delivery of false beliefs in those circumstances is irrelevant to the epistemic standing of the actual belief in question. Indeed, this is an important ingredient of various reliabilist responses to scepticism (e.g. Dretske, 1970, 1981; Nozick, 1981, ch. 3; Cohen, 1988). Translating into the possible-worlds framework, the issue here is this.

---

[1] Ayers (1991, pp. 133–4) makes related points about the likely indeterminacy of pure reliabilists' notion of a method; and he also stresses the need to give considerations of rationality a more prominent role than reliabilists allow. Ayers's (1991, pt. III) neo-Lockean account of the crucial role of conscious experience in providing perceptual knowledge with a perspicuity, evidence, or rational grounding of crucial epistemological significance seems to me to embody an extremely important insight, which has had a major impact upon my own positive views in this area.

In which possible worlds must the subject's beliefs acquired by the method which he actually uses also be true if his belief is to be a case of knowledge?

The third dimension of the Specification Problem is closely related to this, and concerns the range of 'such matters', in the rough formulation of reliabilism as the doctrine that a true belief that *p* is a case of knowledge if and only if the method by which it is acquired is reliable *on such matters*. The need for restriction here is straightforward. For unless methods are individuated extremely finely, such that it is a necessary condition on two beliefs being acquired by the same method that they have the same content, the absence of any such restriction entails that knowledge—that *p*, say—is inconsistent with actual or even possible (in relevant circumstances) false belief on any other matter. Clearly, if the belief whose status as knowledge is in question has the content that *p*, then there must be a limited range of related contents, beliefs with which, acquired by the appropriate method in appropriate alternative possible worlds, are relevant to the reliabilist's pronouncement. It is the precise determination of this range of contents which constitutes the third dimension of the Specification Problem. Translating again explicitly into the extensional framework set out above, the situation is this. Given a set of possible worlds on the second dimension of the Specification Problem, the first provides a set of the subject's beliefs in those worlds which are acquired by the same method as his actual belief that *p*. The reliabilist must now also specify which of these beliefs—those with *which contents*—are such that his actual belief is a case of knowledge if and only if they are true in the possible worlds in which the subject has them.

I say that the second and third dimensions of the Specification Problem are related because, just as it is overwhelmingly plausible that the solution to the third will be determined by some function of the content of the actual belief in question, reliabilists are also inclined to regard the question of which alternative possible circumstances are relevant—the second dimension—as sensitive, among other things, to this feature of the actual situation. The thought here is that the status of a true belief that *p* as knowledge is dependent upon the capacity of the method by which it is acquired to determine whether or not things like *p* are true only across the easiest or most likely ways in which *such*

Perceptual Experiences Provide Reasons

things might not have been, or might have remained, the case. In fact, this is the heart of the well-know reliabilist and relevant-alternatives responses to scepticism which I mentioned above (Dretske, 1970, 1981; Nozick, 1981, ch. 3; Cohen, 1988).[2] It is an

---

[2] The way in which such responses work is this. With respect to any belief—that *p*, say—which a person, *S*, acquires through perception, the sceptic argues as follows.

(1) *S* does not know that a sceptical hypothesis, *h*, incompatible with *p*, is false.
(2) If he does not know that not-*h*, then he does not know that *p*.
∴ (3) *S* does not know that *p*.

Premise (1) is supposed to be true, because any evidence which *S* may cite in favour of not-*h* can be reproduced, or at least appear to be so, on the assumption that *h* is true. This is how *h* is constructed. Hence all such evidence is insufficient for knowledge that not-*h*. (2) is supposed to be true, because, on the assumption that *S* knows that (*p* entails not-*h*) (which is unproblematic, since the sceptic can simply demonstrate this to him), it is an instance of the general principle of the closure of knowledge under known entailment: if *S* knows that *p* and *S* knows that (*p* entails *q*), then *S* knows that *q*. (3) clearly follows.

The responses in question purport to do justice to the sceptic's first premise. For, with respect to *S*'s belief that not-*h*, possible worlds in which *h* is true are deemed relevant to its epistemic assessment; and since *h* is designed in such a way that, however *S* acquires the belief that not-*h*, he also has this belief in such sceptical worlds, it fails to qualify as a case of knowledge: his belief that not-*h* is in the relevant sense only accidentally true. Nevertheless, this line of thought continues, the sceptical argument fails. For, provided that the method by which *S* acquires the belief that *p* yields truths about this and suitably related contents in the *closest* worlds in some of which *these contents* are true and in others of which they are false, then his actual belief that *p* survives as a case of knowledge all the same. He is reliably right that *p* in the sense constitutive of knowledge. The key here is that, in assessing the epistemic status of *S*'s belief that *p*, the reliabilist is required only to consider a region of logical space which does not extend as far away from the actual world as even the closest sceptical *h*-worlds in which he is mistaken about *p*, although these worlds are to be included in the assessment of his belief that not-*h*. This is precisely the relativity of the notion of reliability to the content of the target belief. Thus, the position provides a motivated rejection of (2), and the argument collapses. The sceptic may be right that we do not know that his outlandish hypotheses are false; but he is wrong to conclude from this that we do not know such commonplace truths as those which we normally come to believe on the basis of veridical perception.

I believe that this line of response fails on its own terms as a satisfying response to scepticism (see Craig, 1989). I also argue in what follows that the reliabilism which underlies it is unacceptable. My own response is to endorse the closure principle upon which (2) is based, and to deny (1). See 7.3 for a development of this strategy.

extremely delicate issue, though, precisely how to capture this interaction between the questions of which possible worlds and beliefs with which contents to consider, which is packed into the idea of a method of belief acquisition being 'reliable on such-and-such matters'.

I do not intend to carry this discussion any further. I just want to register at the outset how much is involved even in stating a prima facie plausible, yet sufficiently specific, version of the pure reliabilist account of perceptual knowledge. The challenge here is to avoid both of two pitfalls: first, giving a statement of the position which is little more than a reformulation of the initial insight that many true beliefs fail to be cases of knowledge because the subject's having such *true* beliefs is *in some appropriate way* accidental; and second, giving a statement of the position which does take seriously the need to fill out its details sufficiently to propose solutions on at least some of the dimensions of the Specification Problem, yet which thereby renders itself subject to various intuitive counterexamples, which can only be avoided, if at all, by what appears to opponents, or even neutral observers, to be *ad hoc* tinkering.[3] In the first case, the theorist fails entirely to engage with the crucial details of the Specification Problem at all, and therefore does nothing to explicate the unity of the target set of non-accidentally true beliefs, other than drawing on a *prior* notion of *epistemically* non-accidental true-belief acquisition, that is, the acquisition of knowledge. In the second case, his laudable attempt to engage with the Specification Problem altogether undermines the plausibility of the resultant position as a philosophically illuminating elucidation of the nature of human knowledge as we understand it. What is required, of course, is an independently motivated solution to the Specification Problem, which provides a detailed account of what should be said about each of its three dimensions and their complex interactions, and which generates a formulation of the overall reliabilist position about which it is reasonable to be confident that no genuine counterexamples can be constructed. This is a very substantive undertaking, which

---

[3] Sosa (1988) makes a similar point about the *ad hoc* nature of standard reliabilist treatments of the Specification Problem. See also Sosa, 1991, chs. 8 and 16.

proponents of the position have in my view so far failed successfully to carry off.[4]

However that may be, there is a more serious general objection to any version of the reliabilist position, which concerns the minimal role assigned to conscious perceptual experiences. Pure reliabilism has it that experiences simply serve as one among many elements of causal processes reliably terminating in true beliefs about the world around the perceiver. The inclusion of such experiences as elements of the relevant processes may be germane to these being processes of *perception,* rather than deduction, say, or mere guesswork; but the epistemic status of their products rests solely upon the reliability of these processes. Thus, any such view explicitly ignores the role of perceptual experiences as providing *reasons* for empirical beliefs, recognizable as such by the subject, and crucial to their standing as cases of knowledge, which I argued above is a necessary condition upon a person's genuinely having such beliefs about the world around him at all. I shall work my way up to a more explicit presentation of this fundamental difficulty by considering and suc-

---

[4] See Peacocke, 1986, ch. 9, for what is in my view the best available attempt to meet this challenge on behalf of reliabilism, an attempt which nevertheless fails for the reasons which Peacocke himself brings out in the following chapter.

Several of the issues raised by the Specification Problem face opponents of pure reliabilism too. For, even granted that perceptual experiences provide reasons *for the subject* to believe what he does about the world around him, in a way which cannot be captured by considerations of reliability alone, the conditions under which such experiences constitute a source of *knowledge* plausibly have some connection with reliability. A full discussion of these matters would take me too far afield to be appropriate here. Further development of the following brief sketch of my response is to be found in Chs. 6 and 7, esp. 7.3. The fundamental notion in this area, in my view, is that of a person's perceiving that *p*, for essentially experiential and irreducibly demonstrative contents, '*p*'. This entails, but cannot be analysed in terms of, the reliability, in certain respects, of his perceptual systems. The only situation in which it does not constitute a source of knowledge that *p* is that in which he mistakenly fails (perhaps with sufficient confidence) to endorse the content in belief. Nevertheless, there are cases in which he is in a subjective condition which he cannot distinguish infallibly from that of perceiving that *p*, which gives rise to certain beliefs about the world, perhaps some of which are true, which fall short of knowledge, because the relevant subjective condition is *not* one of perceiving that *p*. Although the subject takes himself to have a reason to believe what he does in such cases, he does not (or at least his present subjective condition does not provide one).

cessively refining what strikes me as a strong intuitive objection to the pure reliabilist's account of perceptual knowledge.

Although the reliabilist may distinguish the various perceptual methods of belief acquisition from certain non-perceptual methods by reference to the involvement in each of the former of conscious experiences, and perhaps also distinguish amongst the perceptual methods of belief acquisition on the basis of the types of experiences involved, the nature of these experiences as experiences of certain specific kinds, or even as experiential at all, is quite irrelevant to the epistemic assessment of the beliefs to which they give rise. All that matters is their being part of an overall process which reliably produces true beliefs. Hence perceptual beliefs are epistemically on a par with the products of de facto reliable blind guesswork. Yet we would surely resist the idea that a person's ungrounded hunches about the weather in Blackpool, say, on waking each morning, constitute knowledge as they stand, however reliable these may turn out to be.[5] The presence of experiences in the perceptual case, on the other hand, intuitively serves somehow rationally to ground the subject's beliefs about what is going on around him. They make *just those beliefs*, rather than any others, reasonable for him in those circumstances, in a way which is crucial to their standing as cases of knowledge. This appears to be an epistemically essential feature of normal perception, which cannot be captured by any form of pure reliabilism.

A first response to this intuitive objection would be to supplement the pure reliabilist position as follows. The epistemic standing of the products of a particular method of belief acquisition which is reliable on the relevant matters depends further

---

[5] I realize that pure reliabilists may be inclined to bite the bullet here, and insist that, since reliability is *all* that is epistemically relevant in addition to actual truth, such hunches are rightly to be counted as knowledge. Perhaps they might add that the presence of conscious experiences in normal perceptual cases contributes to the subject's confidence that he knows, by providing a reliable indicator that he is using a reliable method. This has no bearing on the epistemic status of perceptual beliefs themselves, though, and so the present objector's contrast with blind hunches is irrelevant. This may be the reliabilist's considered response; but I think that everyone must acknowledge at least a prima facie challenge here; and the present formulation is supposed only to capture an intuitive difficulty for the pure reliabilist view, later to be refined as the objection proceeds.

upon the *cognitive accessibility* to a subject acquiring beliefs in that way of some condition which, as a characteristic component of the process in question, reliably correlates with the truth of the beliefs to which it gives rise, although this property of the condition in question—that it is reliably correlated with the truth of such beliefs—need not itself be similarly accessible to the subject (Alston, 1988). The thought here is this. Precisely because it wrongly places knowledge acquisition epistemically on a par with de facto reliable blind guesswork, the *pure* reliabilist account is insufficient as it stands. What must also be the case, if a method of belief acquisition which is reliable on certain matters is to be a source of genuine knowledge, is that its specification should make reference to the occurrence in the causal process reliably leading to true beliefs on such matters of some condition or other to which the subject himself has cognitive access. This is what distinguishes a true belief reliably acquired through perception, which is normally a case of knowledge, from an ungrounded hunch, however reliable the method involved might be, which is not. For what makes the former an instance of the method of belief acquisition that it instantiates is the occurrence of a perceptual experience, of a type that reliably correlates with the truth of the belief to which it gives rise, which is *cognitively accessible to the subject*.[6]

A modified reliabilism along these lines is, of course, only as clear as its central notion of *cognitive access*. Yet it is far from clear to me exactly what could be intended by this in the present

---

[6] The classic statement of this kind of position is by Alston (1988). He makes very clear the status of his view as an intermediary between the pure reliabilism which I have been criticizing and any full-blown traditional internalist account of justification, which demands that '*all* of the factors needed for a belief to be epistemically justified for a given person be *cognitively accessible* to that person, *internal* to his cognitive perspective' (Dancy and Sosa, 1993, p. 132, first emphasis mine). The present position differs from pure reliabilism in requiring the subject's cognitive access to some component of the belief acquisition process, which thereby constitutes his *ground* for the belief in question, and rules out reliable guesswork/hunches. It differs from strict internalism in claiming that it is neither necessary nor sufficient for justification that the *adequacy* of this ground should be cognitively accessible to the subject. Instead, its adequacy is held to consist entirely in its objective truth-conduciveness, or the de facto reliability of the process of belief acquisition of which it is a characteristic part. I discuss the standard variants of more strongly internalist positions explicitly in 4.2 and 4.3 below.

context.[7] Indeed, I shall argue in the next section (4.2) that there are principled objections to any account on which a person's cognitive access to, in the sense of introspective knowledge of, his own experiences is supposed to be epistemically prior to, and in some way foundational with respect to, his perceptual know-ledge of the mind-independent spatial world around him. In any case, I think that the present proposal faces a dilemma on any plausible account of cognitive access. For consider the question whether the condition of the subject's believing that p—where this is the very belief whose status as a case of knowledge is in question—is an admissible object of cognitive access for the pur-poses of the suggested supplement to pure reliabilism. Can a belief itself be its own ground in this sense?

Suppose, on the one hand, that it can. Then nothing has been done to rule out the problematic cases of de facto reliable blind guesswork, or ungrounded hunches. For in such a case, in which the subject does indeed have cognitive access, in the relevant sense, to the belief which he acquires by these means, he has cog-nitive access to a condition which, as a characteristic component of the process in question, reliably correlates with the truth of the beliefs to which this process gives rise. The reliability of the guesses or hunches involved implies precisely this: that the exist-ence of beliefs acquired in this way is a reliable symptom of their truth. He is unlikely to be aware of this correlation, of course; but this is explicitly excluded as any part of the proposed con-dition. So it follows that true beliefs acquired in this way are classified as cases of knowledge. Yet the purpose of the modifi-cation to pure reliabilism currently under consideration is sup-posed to be to rule out such cases, which intuitively fail as candidates for knowledge.

Suppose, on the other hand, that it is stipulated that the con-dition, cognitive access to which is required for the status of certain true beliefs as cases of knowledge, must be distinct from and causally prior to the beliefs themselves to which it gives rise. In that case, there are intuitive counterexamples to the

---

[7] Alston himself admits that this may be ineliminably imprecise, due to imprecision in the concept of justification. He contents himself with the idea that 'to be a justifier of a belief, its ground must be the sort of thing whose instances are fairly directly accessible to their subject on reflection' (1988, p. 275).

supplemented reliabilist view of the opposite kind: plausible cases of knowledge whose status as such is denied. For example, if a person is asked what day it is, she can normally reply correctly and *knowledgeably*. Yet there need be no obvious candidate for a condition of hers which satisfies all three of the following modified reliabilist's conditions. First, it is a characteristic component of the method by which she acquires her true belief that the day in question is a Tuesday, say, which is a reliable method on such matters; second, it is a distinct condition upon which her believing that the day is a Tuesday causally depends; and third, it is a condition to which she has cognitive access. Hence the present account wrongly rules her belief out as a case of knowledge. There are obviously numerous further counterexamples along similar lines (see e.g. Wittgenstein, 1975, esp. §§ 568–79, on knowing one's own name). Thus, it seems to me that the proposed supplement to pure reliabilism is an unacceptably *ad hoc* response to the intuitive objection from de facto reliable guesswork and hunches, which loses any initial plausibility which it may have upon detailed investigation.

There is a further objection to this way of developing the pure reliabilist position. For it makes no demands upon the intrinsic *appropriateness* of the condition which is cognitively accessible to the subject—his conscious perceptual experience in our central case—to the particular belief to which it gives rise. All that is required is that this condition is a component of a process which reliably leads to truths on such matters. So, although, thus modified, reliabilism is capable of making an epistemologically relevant distinction between beliefs acquired through normal perception and de facto reliable guesswork and hunches, the former remain on a par with other cases which intuitively fail to constitute knowledge. The simplest such case would be one in which a person's perceptual experiences are modified in some systematic way, perhaps by providing him secretly with colour-inverting lenses, yet in which, for some reason or other, he continues to form correct beliefs about the colours of the things around him.[8] Intuitively, in such a case, provided that he is igno-

---

[8] As will become clear, I actually think that this case is incoherent; but the question of how it is to be handled, or ruled out as impossible, brings important issues into focus. So I urge a suspension of disbelief for now.

rant of the change, the subject's true belief that there is something green in front of him, when he has an experience presenting a red object there is not a case of knowledge. Yet this meets the original pure reliabilist condition, if normal colour perception does;[9] and it also meets the supplementary condition currently under consideration, for the subject still has cognitive access to his colour experiences.

A slightly different case is suggested by Peacocke (1986, p. 154).

A noninferential belief 'That liquid (perceptually presented) is water' may be knowledge, when based on the experiences of looking and tasting. But the same method by itself is not sufficient to make the belief 'That liquid (perceptually presented) is H_2O' knowledge: when the method does not involve inference or memory, looking and seeing would be quite irrational as a method of reaching the belief that that liquid is H_2O. If we can conceive of someone reaching the belief by that method, the belief would not be knowledge. We can elaborate the example in such a way that in nearby possible worlds, only H_2O has that distinctively neutral taste; with this elaboration, we can obtain an example in which . . . [the most plausible purely reliabilist conditions] are met. . . . But this would still not make the belief that that liquid is H_2O into a piece of knowledge.

This case also meets the supplementary condition that the method should comprise some condition which is cognitively

---

[9] An immediate response should be resisted at this point. It might be claimed that such a case cannot possibly meet the pure reliabilist condition. For had some compensating adjustment not been made elsewhere in the system, he would falsely have believed that the green object in question is red. So the truth of his actual belief is too accidental for it to be a case of knowledge. According to this reliabilist strategy, then, the fact that his actual method of belief acquisition produces false beliefs in possible worlds in which it is modified in this way—that is, by reversing the compensating adjustment which is in fact made, such that it produces beliefs that things are red when they cause experiences as of red things—is sufficient to rule out his belief as a case of knowledge. In that case, though, it ought to be enough to undermine the epistemic status of any of a normal subject's perceptually based colour beliefs that she would have false beliefs about the colours of things if something like the adjustment which is made to the subject in my example to compensate for his colour experience inversion were made to her in the absence of any such inversion. Thus, the present reliabilist response has untenable sceptical consequences. The case must therefore be handled differently; and my interest in discussing this objection is in what exactly the options are here.

accessible to the subject: in this case, his experience of seeing and tasting the liquid in question. So, again, the modified reliabilist is compelled wrongly to classify it as a case of knowledge.

I can see three possible replies to this line of objection. The first (4.1.1) offers a further supplement to the reliabilist account; and I shall argue that this itself is highly problematic. The second (4.1.2) attempts to rule out the possibility of such counter-examples involving what I shall call *inappropriate experiences*; but it does so in a way which is both subject to difficulties of its own and incompatible with my thesis (R). The last reply (4.1.3) also puts pressure upon the coherence of counterexamples along these lines, and in a way which I find far more conducive; but, precisely in being a more plausible parry to the examples, it implies a total rejection of the characteristically reliabilist approach to the epistemology of perception. I shall consider each of these in turn.

4.1.1 *Belief in Reliability*

First, inspired by the role of the subject's ignorance of his new lenses in the first example, and by Peacocke's exclusion of inference and memory from the method involved in the second, a further supplement might be proposed to the reliabilist position. What rules these cases out as cases of knowledge, it may be said, is the fact that the subjects have no idea whatsoever of the correlation between the experiences in question and the truth of the particular beliefs to which they give rise. In normal perception, on the other hand, in so far as this really is a source of genuine knowledge, the subject at least believes that the experiences he has are a good guide to the truth of the beliefs which he forms on their basis. Thus, the conjunction of the pure reliabilist condition and the first supplement above is insufficient for knowledge. A correct account must include (at least) the following three clauses.

(1) The belief is acquired by a method which is reliable on such matters.

(2) This method characteristically comprises a component which is cognitively accessible to the subject, and thereby constitutes his *ground* for the piece of knowledge in question.

(3) The subject believes that grounds of this kind are reliable indicators of the truth of his belief.[10]

In this way, it will be maintained, the doubly modified reliabilist account is able not only to exclude cases involving inappropriate experiences, like those outlined above, but also, intuitively correctly, to admit as cases of knowledge the following variants of them: first, the case in which the subject is aware of the effects of his colour-inverting lenses, and reliably arrives at true beliefs about the colours of things around him by an appropriate reinverting transposition from his colour experiences; and second, the case in which the subject understands that water is H_2O, and arrives at his belief 'That liquid (perceptually presented) is H_2O' from his prior noninferential belief 'That liquid (perceptually presented) is water' on that basis.

Nevertheless, there are serious difficulties with the proposal. To begin with, condition (3) needs to be stated very carefully indeed if it is not to be implausibly strong. For there are many knowing subjects, for example small children, who lack the conceptual resources required to raise, never mind answer, remotely sophisticated epistemological questions concerning the adequacy as grounds of the various grounds which they have for their beliefs, or the reliability of these grounds as indicators of the truth of such beliefs.

At the same time, though, the motivation for this additional clause suggests that there may also be a sense in which it is currently too weak. For, if the subjects' beliefs about the reliability of their experiences as indicators of the truth of the relevant beliefs, in the two examples set out above, are themselves utterly without justification, then it may well be wrong to readmit the cases as cases of knowledge. Suppose, for example, that the subject in the first example simply retains his *previously* justified belief that beliefs about the colours of things which he forms as a result of his colour experiences are generally true. This is no longer justified unless it is sustained by his knowledge of the operation of the inverting lenses and of the appropriateness of

---

[10] This condition is closely related to Dretske's fourth condition upon what he calls 'primary epistemic seeing' (1969, p. 88). Although this was my inspiration for considering the present development of the reliabilist view, I do not mean to imply that everything which I say here applies equally to his account of perceptual knowledge.

the reinverting transposition which he makes as a result, in moving from his experiences to his beliefs. So his reliably getting the colours right is again intuitively too chancy to count as a source of knowledge. Similarly, a quite unjustified belief, on the part of the second subject, that the characteristic appearance of water is a reliable sign of the presence of H_2O would render dubious the epistemic status of his belief 'That liquid (perceptually presented) is H_2O'.

The suggestion that (3) above should be rewritten to require of the subject *knowledge*, or *justified* belief, that his grounds are reliable, though, both makes the first difficulty above even more pressing, and notoriously opens the door to scepticism. For, in the first place, it is even less plausible to require of infant knowers that they have knowledge of, or justification for, any epistemological views which they may have about the reliability of their various modes of belief acquisition. In the second place, the challenge to a person to provide a justification for his belief in the reliability of his basic methods of belief acquisition prior to, and therefore nowhere drawing upon, his possession of any knowledge acquired through their successful operation, is notoriously difficult to meet (Alston, 1993; and see 4.2 below).

4.1.2 *Experiential Content Is Determined by Belief Content*

A second possible reply to the objection from experiences which are intuitively inappropriate grounds for the true beliefs to which they reliably give rise is this. First, the range of application of the proposed theory must be qualified somewhat. In particular, if the method of belief acquisition to which it is applied comprises perceptual experiences as its component grounds— that is, those elements of the process which are, as the theory requires them to be, cognitively accessible to the subject—then the only beliefs which can properly be evaluated directly for their epistemological standing are those with *observational* contents. A *further* method, involving some kind of inference, is required to proceed from these beliefs to those with more theoretical, non-observational, contents, which therefore requires further cognitively accessible grounds, and a second application of the overall theory. Of course, it is notoriously difficult, and

indeed may well be impossible in principle, to make the obser-
vational/theoretical distinction satisfactorily; but I shall waive
that major worry for the sake of the argument. Suffice it to say
that the point of this first move is to focus the objection from
inappropriate experiences exclusively upon cases like my first
one above, of colour-spectrum inversion, by negotiating away
the second kind of counterexample, due to Peacocke. For it is
clearly at least part of the problem in the latter case that the
content of the belief in question contains the relatively non-
observational concept 'H$_2$O'. Having so focused the objection
by these independent means, it is then quite plausible to claim
that any remaining counterexamples to the present modified
reliabilism of the inappropriate experiences variety are merely
apparent because the situation which they describe is incoherent.

Thus, the second move of this second reply (4.1.2) is to set out
a rationale for this rejection of any remaining (apparent)
counterexamples as incoherent. This, it will be claimed here,
consists in the fact that the intrinsic nature of perceptual experiences is simply determined by the contents of the beliefs to which
they normally give rise. Hence, in the case outlined above, a
colour inversion is achieved if and only if there is a corresponding inversion in the beliefs which the subject is inclined to form
on the basis of perception about the colours of things around
him. So his perception is a reliable method of acquiring beliefs
about such matters if and—this is what matters here—only if the
experiences involved are appropriate, in the relevant sense, to
the truth of the beliefs in question. The putative case in which
he reliably gets the colours of things right on the basis of colour
experiences which are inappropriate, in this sense, is therefore
impossible. Either the subject continues to be reliably right in his
beliefs, in which case his experiences thereby remain uninverted;
or a spectrum inversion is achieved, but only by systematically
inverting his colour *beliefs* with respect to the facts, in which
case he is no longer reliably right about the colours of things
around him.

Although I share the conviction that there is something very
dubious about the example of an experiential inversion which
leaves the process of perceptual belief acquisition otherwise
unchanged, I do not think that this can be the right way to
exclude it. So it cannot be the right way to respond to the current

line of objection to the (singly) supplemented reliabilist position
either. For the thesis that the intrinsic nature of perceptual
experiences is *determined* by the contents of the beliefs to which
they normally give rise is both subject to compelling counterexamples and incompatible with my thesis, (R).

First, then, there are famous examples of what Evans (1982,
p. 123) calls the *belief-independence* of experiences: the fact that
a person's having a perceptual experience of a certain type is
independent of whether or not he believes that the experience is
veridical, or that the world is as experiences of that type normally indicate. The Müller–Lyer illusion makes this vivid. The
experiential appearance that the two lines are of different
lengths persists however well the subject understands the illusion, and regardless of her belief, which may well be knowledge,
that they are in fact of the same length. So the intrinsic nature of
experiences cannot be fixed by the beliefs about the world to
which they normally or reliably give rise.

Second, the present reply directly contradicts my claim that
the determination relations between experiences and beliefs run
in the opposite direction. I have argued that certain empirical
beliefs have their contents fixed by the reason-giving relations in
which various perceptual experiences stand with them. It is then
incoherent to claim that these same belief contents in turn fix the
way the world is presented in the experiences which generally
produce them. So this cannot be the basis of an adequate reply
to the objection from epistemically inappropriate, but de facto
truth-conducive experiences.

4.1.3 *Belief Content Is Determined by Experiential Content*

This last criticism suggests a third reply to the objection from
inappropriate experiences. It may be possible to undermine the
putative counterexample, of a spectrum inversion which leaves
reliable perceptual belief acquisition intact but nevertheless fails
as a source of knowledge, by quite different means: on the basis
of thesis (R) itself. I have three points to make about this suggestion.

First, (R) is not capable immediately of ruling out the possibility of any such counterexample as incoherent. For, unlike

the previous claim, it does not entail that the normal causes of all perceptual beliefs are necessarily experiences appropriate to their contents, in the relevant sense. So it does not rule out the possibility of a reliable method of belief acquisition which intuitively fails to be a source of knowledge because it involves misleading or inappropriate experiences, and whose truth conduciveness is therefore unacceptably accidental. All that follows, rather, is that in certain basic cases—at least those in the set E, defined above—the beliefs to which perceptual experiences give rise thereby have their contents determined in such a way that these experiences provide reasons for them. In these cases, then, such experiences are epistemologically appropriate to the beliefs to which they give rise. Hence counterexamples of the kind currently under consideration to the modified reliabilist position are impossible. Nevertheless, the present reply, as it stands, leaves *some* scope for such counterexamples, as non-basic or deviant cases; it cannot legislate them out of existence altogether.

Second, in so far as it does have force in ruling out cases of reliable belief acquisition on the basis of inappropriate experiences, on the other hand, this third reply (4.1.3), unlike the second above (4.1.2), is immune to counterexamples from the belief-independence of perception of the Müller–Lyer variety. For the set of central cases, in which the contents of empirical beliefs are determined directly by experiences in such a way that the experiences in question provide reasons for them, will contain (at most) those in which there is no influence of additional, extraneous information, or independent further reasons. Yet this is not the case with respect to a subject of the Müller–Lyer illusion who believes that the lines are not of different lengths, *because she understands how the illusion works, or knows that it is an illusion with the features which it has.* The role of this latter knowledge and understanding, in the context of which we can easily make sense of the case, is precisely to provide the subject with such further reasons to overrule, as it were, the prima facie rational force of experience.

These first two points are clearly related. For it is precisely that latitude in the relations between experiences and beliefs imposed by (R) which prevents the proponent of the present reply from ruling out altogether the possibility of reliable perceptual belief acquisition on the basis of epistemically inappropriate experiences, which at the same time allows such a theorist to accommodate belief-independence. Furthermore, although this reply stops short of a total rejection of all such cases of reliable but inappropriate perception as incoherent, it nevertheless has significant force in ruling out its wilder variants. For what enables its handling of a knowing subject of the Müller–Lyer illusion, is the presence in this case of further, independent reasons, extraneous, and in addition, to the perceptual experience itself. Indeed, this is the heart of the explanation which a proponent of (R) will give of the belief-independence of experience generally. For, according to (R), in the absence of any such extraneous information, or independent reasons against, a perceiver will normally move to a belief whose content is determined in such a way that her experience provides a reason for her to endorse it in judgement. So, in cases where there are no such independent, competing reasons, the subject's failure to acquire the appropriate belief is at least a case of some irrationality; and the claim that she does move to a belief, but that this belief has an inappropriate content, *is* incoherent. *In this case*—in the absence of independent undermining reasons—if she ends up with a belief on the basis of her experience, then this just *does* have a content, for the endorsement of which her experience provides a reason. This is the force of (R). Yet, in so far as the colour inversion case envisaged above is *not* to be one in which an additional inferential method is applied to the deliverance of a perceptual-experiential instrument, as it were, where the subject infers that there is something green in front of him from his experience presenting a red object there and his knowledge of the operation of his inverting lenses—in which case it is no longer intuitively epistemologically problematic—then there are no such extraneous reasons. Hence that version of the case is, by my intuitions correctly, ruled out as incoherent.

My third point about this third reply (4.1.3), is that the way in which it invokes (R) makes it inconsistent with the basic reliabilist contention. For, as I argued in Chapter 3, the determination of genuine empirical contents for beliefs by their relations with perceptual experiences requires that these are *reason-giving* relations. Hence they are relations of a type which make an autonomous contribution to the epistemic assessment of the beliefs involved, over and above anything which can be captured purely in terms of the reliability of the method of their acquisition. According to the reliabilist, either pure or modified, the fundamental dimension of epistemic appraisal is to be spelt out in terms of the notion of reliability. Yet any appeal to (R) brings with it an essential role for a prior and independent notion of reason-giving relations between experiences and the beliefs to which they normally give rise. So (R) is directly in conflict with the reliabilist position. Put another way, the reliabilist's need for a filter to exclude epistemologically inappropriate experiences as grounds for empirical beliefs, however reliable the method of belief acquisition may be as a component of which these occur, is precisely a need for a notion of *reason-giving* relations between perceptual experiences and beliefs: these are the relations which (R) insists are crucial for empirical content-determination. Furthermore, these relations play an essential role in the epistemic assessment of beliefs acquired through perception, which is independent of anything which can be captured in terms of the notion of reliability. For the problem of inappropriate experiences creates a need, precisely, for an *epistemologically significant* distinction between perceptual methods of belief acquisition which are perfectly on a par with respect to their reliability on the matters in question.

Thus, (R) is incompatible with reliabilism, as I construe it. For (R) introduces epistemologically essential relations between experiences and beliefs which are quite independent of considerations of reliability in the relevant method of belief acquisition. So, assuming that my argument (Chs. 2 and 3) for (R) is sound, then I have established that reliabilism is false. In ignoring the reason-giving relations between perceptual experiences and empirical beliefs, the reliabilist rules out the very possibility of such beliefs, with genuine empirical contents at all. Like all epistemologists belonging to the tradition which I am opposing in this book, he simply takes the existence of such beliefs for granted, with all their perfectly determinate contents in place, and asks what has to be the case with respect to the ways in which they are produced if they are to be cases of knowledge. Yet (R) entails that if these beliefs are really to be beliefs *of an understanding subject*, about particular things in the mind-independent world around him, to the effect that they are determinately thus and so, then the reliabilist's answer to this question has to be incorrect. If my overall discussion so far in the present section (4.1) is at all on the right lines, then the reliabilist's predicament is in fact even worse than this. For it appears that there is in any case a motivation *from within his own position* for the very thesis, (R), which undermines it.

In the following two sections, I outline and reject two very influential attempts to articulate a theory of perceptual knowledge which, unlike reliabilism, respects (R), and aims to supply an account of what it is in virtue of which (R) is indeed true. These are *classical foundationalism* (4.2) and *classical coherentism* (4.3) respectively.

4.2 *Classical Foundationalism*

The first reply which I considered above (4.1.1) to the objection from epistemologically inappropriate experiences insists upon supplementing the modified reliabilist account with a further, reflective condition, according to which the subject himself must have a view about the reliability of his grounds as indicators of the truth of the beliefs in question. I criticized the proposal in so far as this further condition might be met by an ungrounded hunch on the subject's part about the reliability of the relevant method of belief acquisition; and I also mentioned, only to leave hanging, the sceptical problems which are raised by the claim that this reflective view must itself be a piece of knowledge, or justified belief. One position which insists upon precisely this latter, heroic, picture has been extremely influential in discussions of perceptual knowledge at least since Descartes. Following Dancy (Dancy, 1988, intro., pp. 11 ff.), I call it *classical foundationalism*. I shall now take a more detailed look at this position, in order to clarify the way in which it attempts to elucidate the truth of (R), and to bring out both its unacceptable sceptical implications and another major difficulty which it shares with a number of other traditional approaches to the topic. I hope that this will help further in determining the direction in which to seek a correct account of how exactly it is that (R) is true.

According to classical foundationalism, true beliefs which a person forms about the external world on the basis of perception are normally knowledge because:

(G) the way things appear to her in experience is 'given';

and

(L) she knows, or is in a position to know, that being appeared to in this way is a reliable indicator that things are as she believes them to be out there.

(G) provides her with *foundational* introspective knowledge about the nature of her experience, in need of no inferential justification whatsoever. (L) combines with this to put her in a position to deduce the likely truth of her empirical belief. So her experience provides a reason for this belief, that p, say, in the sense that it gives her knowledge—that things appear thus to her—from which she is in a position to infer that, in all likelihood, p. Thus, classical foundationalism underwrites (R). Note, especially, that the fact that her belief that p is reasonable in these circumstances is something which she is herself in a position to appreciate. For she knows, or is in a position to know, that her current experience reliably indicates its truth. That is to say, (R) is vindicated in the sense in which it is intended, in which reasons' status as such is something which is apt to figure in the subject's reflective thinking about her situation. Unlike reliabilism, then, the difficulties with classical foundationalism are not due to any formal incompatibility with (R). Rather, it is the way in which (R)'s truth is supposedly secured which renders the position untenable. Indeed, I shall argue that both (G) and (L) are problematic. I begin with three objections in connection with (G).

4.2.1 *Conceiving of Others' Experiences on the Model of One's Own*

First, if simply having the experience is to provide knowledge of the way things appear to someone, then her conception of what it is to be appeared to in that way can draw upon nothing more than what is involved in the presence to her of the conscious experience itself. Yet if this is to be knowledge that things are thus and so *for her now*, then she must have some conception of what it would be for things to be just that way for a person other than herself, or at another time. But this is incoherent. It would be for her to conceive of the presence of just that conscious experience, in the absence of that very experience (see Wittgenstein, 1958, §§ 293–302).

In order to state the incoherence involved here as clearly and precisely as possible, I shall make a brief comment about each of three likely ripostes to the argument as it stands. In the first place, why is the subject's conception of what it is to be appeared to in the relevant way, *F-ly*, say, restricted in its content simply to the present occurrence of the experience itself, if the experience is to give her the required foundational introspective knowledge? This is because, if her conception of what it is to be appeared to *F-ly* were not restricted in this way, then, given just the present occurrence of the experience in question, she would require further grounds to suppose that the way she is being appeared to is indeed *F-ly*, as opposed to some other way, further grounds, that is to say, to suppose that the additional features of her conception of being appeared to *F-ly* are actually met. Yet the whole point of the foundationalist's position is that such additional grounds are quite unnecessary in this case. So the restriction is crucial. In the second place, why does her knowledge that she is now being appeared to *F-ly* require her grasp of what it would be for someone other than herself, or at another time, to be appeared to in just that way? This is an application of Evans's Generality Constraint (1982, sect. 4.3), which states that a thought, that *a* is *F*, say, is *structured* in the sense of being 'a complex of the exercise of several distinct conceptual *abilities*' (p. 101, his emphasis), which must each be exercisable in combination with appropriate others in the thoughts that *a* is *G*, *a* is *H*, and so on, and that *b* is *F*, *c* is *F*, and so on. Thus, exploiting the second series of commitments in our particular case, a person's thought that she is being appeared to *F-ly* is a complex of her ability to think of herself and her conception of what it is to be appeared to *F-ly*, where this has at least the implication that there should be no conceptual bar to her grasping what it would be for someone *else* to be appeared to *F-ly*. Similarly, her thinking that she is now being appeared to *F-ly* entails that there should be no conceptual bar to her entertaining the thought that someone (herself or another) *was*, or *will be*, appeared to F-*ly*. In the third place, why must the classical foundationalist accept that the content of a person's foundational introspective knowledge is that *she* is *now* being appeared to F-*ly*, in the sense in which this imposes such commitments of generality? In response, I claim that unless this is so, her supposed knowledge that being appeared to F-*ly* is *a reliable indicator* that the world is thus and so around her is incoherent. For this is the idea that the way things are with her now is such that, in the majority of cases in which things are like that with her or another person on other occasions, the world around the relevant person is indeed thus and so. Perhaps, it may be objected, the generality required to make sense of the notion of a reliable indicator may not necessarily be intersubjective. Perhaps; but intrasubjective reliability still requires generality over time; and this is all that the argument needs.

So, what exactly is the incoherence supposed to be here, in the classical foundationalist's conception of a person's foundational, introspective knowledge of her experiential appearances? It is this. Given what has been said, the subject's conception of what it is to be appeared to F-*ly* must both be such that it draws upon nothing more than the presence of her conscious experience in being appeared to in this way, and be such that there is no conceptual bar to her grasping what it would be for someone other than her to be appeared to in this way, or for herself to be appeared to in this way at another time. Yet the first requirement produces precisely the conceptual bar precluded by the second. For it entails that she can have no conception of being-appeared-to-F-*ly*'s being instantiated in the absence—*to her*—of the very conscious experience from which this conception is a construct; but this is exactly what is required for a genuine conception of its being instantiated *by someone else*, or by her *at another time*. For her, its being instantiated is simply a construct out of her present conscious state. Yet its being instantiated by another or at another time is not: indeed these are logically independent of her present conscious state. This is what she cannot possibly appreciate. So she has no genuine conception of these alternative states of affairs. The classical foundationalist's conception of introspective knowledge which figures in (G) above is therefore incoherent.

4.2.2 *Is Foundational Introspective Knowledge Conceptual or Not?*

My second objection to (G) is closely related to this first one. It is really just a slightly different way of coming at the same problem, via the first series of commitments imposed by Evans's Generality Constraint. If the perceiver's foundational introspective knowledge is to be provided simply by her being appeared to as she is, then it is subject to inconsistent demands. On the one hand, its role as an inferential reason for her perceptual belief about the world requires that it is *conceptual*, in the sense that it consists in her application to her current condition of a determinate concept, of being appeared to *F-ly*, as opposed to any other way. On the other hand, its epistemologically foundational status requires that it is independent of any application of such concepts of determinate appearances (see Sellars, 1963, sect. 1).

Again, there are various ripostes to consider in filling out this argument. I shall make a brief comment about two of the most obvious ones. In the first place, why must a perceiver's introspective knowledge be conceptual in this sense? It is because this knowledge is supposed to constitute the factual premise of an inference to the likely truth of her belief about the world. In this role it has to engage with the second premise, supplied by her general knowledge of the reliability of appearances *of just that type* as indicators that the external world is thus and so, which it can only possibly do if it comprises an application of the appropriate concept. Why, in the second place, do I claim that her knowledge that she is being appeared to *F-ly* must at the same time be independent of any application of concepts of determinate appearance types? Otherwise, I contend, it will itself be subject to challenge, and therefore in need of justification of the kind which the foundationalist insists is unnecessary and inappropriate. For, suppose that this introspective knowledge does comprise a determinate appearance concept. In that case, it will be possible to raise with the subject herself the question whether she is really being appeared to in just that way or in some other way which may be mistaken for it. If, on the one hand, the foundationalist rejects this question by claiming that any such mistake is logically impossible, then

he thereby contradicts the present hypothesis that her introspective knowledge comprises a genuine concept, with respect to
which a distinction between its seeming to apply and its actually
applying is therefore at least logically possible. If, on the other
hand, the possibility of such a mistake is granted, then the
request for the subject's reason to suppose that she is being
appeared to *F-ly* as opposed to some other such way is perfectly
legitimate, and the foundationalist's crucial claim that introspective knowledge is epistemologically foundational in the
sense that it neither needs nor can be given any justification is
undermined. Thus, the classical foundationalist is indeed compelled simultaneously to assert and to deny that introspective
knowledge is conceptual in the relevant sense. So his position is
incoherent.

4.2.3 *Do Experiences Provide Reasons for Introspective Beliefs?*

A third objection to (G) is also suggested by Sellars (1963, sect.
VIII). As I have set up the position, classical foundationalism
aims to respect (R), by showing how perceptual experiences provide reasons for empirical beliefs. They are supposed to do this
by providing the subject with foundational knowledge of their
own nature, from which she is in a position to infer the likely
truth of the way she takes things to be in the world around her,
by appeal to an experience–world linking principle to the effect
that being appeared to in such and such a way is a reliable indicator that things are thus and so out there. The characteristically
foundationalist feature of the position, though, the idea that this
introspective knowledge is in no way dependent for its status as
knowledge upon any further knowledge or inferential
justification of any kind, is motivated by the worry that otherwise there would have to be an unacceptable infinite regress or
closed circle of justification, which would undermine perceptual
knowledge altogether. I do not want to get into any detailed discussion of this argument here. For there are numerous such discussions elsewhere (e.g. Dancy and Sosa, 1993, pp. 209–12; and
see also the references in the bibliography of that entry in the
Dancy and Sosa *Companion*); and the objection which I want to
consider is anyway independent of the details. Instead, I shall

just articulate the four features of foundationalist thinking at this point which are most relevant. First, the status of a belief as a piece of knowledge depends upon its being justified in some way. Second, inference is a source of justification in the following sense: a belief is justified if it is, or can be, inferred from other justified beliefs. Third, some justification must be *non*-inferential, since otherwise there would be an unacceptable infinite regress or vicious circularity of justification; so no belief would be genuinely justified; and therefore there could be no knowledge. Thus, fourth, in the case of perceptual knowledge, experience itself provides non-inferential justification for a person's foundational introspective knowledge of the way things currently appear to her. Finally, then, my third objection to (G) concerns how exactly the justificatory role of experience with respect to this foundational knowledge is to be understood.

Let us grant for the sake of the argument that a person's being appeared to *F-ly* reliably gives rise to her belief that she is. The problem is this. How can the classical foundationalist consistently claim, as he must, that this belief is really a case of knowledge, which must therefore be *justified* by its relation with the subject's experience? For he faces a dilemma over the question whether this justification depends upon the fact that her being appeared to *F-ly* provides a *reason*, in my sense of something essentially recognizable as such, for the introspective belief in question, that she is indeed being appeared to *F-ly*.

If, on the one hand, the foundationalist answers that it does, then he faces a challenge to explain how experience can possibly provide such a reason *other than* by itself consisting in or somehow providing a further justified belief from which the subject's introspective knowledge that she is indeed being appeared to *F-ly* can be inferred. For, recall, it is crucial to the position that the justification provided by experience for this foundational knowledge should be *non-inferential*. What is required, therefore, is an account of what is involved in a person's having the experience of being appeared to *F-ly*, from which it follows that her simply having this experience provides her with a non-inferential reason to believe that she is, where this essentially involves her being capable of recognizing the status of her reason as such in her reflective thinking about her situation. I am aware of no serious attempt to meet this challenge.[11] Indeed, the foundationalists which I know of who say anything much about the justificatory relations between experiences and introspective knowledge of experiences appear implicitly to opt for the second horn of the present dilemma, identifying reasons, in the relevant sense, only with justified beliefs from which the beliefs for which they are reasons can be *inferred—inferential reasons*, that is— and aiming for a *non*-reason-giving, reliabilist-style justification at the foundational level (see e.g. Chisholm, 1989; and Van Cleve, 1979). Furthermore, the most natural foundationalist conception of what is involved in a person's having an experience of a certain kind is extremely undemanding. As Sellars puts it, this is normally equated simply with '*being conscious* [in such and such a way], as a person who has been hit on the head is *not* conscious, whereas a new-born babe, alive and kicking, *is* conscious' (1963, p. 131, his emphasis). Yet, given the demands upon having a reason of the required kind, this makes the challenge posed by the first horn of the dilemma especially difficult to meet.[12]

On the other hand, the foundationalist may insist that the way in which a person's experience justifies her foundational introspective knowledge does not depend upon the claim that her being appeared to *F-ly* provides a reason, in this demanding sense, for her belief that she is. In the absence of substantial further argument, though, this undermines the motivation for his own position, and also faces problems from my earlier argument for (R). For the only clear alternative account of the justification

---

[11] No attempt, that is, within the classical foundationalist context, in which the justification of introspective knowledge of mind-dependent appearances is essentially prior to any justification for perceptual knowledge about the mind-independent world. Outside this context, discussion is also quite rare. See Peacocke, 1998a, for an account which suggests exploiting the *conscious* nature of outward-facing perceptual appearances in this regard. Roessler (1996, esp. ch. 2) presents a position on which the subjectively recognizable reasons for a person's self-ascriptions of beliefs are derived from the reasons which he has for the first-order beliefs themselves. It may be possible to extend this idea to give an account of a person's genuine reasons for his self-ascriptions of perceptual experiences of certain types, on which these are derived in a similar way from the reason-giving role of the experiences in question with respect to such first-order empirical beliefs.

[12] See Ch. 5 for explicit discussion of certain constraints upon having a reason of this kind, which further bolsters this claim.

of introspective knowledge by experience which is available is *reliabilist* in nature, along the following lines. A person's belief that she is being appeared to *F-ly* is justified by her experience of being appeared to *F-ly* because the process by which the latter causes the former is highly reliable on such matters: introspection is a reliable source of belief about the nature of perceptual experiences. Given some such reliabilist account of justification at the foundational level, though, why should the foundationalist object to a more direct application of the very same strategy in accounting for the justification of perceptual belief about the mind-independent world itself? That is to say, why should the foundationalist not in that case simply endorse a reliabilist account of perceptual knowledge of the kind which I discussed in the previous section, dispensing with the detour via (G) and (L) above altogether? It might then be added that this particular reliabilist justification applies only to direct perceptual knowledge of the observational properties of things, and that all other empirical beliefs are therefore justified only indirectly, by inference of some kind from these basic beliefs. So there could still be a foundationalist structure to the position.[13]

The classical foundationalist obviously needs to resist this revision. For the result is to render his account of basic perceptual knowledge indistinguishable from the reliabilism which I rejected above, and therefore likewise directly in conflict with (R). So he must insist upon the crucial role of (G) and (L), as outlined above, even whilst acknowledging that the justification given by a person's experience to her foundational beliefs about the nature of this experience is purely reliabilist. I shall make two points against this proposed combination of classical foundationalism with reliabilism at the foundational level, although my discussion of the first is somewhat extended.

My first point, then, is that the standard foundationalist motivation for the appeal to (G) and (L) in the justification of perceptual knowledge is some form of *internalism* about justification. Crudely, this is the idea that everything which is involved in a belief's being justified for a person should be cognitively accessible to her. In other words, if a belief is to be

---

[13] Sosa (1991, esp. pts. II and III, 1994, 1997*a*, and 1997*b*) develops a position along these lines.

justified in virtue of its relation with another belief, or an experience, then the status of this further belief or experience as providing a justification for the justified belief in question must in some way be recognizable by the subject. Thus, justification is provided only by reasons in my demanding sense.[14] Hence the crucial role of (G) and (L) in the justification of perceptual knowledge about the mind-independent world. For, on this account, a person's perceptual experiences provide reasons for her empirical beliefs only through her recognition of this reason-giving role in her introspective knowledge of their nature, along with her general knowledge of the reliability of experiences of these kinds as indicators of the truth of the beliefs in question. But then how can the foundationalist consistently accept that this internalist condition *fails* at the foundational level, with respect to (G) itself, in connection with the justification by experiences of introspective beliefs themselves? A parallel line of argument surely suggests the following requirements upon the justification of introspective knowledge:

(GI) the way things introspectively *appear* to her is 'given';

and

(LI) she knows, or is in a position to know, that being introspectively appeared to in this way is a reliable indicator that her experience is as she believes it to be.

Yet the present foundationalist is committed to rejecting internalism entirely at this point, and appealing simply to the de facto reliability of introspection for the justification of a person's knowledge of how she is being appeared to in perceptual experience instead. I can see the following two considerations to which he might appeal in explaining this difference in standards with respect to the requirements upon justification. Neither is satisfactory in my view.

First, he may cite the putative fact that self-ascriptions of appearances are incorrigible: necessarily, if a person sincerely believes that she is being appeared to *F-ly*, then she is. By contrast, perceptual beliefs are obviously corrigible: one can

---

[14] See 5.2 for more on this recognition requirement upon genuine reasons *for the subject.*

perfectly sincerely arrive at a false belief about the world through perception. This, it may be claimed, is why the latter—perceptual belief about the world—stands in need of internalist, reason-giving justification, whereas the former—introspective belief about the nature of perceptual experience—does not. I am myself far from convinced that these self-ascriptions are incorrigible in this sense; and in any case, how would it help to establish that a non-internalist justification is satisfactory to give them their status as self-*knowledge* even if they were? The foundationalist's motivation for the crucial role of (G) and (L) in his internalist account of the justification of perceptual belief about the mind-independent world is quite independent of the hit rate (in the sense of the proportion of truths delivered) of the relevant perceptual method of belief acquisition. This motivation would remain even if God had ensured that certain perceptual beliefs were incorrigible. For, as it stands, this fact would be wholly inaccessible to the subject. The internalist intuition, on the other hand, is that justified belief is reasonable belief in the sense that the subject has some grasp of how it is that she is, or may well be, right in holding the belief which she does. So it is extremely difficult to see how it might be supposed to be silenced by the fact, even if it were one, that introspection of perceptual appearances is incorrigible. Put another way, the internalist thought which drives classical foundationalism, as I understand it, is that justified belief is superior to accidentally true belief *from the subject's point of view*. So the de facto hit rate of the method in question on its own does nothing to undermine its force.

Second, a more radical suggestion might be made, both in explanation of this supposed incorrigibility, and in justification of its epistemological significance. Introspective knowledge, it may be said, is susceptible to non-internalist justification, which obtains quite independently of any recognition upon the subject's part of the reliability of introspection as a source of belief about perceptual appearances, because a person's judgement that she is being appeared to *F-ly constitutes* her being so (see C. Wright, 1989; and Heal, forthcoming, for the suggestion that a person's direct self-ascriptions of certain mental states are constitutive of her being in the self-ascribed state). Call this the *Constitution Thesis*. Certainly it rules out the possibility of error, but not in any way which obviously overrules the requirement that the subject grasps how she is right in introspection, if this internalist condition is held to apply in the case of perceptual beliefs about mind-independent reality. This can be brought out by considering the case of promising (see Heal, forthcoming). The thought behind the present appeal to the Constitution Thesis is that promising provides a model for the epistemology of introspective self-ascriptions of appearances. For sincerely to say 'I promise' is to make a claim about what one is doing which at the same time constitutes the state of affairs which makes it true. Thus, it is held, the claim automatically qualifies as a case of knowledge. I think that this model works the wrong way for the foundationalist, though. For, although it may be true that if a person actually makes a promise by saying 'I promise', then he knows that he does, anyone with remotely internalist sympathies will insist that this is *not* simply because saying 'I promise' *alone* constitutes promising, as a result of which it is mysteriously supposed to expresses the subject's *knowledge* of doing so. (Consider a child merely imitating these noises.) Rather, the explanation would be that saying 'I promise' constitutes promising only if the speaker knows this to be so. So a consistent foundationalist attempting to exploit this move should equally insist that a person's making the self-ascription constituting her being appeared to *F-ly* is only expressive of knowledge if she knows, or can know, the Constitution Thesis itself. Furthermore, the Constitution Thesis is itself highly controversial. Indeed, I am myself highly sceptical about it, although this is not the place to go into that debate in any detail.[15]

The second point against the foundationalist appeal to a reliabilist account of the non-inferential justification of introspective knowledge by experience is this. An analogue of the argument which I gave above for (R) could equally be employed at this point, to show that if the 'justificatory' relation between experiences and introspective beliefs is supposed to be merely reliabilist, and is therefore not reason-giving in the demanding

[15] Evans (1982, sect. 7.4) outlines the alternative account of experiential self-knowledge which I favour. See Roessler, 1996, esp. ch. 2, for a development of this account and a critical discussion of the opposing approach which draws upon the Constitution Thesis.

sense in which I am using this notion, then the subject is left quite ignorant about which way of being appeared to being appeared to *F-ly* actually is. So her purportedly foundational introspective knowledge could be no such thing, and would be quite useless in her project of justifying her knowledge of the world around her, on the present conception of what this involves. First, it is clear that, according to the current proposal, her belief that she is being appeared to *F-ly*, as opposed to some other way, has its content in part determined by its relation with her actually being appeared to in just that way. This experience provides the only possible way in which she could know what it is to be appeared to in just that way. Second, on the assumption that this content-determining relation is not a reason-giving relation, it follows that she has, and could have, no reason not to believe that she is being appeared to in some quite different way, *G-ly*, say, as opposed to *F-ly*. Thus, she does not really understand these as different experiences at all. She has no conception of what it is to be appeared to *F-ly*, as opposed to *G-ly*, or any other way. So she is certainly incapable of knowing that she is being appeared to, determinately, *F-ly* (as opposed to *G-ly* or any other way). Contraposing, if she is to have determinate beliefs about the way she is appeared to in perceptual experience, on this model, then the relations between experiences and introspective beliefs must be genuinely reason-giving. A purely reliabilist account of the justification of such beliefs by these experiences is therefore untenable.

For these three reasons (4.2.1–4.2.3), the classical foundation-alist's commitment to (G), above, is seriously problematic. (L) is no better off, in my view. For the foundationalist's conception of the perceiver's epistemic predicament obstructs all of the stand-ard proposals for her knowledge of the relevant mind-to-world linking principle, of the form 'being appeared to *F-ly* is a reliable indicator that *p*'. Bracketing all of the difficulties with this idea which I have just been presenting, we are to consider a per-son whose perceptual experience constitutes her direct, non-inferential knowledge simply of the way things appear to her. Coming to know that being appeared to in such and such a way is a reliable indicator that things are externally thus and so from this position is equivalent to giving a successful head-on refuta-tion of external world scepticism *on the sceptic's own terms*. Yet the history of epistemology constitutes convincing evidence that this cannot be done. The three candidate accounts—induction, inference to the best explanation, and transcendental argument—are all unsuccessful (see Alston, 1993, for a useful survey of their difficulties). I cannot go into these failings in any detail here; but I shall say just a little about the principal problems faced by each approach in turn.[16]

4.2.4 *Induction*

As Hume famously argues (1978, pp. 187–218), any attempt by a perceiver to establish the mind-to-world linking principle required by (L), that being appeared to F-*ly* is a reliable indicator that p, by induction will be circular. For this requires, as an inductive base, her knowledge of the repeated past correspondence of her F-type appearances with the fact that p. Yet such knowledge clearly requires her knowledge that p on the appropriate past occasions, which is necessarily perceptual, and therefore in its turn requires her knowledge of precisely the mind-to-world linking principle in question. Perhaps, it may be replied, knowledge of a different linking principle underwrites her knowledge that p on these previous occasions. But then we can raise the question of how she acquires knowledge of this second linking principle; and the argument begins again. Thus, by repeated application of this objection, the appeal to induction is either circular or viciously regressive. Either way, it is unacceptable.[17]

4.2.5 *Inference to the Best Explanation*

Can the reliability of perceptual appearances as indicators of the way things are in the mind-independent world be inferred as the best explanation and predictor of certain regularities within experience itself, themselves known directly by introspection?

---

[16] The discussion which follows is greatly indebted to Alston (1993), especially in connection with the possibility of a perceiver arriving at knowledge of the appropriate mind–world linking principles by inference to the best explanation.

[17] See 4.3 below for my discussion of Sellars's attempt to avoid this line of objection to a person's appeal to induction at just this point in his own coherentist account of perceptual knowledge.

Again, my discussion will be extremely brief; but I have three worries about this proposal.

First, it is far from clear precisely what the experiential data are supposed to be, which are held to be best explained and predicted by hypotheses of the required form: F-type perceptual appearances reliably indicate that, mind-independently, p, say. Second, in what sense, exactly, are hypotheses of this form supposed to be the *best* explanation and source of prediction with respect to such data? Third, even if some notion of superiority in prediction and explanation could be formulated which would uniquely favour the target hypotheses over every possible alternative, it has also to be established that their superiority in this sense is a good ground for judging that such hypotheses are true. Furthermore, this has to be established quite independently of any appeal to induction from the truth-conduciveness of explanatory and predictive superiority in this sense in connection with familiar scientific hypotheses about the perceived physical world. For this would obviously be to beg the question at this point, by assuming the unproblematic availability to us of perceptual knowledge about the world around us. Of course, these are simply three challenges to the proponent of this abductive account of a person's knowledge of the mind-to-world linking principles required by the second clause, (L), of the classical foundationalist's position. But I am myself wholly unconvinced by any of the attempts of which I am aware to meet them.

4.2.6 *Transcendental Argument*

It has also been suggested that the reliability of perceptual appearances as an indicator of the way things are in the world around a person can be established by transcendental argument, as a necessary condition on the possibility of her having experience, thought, agency, or some other basic capacity which she knows more directly that she has. The form of argument would be this.

(1) I am F.

(2) It is a necessary condition on the possibility of S's being F that S's perceptual appearances are reliable indicators of certain worldly affairs.

∴ (3) My perceptual appearances are reliable indicators of certain worldly affairs.

Any such argument faces a general difficulty though. For the possibility of a person's knowledge, by philosophical argument, of (2), tends to undermine her supposedly unproblematic knowledge of (1), unless one of these already presupposes her knowledge of (3). For now, I shall just illustrate this claim in connection with a particular version of the strategy. I return to a more detailed discussion of the principles underlying this response in Chapter 8 below (8.2 and 8.3).

My example comes from Burge, 1993.

(T1) I am thinking that there are physical entities.

(T2) *S* can think thoughts involving the concept of physical entities only if *S* bears causal-perceptual relations to physical entities.

∴ (T3) I bear causal-perceptual relations to physical entities.

I assume for the sake of the argument that bearing causal-perceptual relations with things entails that the subject's perceptual appearances due to such things are reliable indicators of their presence and certain of their properties. So, if this argument really can be the *source* of a person's knowledge of (T3), then the classical foundationalist's commitment to (L), above, is defensible. Furthermore, I shall also grant that premise (T2) is true and knowable a priori by philosophical argument. Still, the classical foundationalist has a problem. For how is he to account for the subject's knowledge of premise (T1), which is supposed to inform her (the subject), via the above argument, what it is of which the appearances in question are a reliable indicator? Surely, it will be replied, this is a perfectly unproblematic piece of self-knowledge. A person just is normally in a position to know the contents of her own thoughts. Of course, there are major philosophical disagreements about what exactly this involves, and how it is best to be understood; but denying the phenomenon is not a plausible option.

This may be so. Yet it seems to me that the classical foundationalist attempting to exploit the present strategy in defence of (L) faces a dilemma at just this point. Either a person's perceptual experiences of physical entities—that is, on the present account, the appearances to which such entities give rise—*themselves* provide her with reasons to believe that there are *physical entities* in her environment, as opposed to something of a quite different nature—non-physical 'things in themselves', a mad scientist, or an evil demon, for example—systematically causing her experiences, or they do not. If, on the one hand, they do not provide such reasons, and are in this sense entirely neutral on their cause, then there are no determinate facts of which she is in a position to know *on the basis of this argument* that her experiences are reliable indicators. Using the form of words 'physical entities' for whatever actually turn out to be the causes of her experiences, she may know that such experiences reliably indicate the presence of just such entities. In other words, she may know that the sentence 'These appearances reliably indicate the presence of physical entities' is true. But she has not the slightest idea which truth this sentence expresses. For she has no idea what 'physical entities', so construed, are. So she has no determinate idea of what it is of which her perceptual experiences are a reliable indicator. She is certainly not in any position to claim that they reliably indicate the presence of—real—*physical entities*, as opposed to anything else.[18]

If, on the other hand, possession of the relevant experiences suffices in itself to provide the subject with reasons to believe that there are physical entities of such and such kinds in her environment, then the transcendental argument is completely unnecessary; and the classical foundationalist appeal to (G) and (L) otiose. For the point of the argument is supposed to be to provide the subject with knowledge of a mind-to-world linking principle which *transforms* her introspective awareness of her own perceptual appearances into a reason for believing that the world around her is thus and so. Yet on this horn of the dilemma, her experiences themselves are assumed already to provide her with just such reasons. So the detour via (L), and the whole classical foundationalist enterprise, is unnecessary.

I conclude that the classical foundationalist's *inferential*

---

[18] This line of argument is clearly closely related to my Switching Argument of 3.1 ff. above, for the necessity of reason-giving content-determining relations between perceptual experiences and empirical beliefs.

account of perceptual knowledge—on which knowledge of the mind-independent world is supposed to be derived from more basic knowledge of the world-independent mind, (G), by appeal to a mind-to-world linking principle, (L)—is completely unacceptable.

4.3 *Classical Coherentism*

The classical foundationalism which I have just been discussing makes a genuine attempt to endorse and elucidate my thesis (R), that perceptual experiences provide reasons for empirical beliefs; and it does so on the intended reading on which a person's reasons are necessarily recognizable as such from the subject's point of view. The key component in its account of how this condition upon recognition is satisfied is the requirement of *second-order* knowledge, on the part of a knowing perceiver, of the reliability of her first-order method of perceptual belief acquisition. Crudely, the picture is this. A person's perceptual system is a reliable mechanism for the production of beliefs about the world around her. True beliefs acquired in this way constitute knowledge provided that she knows, or can know, that the relevant ground-floor method is indeed reliable. In such cases, her experiences provide reasons for the relevant beliefs. Nevertheless, her second-order knowledge is independent of the first-order method whose reliability is in question in the following sense. She might have acquired the same beliefs in the same way—by just this method—without it. It is knowledge about the reliability of a general procedure, of which her acquisition of this particular belief is an instance, where the same general procedure might equally have operated, equally reliably, without any such reflective knowledge.

I call any account with this structure a *second-order* account of the truth of (R). Its defining feature is the idea that the recognition requirement upon the provision of reasons for empirical beliefs by perceptual experiences is a matter of the subject's second-order reflection upon the credentials of her first-order method of belief acquisition, where the first and second orders are independent in the sense given above: she might equally have acquired the same belief by just the same first-order method yet not have had the second-order knowledge in question. Note that there is already a tension here with my argument for (R). For the crucial claim there is that the very existence of determinate empirical beliefs depends, at least in the most basic cases, upon the actual provision of reasons for such beliefs by the perceptual experiences upon which they causally depend. Yet a second-order account of the kind currently under consideration appears committed to the view that satisfaction of the recognition condition upon this provision of reasons is in every case quite independent of the existence of the determinate empirical beliefs themselves. In the end, I think that precisely this tension is what is fatal to any second order approach. A proponent of (R) must instead seek a *first-order* account of its truth, on which satisfaction of the recognition requirement is integral to the subject's very possession of the empirical beliefs in question, essential to her grasp of their determinate contents. But there are two reasons to pursue the possibility of a second-order account further than this bald point. First, the present criticism is far from conclusive as it stands. It notes a prima facie tension between the second-order approach to accounting for the truth of (R) and my argument in favour of the thesis itself. Yet there are many more responses to this situation than a compliant rejection of the second-order approach altogether. Perhaps the apparent tension is only illusory; or, although (R) is true, my argument wrongly locates its source. I disagree with these alternatives, but further argument is required to complete the case. Second, significant illumination is to be gained by working though, in detail, the way in which this tension ultimately leads to the refutation of influential variants of the second-order strategy. The previous section addressed this matter in connection with classical foundationalism. The present section turns to what I shall call *classical coherentism.*

Sellars (1963) proposes an alternative second-order account to the classical foundationalism which he convincingly rejects. He accepts that perceptual knowledge depends upon the provision of reasons for the beliefs in question by experiences, in the sense that a perceiving subject is in a position to recognize how it is that she is right about the way things are in the world around her. He also agrees with the classical foundationalist that this recognition is necessarily the product of the subject's second-order reflection upon the reliability of her first-order belief acquisition, where the first and second orders are independent of each other in the relevant sense: she might have acquired the same belief, on any particular occasion, in the same way, without any such reflective knowledge. Yet he rejects the idea that knowledge of the external world is in any way inferred from foundational introspective knowledge merely of appearances, by means of a mind-to-world linking principle. Rather, on Sellars's view, a person's true utterance of 'This is green', say, on the basis of perception, constitutes an expression of perceptual knowledge simply provided that she knows that utterances of 'This is green' are reliable indicators of the presence of green objects in standard conditions of perception: in that case she has the required reason for her belief.[19]

The status of any utterance as expressive of knowledge, then, depends upon the subject's knowledge that such utterances are reliable indicators of their truth. Without any foundational knowledge (e.g. from introspection of perceptual appearances), in need of no further justification whatsoever, though, an objection immediately threatens: '[I]t might be thought that there is an obvious regress in the view we are examining. Does it not tell us that observational knowledge at time t presupposes knowledge of the form *X is a reliable symptom of Y*, which presupposes *prior* observational knowledge, which presupposes *other* knowledge of the form *X is a reliable symptom of Y*, which presupposes still other, and *prior*, observational knowledge, and so on?' (Sellars, 1963, pp. 168–9). Sellars's own reply to this objection is revealing, and worth quoting in full.

This charge, however, rests on too simple, indeed a radically mistaken, conception of what one is saying of Jones when one says that he *knows* that-*p*. . . . The essential point is that in characterizing an episode or a

---

[19] Note Sellars's shift from the question of which beliefs constitute knowledge to that of which utterances express knowledge. I think that he has two related reasons for this. First, he regards the concept of belief as parasitic upon that of knowledge: an utterance expresses *mere* belief (as opposed to knowledge) if it is a failed attempt at expressing knowledge. Second, his preference for a third-person over a first-person approach in the philosophy of mind places the expression of mentality conceptually prior to the introspection of it. For present purposes, we can simply adopt his reformulation of the issue and leave it at that. Nothing in my discussion depends upon this shift of focus.

state as that of *knowing*, we are not giving an empirical description of that episode or state; we are placing it in the logical space of reasons, of justifying and being able to justify what one says.

37. Thus, all that the view I am defending requires is that no tokening by S *now* of 'This is green' is to count as 'expressing observational knowledge' unless it is also correct to say of S that he *now* knows the appropriate fact of the form *X is a reliable symptom of Y*, namely that . . . utterances of 'This is green' are reliable indicators of the presence of green objects in standard conditions of perception. And while the correctness of this statement about Jones requires that Jones could *now* cite prior particular facts as evidence for the idea that these utterances *are* reliable indicators, it requires only that it is correct to say that Jones *now* knows, thus remembers, that these particular facts *did* obtain. It does not require that it be correct to say that at the time these facts did obtain he then knew them to obtain. And the regress disappears.

Thus, while Jones's ability to give inductive reasons *today* is built on a long history of acquiring and manifesting verbal habits in perceptual situations, and, in particular, the occurrence of verbal episodes, e.g. 'This is green', which is superficially like those which are later properly said to express observational knowledge, it does not require that any episode in this prior time be characterizable as expressing knowledge. (At this point, the reader should reread section 19 above . . .) (Sellars, 1963, p. 169)

Sellars is referring to the passage where he says:

[O]ne can have the concept of green only by having a whole battery of concepts of which it is one element. . . . [W]hile the whole process of acquiring the concept of green may—indeed does—involve a long history of acquiring *piecemeal* habits of response to various objects in various circumstances, there is an important sense in which one has no concept pertaining to the observable properties of physical objects in Space and Time unless one has them all. (p. 148)

It is not easy to make out exactly what is going on here; but it seems to be this. A person, Jones, is conditioned by his training to make certain utterances in certain circumstances. Unbeknownst to him at the time, these are generally circumstances in which the utterances—interpreted as statements about the things around him—are true. His utterances of 'This is green', for example, correspond with the presence of green objects in his environment in standard conditions for perception. (The precise mechanism of the conditioning is, I take it, not crucial to Sellars's story.) Later, through learning the language of physical objects in space and time, he (Jones) comes to understand his relations with such things, enabling him to recognize his previous utterances as true statements about them, or, at least, as coincident with the presence of green objects in his environment in standard conditions for perception. Hence he has evidence that such utterances are reliable in this sense. When he is now inclined (truly) to say, 'This is green', he thereby expresses knowledge that the thing in question is green. For he now knows how it is that he is right: such statements are a reliable symptom of their truth in appropriate conditions like these. He can therefore give a reasoned defence of his present utterance as a true statement about the way things are in the world.

4.3.1 *Self-Knowledge*

An obvious worry about this is that Jones's knowledge that utterances of 'This is green' are reliable indicators of the presence of green things around him contributes to this reasoned defence only if he knows that he is making them when he is. A natural reply might be that knowledge of one's own deliberate utterances is somehow 'given' in the act of making them. Saying 'This is green', and meaning it, itself involves non-inferential knowledge that one is doing so. Whatever truth there may be in this idea, though, it is not something that Sellars can take for granted. For doing so effectively transforms his position into a notational variant of classical foundationalism. The result is an account on which perceptual knowledge is a matter of inference from foundational knowledge of the content of the knowledgeable utterance itself by means of a utterance-to-world linking principle. True statements which a person forms about the external world on the basis of perception are normally expressive of knowledge, on this view, because

(GU) the fact that he makes an utterance with a certain content is simply 'given';

and

(LU) he knows, or is in a position to know, that such utterances are a reliable indicator that things are as he thereby states them to be out there.

Since this position is subject to precisely the objections which Sellars himself presses against the original (G), and which I develop above, and also to variants of the standard sceptical difficulties with (L) in this context, which I also outlined above, he has instead to give an independent account of a person's knowledge of what he is saying in making an utterance expressive of observational knowledge. A possible suggestion would be this. Jones says, 'This is green'. Asked what he said, he answers, 'This is green' or 'I said: This is green'. He knows that such utterances are reliable indicators of what he says. For he can now cite their past truth as evidence, although they did not previously express any self-knowledge. Hence, his second utterance now expresses knowledge that he made the first. This is effectively to apply the proposed account of perceptual knowledge once again, to his *hearing* the initial utterance, supposedly expressive of (visual-observational) knowledge that some object in front of him is green.

Even if Sellars's account of observational knowledge were satisfactory in other respects, I do not think that this suggestion is at all compelling. First, there is an obvious danger of a further regress. For Jones's second, self-ascriptive utterance qualifies as expressive of knowledge on this account only if he also knows that he is making it, and we are back with the original worry about how this latter knowledge is to be accounted for. On the present suggestion, a further application of the theory is required, and so on ad infinitum. Second, assimilation of knowledge of the fact and content of one's own utterances to external perceptual knowledge looks very unlikely to be able to capture the evident first person authority involved in the former. Of course, this matter is itself highly contentious. Nevertheless, a theory which appears incapable in principle of marking any interesting epistemological contrasts between normal external observation and any of the following is surely to be regarded unfavourably from the start: (1) a person's knowledge that he is speaking when he does so deliberately; (2) his knowledge of which words he utters in such a case; (3) his knowledge of the content of what he thereby says. Yet the current suggestion places Sellars's account in precisely this position.

BonJour makes an alternative suggestion at just this point, as part of his own development of Sellars's coherentist account of the epistemology of empirical observation, which, as I explain below, diverges significantly from the original at a number of key stages in responding to the current line of objection.[20] His suggestion here is this. If there is to be a genuine question about whether a person's empirical belief that *p*, say, is justified, or whether his utterance of *s*, say, is expressive of observational knowledge, then it must be the case that he does indeed believe that *p*, or utter *s*. This is a *presupposition* of coherently raising the question. Hence it can simply be taken for granted in answering it. The required account of his reason for believing or saying what he does can legitimately assume that he does so. No justification need therefore be given for this premise in the overall story justifying his belief or utterance. So the most recent difficulties for Sellars's views about a person's self-knowledge of his own utterances or beliefs simply do not arise.

I find this move completely unsatisfactory. According to both Sellars and BonJour, the subject's self-ascription of the belief or utterance in question provides a crucial premise of an argument to the likely truth of this belief or utterance, which is supposed explicitly to articulate the reasons by appeal to which he is able to defend it, epistemologically speaking, as (expressive of) a piece of knowledge. Any such argument constitutes a satisfactory defence of this kind in the current context, though, only if the subject is himself justified in supplying its premises. For how else could it constitute a genuinely *reasoned* defence of the belief or utterance in question? It is quite irrelevant to this that there may be a pragmatic presumption in favour of the truth of the relevant self-ascription involved in actually raising the question of its epistemological status. For, I take it, the status of a belief or utterance as (expressive of) knowledge is prior to, and quite independent of, the issue of whether or not any question as to this status is actually raised. Yet BonJour's move quite clearly denies that the subject has, or can have, any justification for the relevant self-ascription. Thus, it seems to me quite inadequate.

Waiving these worries about the subject's knowledge of his own utterances (or beliefs) for the sake of the argument, two

[20] See BonJour, 1985, pt. II. The present suggestion is what he labels the 'Doxastic Presumption' (sect. 5.4). His other major deviation from Sellars is made during chs. 6–8.

related questions bring out what is perhaps a deeper difficulty
with Sellars's own overall view. First, how is Jones supposed to
acquire his concepts of external physical objects? Second, how
are these supposed to bring him to recognize the truth of his *past*
utterances of 'This is green', as statements about the world
around him at that time? I shall take these in turn (4.3.2 and
4.3.3), and then go on to discuss BonJour's revision of Sellars's
classical coherentism itself in more detail (4.3.4).

4.3.2 *Acquiring Concepts of Physical Objects in Space and Time*

Jones's initial utterances are just 'verbal habits': noises which he
does not yet understand, which he has benevolently been brain-
washed—somehow—into making when there is something
green (visibly) around in standard conditions of perception,
without any idea of what he is up to or how he might be right.
How, first of all then, are any further noises which he learns to
make in this way supposed to become expressive of a genuine
conception of the physical objects and properties standardly
prompting these verbal habits? A person can acquire theoretical
concepts as part of a coherent explanation of certain observed
data; and in suitable circumstances these can be used in expressing knowledge about the things in question. But Sellars's account
explicitly denies that there are any such data, known in advance
of any observational knowledge of external things, in explanation of which a theory of physical objects in space and time is
exploited. The only alternative which I can envisage to this data
theory model is that Jones acquires the public language of physical objects on the basis of his prior, non-linguistic, perceptual
demonstrative *knowledge* about them, upon which the conven-
tional linguistic categorization gets to work. This account is
developed in detail in 8.1, but its key idea in the present context
is that Jones's initial utterances are not to be regarded as blind
verbal habits at all, but rather as expressions of direct perceptual awareness that *that thing is thus*. As such, though, on
Sellars's own account, they already require some knowledge on
Jones's part of how he is right about the way that thing is. For
Sellars explicitly endorses the idea that observational knowledge
requires reasons in just this sense. Hence the current account is
ruled out as a strategy by which he can avoid the obvious dan-

ger of regress with which we began. So neither model yields an adequate explanation for Sellars's purposes of how Jones is supposed to come by the concepts of physical objects in space and time which are essential to his expression of observational knowledge about the way particular things are in the world around him.

This first difficulty for Sellars's position is closely connected with my original argument for (R). For the point which I am pressing here is precisely the indispensable role in a person's genuine understanding of his most basic beliefs about the world of mind-independent spatial particulars, of essentially experiential perceptual demonstratives, through which his experiences provide reasons for these empirical beliefs. As a result of his exclusive focus upon a person's reflection upon the process by which he acquires certain beliefs, in particular, the need for knowledge of its reliability, which is characteristic of second-order accounts of (R) quite generally, Sellars fails entirely to get to grips with the crucial issue of what is involved in the subject's having such beliefs in the first place, in his actually grasping their empirical contents. Yet, as I shall argue, this is the correct locus for a proper account of the truth of (R).

4.3.3 *Recognizing the Truth of Past Utterances*

A second and closely related difficulty for Sellars concerns his suggestion that learning the language of physical objects in space and time provides Jones with memory-based knowledge that his earlier utterances were true statements about the condition of external things when they were made. It is one thing to admit, as he puts in a footnote to the passage quoted above, 'that one can have direct (non-inferential) knowledge of a past fact which one did not or even . . . *could* not conceptualize at the time it was present' (1963, p. 169). It is quite another thing to hold that this is possible even if there is no sense whatsoever in which such a fact was actually present *to the subject* at the earlier time.[21]

---

[21] See Martin, 1992, for an argument from the possibility Sellars insists on here, of 'direct (non-inferential) knowledge of a past fact which one did not or even . . . *could* not conceptualize at the time it was present' (1963, p. 169), to the need to recognize the existence of a more primitive perceptual mode of presentation to the subject at the earlier time of the facts later conceptualized in memory.

This is what is required though. For, on Sellars's view, memory of the truth of past utterances, as statements about external states of affairs, is supposed to provide the knowledge of the reliability of such utterances generally which transforms a present instance into an expression of observational knowledge, and it is supposed to do this *in the absence of any past knowledge that such states of affairs actually obtained*. Memory that utterances of 'This is green' *were* true justifies knowledge that a present utterance is the product of a reliable process. Yet the remembered utterances were simply the blind verbal reflexes of a person with no perceptual awareness or knowledge of anything green in his environment at all, indeed, no knowledge of anything out there whatsoever.

If a person knows on independent grounds that a particular instrument is a reliable indicator of the current running through an electric circuit, say, then she can use her memory of its past readings to acquire inferential knowledge of what the current then was, which she did not have at the time—perhaps she did not even know what electric current was then. She knew, and still remembers, say, that the needle was on red; and she infers from this, along with her recent knowledge of its reliability as an ammeter, that the current then was dangerously high. Sellars needs something quite different in the case of Jones, though. The sole ground for his (Jones's) belief in the reliability of the 'instrument'—that is, him, uttering 'This is green' in various circumstances—is to be his memory-knowledge of a correspondence in the past between its readings (his past utterances of 'This is green') and the relevant facts (the presence then of green things in his environment in standard conditions of perception); and he is supposed to have this memory-knowledge even though, at those earlier times, he had no knowledge whatsoever that any such facts obtained. In other words, his memory at some time t of what was the case at an earlier time t_0 is supposed radically to depend upon his conceptual sophistication at t in the following sense. He might have known *absolutely nothing* at t_0, about the way things then were in the world around him, or, indeed, about anything else; yet there might nevertheless be a later t_1 at which he is able directly (non-inferentially) to remember that there was a green object in front of him at t_0.

Now, if he were not totally ignorant about the world around

him at t_0, but knew directly on the basis of perception at least that *that thing is thus*, then later linguistic categorization might get to work on this essentially demonstrative knowledge in producing descriptive memory: 'There was something green in front of me'. But Sellars cannot make this move. For, again, on his own account, it requires that Jones knew at t_0 that appropriate utterances—for example, of 'That thing is thus'—are reliable indicators of certain external states of affairs. Yet the whole point of Sellars's reply to the regress objection is to deny that this has to be so. Thus, his overall position rests upon an untenable account of the role of memory in observational knowledge.

4.3.4 *BonJour's Coherentism*

In defence of his own (1985) development of classical coherentism, BonJour would, I think, accuse Sellars of going along too far with his opponents in his attempted response to the regress objection. For Sellars appears to some extent to be endorsing their *linear* conception of epistemic justification. His account of how it is that a given utterance is expressive of observational knowledge consists in presenting an argument which can be given by the subject as a reasoned defence of this utterance, each premise of which is in turn supposedly susceptible of non-regressive, if ultimately mutually supportive, justification, again, by the subject. In connection with his own example the argument would be this.

(1) I said: 'This is green'.

(2) My utterances of 'This is green' are reliable indicators of the presence of green objects in standard conditions of perception.

(3) Conditions are standard for perception.

∴ (4) This (thing in front of me) is probably green.

It would certainly be very odd for someone actually to offer this argument, or anything like it, in response to the question how he knows that there is something green in front of him. So Sellars's reconstruction of a person's reasons cannot be supposed to mirror the reasoning which he is inclined to give upon being questioned about the matter. In any case, I have expressed scepticism about Sellars's ability to provide the subject with a satisfactory justification for (1), and about his appeal to the subject's memory of the past correlation between his utterances of 'This is green' and the presence of green objects in front of him in standard conditions for perception as an inductive justification for (2). Sellars himself says very little about premise (3), although it is clear, given the way in which he formulates the subject's recognition of the reliability of his utterances, that something along these lines is required. The most sympathetic interpretation of his position would be that he is operating with a notion of 'standard conditions' on which it is reasonable for the subject to assume that (3) holds, provided only that he has no evidence to the contrary. Otherwise, it may be that (3) is supposed to be justified as a conjunction of further pieces of observational knowledge—that the lighting is good, that there is nothing obstructing his view, and so on—each handled in the same way, although this brings an obvious danger of circularity. Whatever his view may be here, if I understand his overall approach correctly, then the central idea is that the subject's success in this enterprise would complete the account of his possession of observational knowledge. His ability to carry on giving satisfactory reasons—first the argument itself, then his reasons for each of its premises, and reasons for those, and so on—exhausts the epistemic good standing of the utterance with which the process begins. Although it may perhaps meet and intersect with itself at various points, there is nevertheless an *ordered* chain of inferential epistemic justification. My objection is just that, on detailed investigation, it turns out that this cannot satisfactorily be done, at least not in the way Sellars suggests.

BonJour's dissatisfaction with this approach, on the other hand, is that its adoption of the foundationalist's linear conception of justification inevitably causes trouble for any non-foundationalist position (1985, p. 24). This, he thinks, is the truth in the traditional regress argument in favour of foundationalism. For, given a rejection of foundationalism, the chain of justification is bound to involve closed loops, which *cannot*, from the perspective of an ordered, linear conception, be regarded as harmless. The alternative which he proposes is a holistic, non-linear conception of justification. As I understand it, and this is not exactly the way in which BonJour presents it himself, the key difference is that a person's having a reason for a belief takes on a two-stage structure on the holistic view, in the following sense. It is a matter, first, of certain relations obtaining between the target belief and the whole system of all of her other beliefs; and, second, of her being able, at least in principle, to give a metajustificatory argument for the thesis that a system of beliefs between which such relations obtain, in the long run, and in the face of the continual addition of 'cognitively spontaneous' observational beliefs,[22] is likely to contain mainly true beliefs. On the linear conception, displaying a given belief as derivable from others by inference of some kind is, provided that the premise beliefs are themselves justified, sufficient to justify it. Having justified beliefs from which this can be done *is* having a reason for the belief in question. On the holistic conception, the relations between beliefs displayed at the first stage are not, in and of themselves, intrinsically, reason-giving relations. They can be transformed into such only by the subject's giving, or being in a position to give, a further argument that their obtaining is truth-conducive, in the sense outlined above.

Of course, only certain relations between beliefs will be plausible candidates at the first stage, given the need for this second-stage metajustification. BonJour, unsurprisingly, focuses on consistency, both logical and probabilistic, the presence of inferential connections, and interrelations of explanation and prediction: he calls the extent and strength of such relations the degree of *coherence* of the overall system of beliefs (1985, sect. 5.3). That the required relations are of these kinds, though, does not make them justificatory as they stand, precisely because, presented as such, they would be undermined by the inevitable circular interdependence between them. Rather, they are made genuinely reason-giving by being proven to be such that,

---

[22] These are beliefs which simply occur to, or 'strike', the subject 'in a manner which is both involuntary and quite coercive'; they are neither inferred from other beliefs, nor derived 'from any other sort of deliberative or ratiocinative process, whether explicit or implicit' (BonJour, 1985, p. 117). The subject's ability, *at least in principle,* to give such an argument is a matter, I take it, of its being possible for a theorist of her situation to give such an argument on her behalf, and from her point of view. Having said that, it is not altogether clear, to me at least, exactly which rules govern such a project: how much, or how little, can the theorist himself bring in to the subject's point of view?

although circularly interdependent, a system which remains coherent, in this sense—in the long run and in the face of the continual impact of observation—is likely, to a degree which is proportional to the degree of this coherence and the length of the run, to correspond closely to independent reality.[23] He claims that such a proof can be given, by an inference to the best explanation. Such long-run coherence in the face of the continual addition of cognitively spontaneous observational beliefs needs explaining. It is best explained by the truth of the beliefs in question. Hence the system is likely to correspond with reality (1985, sects. 8.3–8.4).

Although BonJour explicitly denies this, it seems to me that the resultant position is very similar to a classical foundationalist account with an abductive proof of the mind-to-world linking principle required by (L). On BonJour's account, the contents of a person's empirical beliefs and the coherence relations between them are simply given, by the Doxastic Presumption (1985, sect. 5.4), that these can just be taken for granted in the context of a serious challenge to provide a justification for the system of beliefs in question. Then the suggestion is that an inference to the best explanation is available to establish that, provided the subject strives for the maximum coherence in the long run, these beliefs will be, by and large, true. In this light, I think that his explicit admission that no justification is available for the foundational self-ascriptions given by the Doxastic Presumption is fatal. Indeed, in discussing the range of options available in response to the traditional regress argument which often motivates foundationalism, he says the following about the possibility that '[t]he regress might terminate with beliefs which are offered as justifying premises for earlier beliefs but for which no justification of any kind, however implicit, is available when they are challenged in turn' (1985, p. 21): 'If this alternative were realized, then the justification of all empirical knowledge would rest finally on beliefs which were, from an epistemic standpoint, entirely arbitrary and hence incapable of conferring any genuine justification upon their inferential consequences. The chains of inferential

---

23 This is a close paraphrase of his metajustificatory thesis, MJ (1985, p. 171).

justification would be left hanging in the air, ultimately unsup-
ported, and no empirical knowledge would be genuinely
justified' (1985, p. 22). Yet this seems to be precisely his own
predicament, when the essential need for the second stage metajustification is properly appreciated. Thus, his overall position
appears untenable by his own lights.

Furthermore, there are still the objections which I sketched
above to any inference to the best explanation argument in support of the required mind-to-world linking principle. Ad-
mittedly, BonJour has a clearer conception than is offered by
classical foundationalist proponents of this approach of exactly
what the data are supposed to be which are best explained by
this linking principle—which he calls the 'correspondence
hypothesis' (1985, pp. 171 ff.). For he goes into some detail about
exactly what the long-run coherence of a system of beliefs in the
face of observational input consists in. Similarly, I grant that he
is working with a notion of the superior explanatory value of the
correspondence hypothesis, over all its opponents, from which
its likely truth does indeed follow. Nevertheless, I am entirely
unconvinced by his case that this hypothesis is indeed superior
in this sense as an explanation of the data in question.

The crucial argument is complex, but it is intended to establish that the a priori probability of the correspondence hypothesis is greater than that of any sceptical alternative hypothesis
about the relation between a system of beliefs preserving coherence over a long run of observational input and the mind-
independent facts. The key claim is this. It is a priori vastly more
likely that observational input should be coherence-preserving
given the assumption that such cognitively spontaneous beliefs
are caused *in some way or other* by a relatively stable spatio-
temporal world, than is given the hypothesis that their cause
is as suggested by the relevant sceptical alternative. BonJour
makes two points in defence of this claim. First, whereas the
cause of observational beliefs, according to sceptical hypotheses,
is a 'neutral producer of beliefs', with respect to which 'all or vir-
tually all possible patterns of beliefs and of belief causation [are]
equally likely to occur', a spatio-temporal world, 'having as it
does a definite and orderly character of its own . . . would be
expected a priori to cause beliefs in ways which reflected that
character to some degree, not in a completely random fashion'

(BonJour, 1985, pp. 186–7). Hence full coherence-preserving observation is more probable on the latter hypothesis than on the former. Second, the correspondence hypothesis brings with it a biological evolutionary story of how it is that there came to be 'cognitive beings whose spontaneous beliefs are connected with the world in the right way' (p. 187), whereas, focusing simply on those aspects of sceptical hypotheses which are relevant to the generation of spontaneous beliefs, no such account can be given.

Both of these points rely entirely upon BonJour's choice of a particular sceptical hypothesis, though: a Cartesian evil demon hypothesis *with respect to which he explicitly ignores the fact that the demon is a purposive agent* (p. 246, n. 35). Were he instead to consider, as a metaphysically radical alternative to the correspondence hypothesis, Berkeley's God as the cause of the subject's cognitively spontaneous 'empirical observations', then both of his contrasts would vanish. First, relative to the hypothesis that their cause is God, the preserved coherence of her observations is extremely likely. More so, indeed, than relative to the hypothesis that they are caused in some way or another by a spatio-temporal world; for God purposively directs the causation itself. Second, the hypothesis that observation is the direct result of God's will brings with it a very familiar account of how there came to be subjects whose beliefs hang together over time in a highly coherent manner. I am absolutely not endorsing the Berkeleian metaphysics and theology of creation which goes with it. I just want to bring out the fact that BonJour seems powerless to exclude it as an alternative to the correspondence hypothesis. Yet the success of his position requires him to do so.

Thus, like the foundationalist position which his account, in my view, so closely mirrors, BonJour's coherentism is untenable both with respect to a person's knowledge of her own beliefs and their interrelations, and with respect to her knowledge that these are probably a true representation of independent reality.

4.4 Conclusion

Reliabilism is unacceptable because it is incompatible with my thesis (R), and even appears itself to require the truth of this very thesis, which undermines its commitment to the reliability of a method of belief acquisition as the fundamental focus for its assessment as a source of knowledge. Furthermore, if the foundationalist and coherentist versions which I have been discussing are reasonably representative, and I am aware of no significant third alternative, then second-order accounts of the truth of (R) are also unacceptable. These attempt to satisfy the recognition requirement upon the provision by perceptual experiences of reasons for empirical beliefs by the subject's second-order reflection upon the credentials of her first-order method of belief acquisition, where the first and second orders are independent in the following sense: she might equally have acquired the same belief by just the same first-order method yet not have had the second-order knowledge in question. It seems, therefore, that we must, as I suggested earlier, pursue the possibility of a *first-order* elucidation of (R). This will be one on which the truth of (R) emerges *directly* from a correct account of a person's possession of certain beliefs about the mind-independent world around her, of what is involved, that is to say, in her grasping their determinate empirical contents, rather than from any independent requirement concerning her second-order reflection upon her possession of such beliefs.

Articulating such an account in detail, further motivating it, and defending it against objection, are the primary goals of Part II. The key idea will be this. We have already seen that the contents of a person's most basic beliefs about the mind-independent spatial world are essentially experiential. I shall argue that it is precisely for this reason that these contents are such that simply entertaining them provides her with a reason for endorsing them in belief. What her perceptual experiences ineliminably contribute to a person's grasp of these basic empirical contents itself provides her with a reason for her beliefs with those contents.

II

The Rational Role of Perceptual Experiences

5

Reasons Require Conceptual Contents

In Part II, I develop my own first-order elucidation of the truth of (R). I offer a detailed account of how it is that perceptual experiences provide reasons for empirical beliefs, for which I give positive argument, and defence against objection, before tracing out some of its most significant consequences. To begin with, though, we need to get a lot clearer about the nature of reasons themselves, about exactly what is involved in a person's having reasons for beliefs. Doing so provides a workable conception of what (R) demands of perceptual experiences. I shall argue in this chapter for the following claim.

(C) Reasons require conceptual contents.[1]

This is the claim that a person has a reason for believing something only if he is in some mental state or other with a conceptual content: a conceptual state. The crucial term here, of course, is 'conceptual'. As I am using it, the key idea is that a conceptual state of this kind is one whose content is the content of a possible *judgement by the subject*. I propose the following definition. A mental state is *conceptual* if and only if it has a representational content that is characterizable only in terms of concepts which the subject himself must possess and which is of a form which enables it to serve as a premise or the conclusion of a deductive argument, or of an inference of some other kind (e.g. inductive or abductive).[2] Thus, conceptual states are

---

[1] As with (R) above, this claim is central to the epistemology of John McDowell's recent *Mind and World* (1994b); and, again, my argument in this chapter is an extended development of what he says there in this connection: his argument as it strikes me.

[2] Note that this definition does nothing to rule out states with ineliminably *demonstrative* contents, the component concepts of which can only be grasped

capable of providing inferential justifications for the subject and can be given inferential justifications by him: they are 'open to reflection about . . . [their] own rational credentials' (McDowell, 1994*b*, p. 47).

5.1 *The Basic Argument*

Like my argument for (R), the argument which I am about to present in support of (C) has two premises. The first makes explicit the connection between reasons and inference, and hence between giving reasons and identifying contents of a form which enables them to serve as the premises and conclusions of inferences. The second establishes a constraint upon genuine reasons—reasons *for the subject*—imposed by the way in which his own conceptual resources are available for the configuration of his mental states. Recalling the definition of conceptual mental states given above, as those with a representational content which is characterizable only in terms of concepts which the subject himself possesses and which is of a form which enables it to serve as a premise or the conclusion of a deductive argument or of an inference of some other kind, this yields the required conclusion, that reasons require conceptual contents: having reasons consists in being in conceptual mental states. I take each of the two premises in turn.

A reason is necessarily a reason *for* something; and in the sense in which we are concerned with such things, it will be a reason for making a particular judgement or for holding a certain belief (or perhaps for performing an action of some kind at a given time). To give a reason in this context is to identify some feature of the subject's situation which makes the relevant judgement or belief (or perhaps action) appropriate, or intelligible, from the point of view of rationality. It is, paraphrasing McDowell (1985, p. 389), to mention considerations which reveal the judgement or belief (or action) as at least approximating to

by a person actually standing in certain perceptual-attentional relations with their semantic values, or by someone who has done so within the range of his capacity to retain the relevant demonstrative concepts in memory, from the category of conceptual states. This inclusion will be of crucial importance in what follows. See especially Ch. 6, and 8.1.

what rationally ought to happen in those circumstances. Now, making something intelligible from the point of view of rationality in this way necessarily involves identifying a valid deductive argument, or inference of some other kind, which articulates the source of the rational obligation (or permission) in question. This constitutes an explicit reconstruction of the reasoning in virtue of whose correctness this obligation (or permission) is sustained. For *rational* intelligibility, or appropriateness of the kind revealed by giving reasons, just is that mode of approbation which is made explicit by the reconstruction of *valid reasoning* of some such kind to a conclusion that is suitably related to the judgement or belief (or action) for which the reasons are being given.[3] Hence, in making essential reference to the relevant valid inference, giving a reason involves making essential reference to its premises and conclusion, and so, trivially, to the kinds of things which can serve as the premises or conclusion of some kind of inference. In keeping with the orthodoxy as I perceive it, I call such contents *propositions*. This, then, is the first premise of my argument for (C): giving reasons involves identifying certain relevant propositions—those contents which figure as the premises and conclusions of inferences explicitly articulating the reasoning involved.

Second, we are interested here, not just in any old reasons which there may be for making judgements or holding beliefs—such as their simply happening to be true, or beneficial in some mysterious way to the subject's overall well-being—but only in reasons *for the subject* to do these things, to take things actually to be the way he believes them to be. These must be the subject's *own* reasons, which figure as such *from his point of view*.[4] It follows from this, first, that the subject's having such a reason consists in his being in some mental state or other, although this

---

[3] Note here that I intend 'validity' to be interpreted very widely, to capture the correctness or acceptability of inductive and abductive reasoning as well as formal deductive validity.

[4] Notice that it is precisely the provision by perceptual experiences of reasons *in this sense* which is established as necessary for the genuine empirical significance of beliefs by the argument which I gave above (Chs. 2, 3) for (R). In particular, the assumption reduced to absurdity in establishing the second premise of this argument is that the required relations between experiences and empirically significant beliefs might not be reason-giving *for the subject*.

may well be essentially factive. For any actually motivating reason *for the subject* must at the very least register at the personal level in this way. Second, it also follows that it cannot be the case that the proposition, reference to which is required by the first premise above in characterizing the reason in question, can merely be related to this mental state of the subject's *indirectly*, by the theorist in some way. Rather, it must actually *be* the content of his mental state in a sense which requires that the subject has all of its constituent concepts. Otherwise, even though being in some such state may make it advisable, relative to a certain end or need, for the subject to make the judgement or hold the belief (or perform the action) in question, it cannot constitute *his own* reason for doing so. Thus, reasons require what are, by my definition above, conceptual contents: this is thesis (C).

5.2 *Possible Counterexamples*

As with my argument for (R), it is helpful to illustrate what is going on here by considering putative counterexamples to (C). Like the familiar account of our experiences of, and beliefs about, secondary qualities, which I discussed in connection with that earlier argument, a proponent of the counterexample which I shall consider at most length goes along with the present argument most, but not quite all, of the way. Of course, it may be admitted, demonstrating that a person has a reason for believing that p is a matter of identifying a mental state of that person with some appropriate relation to a proposition, that q, say, constituting the premise of an inference of some kind with the conclusion that p. Nevertheless, according to this line of objection, the relevant relation between this mental state and the premise proposition, that q, need not be that this proposition *is* the conceptual content of the mental state in question, which is essential to the subject's having the reason which he has for believing that p. It might be the case, instead, that this mental state has some non-conceptual, but perfectly representational, content, which has to be characterized more indirectly by reference to the premise proposition that q. Yet it may still provide the subject with a reason for believing that p.

Note, first of all, the extent of agreement here with my argument for (C). The subject's having a reason for believing that *p* is admitted to require him to be in some mental state with a representational content appropriately related to a proposition constituting the premise of an inference of some kind whose conclusion is the proposition that *p*, related to the conceptual content of the belief in question by identity. The sole, but highly significant, disagreement lies in the relation envisaged between the relevant premise proposition—that *q*—and the representational content of this mental state involved in the subject's having the reason in question. The present objector denies that *this* is one of identity. Yet it is precisely the idea that this must be the identity relation which completes my argument for the necessary involvement of conceptual mental states in a person's possession of genuine reasons for belief. For the claim that the representational content of the required mental state is (identical to) the premise proposition that *q* just is the claim that the subject has to have all the concepts constitutive of this proposition, which is what is required to make the final connection between his having the reason in question and my definition of a conceptual mental state. Now, recall that it is my insistence that the reason in question should be *the subject's reason* for believing that *p* which is supposed to force this last move of the argument. So this insistence will be the focus of my rebuttal of the proposed counterexample.

Before proceeding to that, though, I should at least acknowledge the possibility of a number of different types of putative counterexample, which effectively resist other, earlier, steps of my argument. Three come to mind. The first denies that giving a reason must somehow make reference to the premise of an inference whose conclusion is appropriately related, most probably by identity, to the content of the belief for which the reason is being given. The second admits this, but denies that a person's having a reason requires his possession of any appropriate mental state. The third admits both, but denies that the mental states required in this way need have representational contents of any kind at all.

I have little to say about the first line of objection, other than to repeat my argument for the first premise of the overall argument for (C) given above. This is the premise which secures the relation between giving reasons and making essential reference to inferences. Giving a reason for a person's believing something, say, *S*'s believing that *p* for example, is a matter of stating a fact about that person which makes her believing that thing intelligible from the point of view of rationality. If this is to happen then the selected fact about *S* must be somehow related to (her) believing that *p*. And since this relation is to make her believing that *p* intelligible *from the point of view of rationality*, it is necessarily a relation which obtains in virtue of the correctness of some kind of reasoning. That is to say, successfully giving such a reason makes essential reference to the premise of an inference of some kind, whose conclusion is appropriately related, most likely by identity, to the content of the belief for which the reason is being given. Given this argument, and in the absence to my knowledge of any proposed alternative conception of reason-giving relations, which is entirely independent of the existence of any underlying reasoning or inference, I submit that there can be no counterexamples of this first type.

The second line of objection concerns the possibility of reasons, possession of which by a person does not require his possession of any appropriately related mental state. This may appear to be a theoretical analogue of the externalist position in the debate between internal and external reasons theorists in the practical case.[5] I think that the appearance would be misleading, though. For even the external-reasons theorist in that debate holds that any actually motivating reason involves a corresponding desire of some kind on the part of the agent (McDowell, 1978*a*, 1995). The debate is rather one about the correct order of explanation, or priority, between the ascriptions of reasons for action and desires (very broadly construed). The *internalist* thinks that a person's 'subjective motivational set', S, of desires and related pro attitudes, is primary, whilst which reasons he thereby has for which actions is secondary, and constrained by appropriate construction from the prior elements of S. The *externalist*, on the other hand, thinks that the primary issue is over what reasons there are for a person to do what, where some of these may *not* be arrived at by appropriate con-

---

[5] See Williams, 1980; Hollis, 1987, ch. 6; McDowell, 1995; and Williams, 1995, pp. 186–94.

struction from any *prior* members of S. Nevertheless, in any case in which it is correct to make a true external-reason ascription in explanation of a person's action, when that reason actually motivates him, there will necessarily be an element of his S corresponding with this reason. His possession of this desire, though, will be a derivative component, or immediate consequence, of his coming to recognize the existence of the reason in question.[6] In any case, it is agreed on all sides of the internalist-versus-externalist debate that *motivating* reasons essentially involve mental states. Likewise, in the theoretical case, it seems to me that whenever it is correct to give a reason as *the subject's* reason for making a certain judgement or holding some belief which he does, then his having that reason essentially involves some mental state or other. For reason giving of this kind is only appropriate when the stated reason's status *as a reason* is casually explanatory; and this in turn depends upon the subject's recognition, or appreciation, in some sense, of its status as a reason, which essentially involves his having an appropriate mental state. So, regardless of one's view about whether or not there is a sense in which the reason exists prior to its motivating recognition by the subject, reason giving of the kind we are interested in essentially involves identifying some mental state of the subject's. Again, in the absence of any concrete proposal, then, I deny that there could be a counterexample of the second kind identified above.

The third type of counterexample is supposed to be one on which a person has a reason for judgement or belief, which, although this does indeed require his possession of a mental state of some appropriate sort, makes no requirement to the effect that this mental state should have any kind of *representational content*. A parallel possibility with respect to reasons for action might be suggested by the following case. Suppose that a person touches a hot surface and withdraws her hand as a result of feeling its heat. It may be claimed that her action is made intelligible

---

[6] See Stout, 1996, for a well-worked-out development of this idea as a means to presenting a 'behaviourist' analysis of belief-desire psychology, by providing a non-mentalist, broadly behavioural, characterization of motivation by external reasons. See especially his introduction, for clear explication of this difference in orders of explanation between himself, on the externalist side, and the internalist orthodoxy.

from the point of view of rationality simply by mentioning the painfulness of the contact. Thus, it might be proposed, the intrinsic nature of that phenomenal, but wholly non-representational, mental state provides her reason for her action.

The case is far from decisive, though. For it might equally be replied that no reason has been given until the subject's desire, or something like it, to get rid of the painful sensation has been mentioned, which obviously has representational content. Certainly, the withdrawal is left unintelligible in the relevant sense if it turns out that she actually enjoys the sensation; and the situation is little better if she has no preference either way. So, a mental state with representational content is after all essential. Similarly, it might be insisted that it is wrong to conceive of the pain itself as entirely non-representational. For this essentially involves the subject's representation of a specific part of herself as being in an inherently undesirable condition.[7] Otherwise, why is her movement *of her hand, in that direction,* rationally intelligible? Again, representational content appears indispensable to reason-giving explanation.

Indeed, my own view is that the notion of *purely phenomenal,* entirely non-representational, mental states—or even such aspects of mental states (see Peacocke, 1983, ch. 1)—is a philosophers' invention of only dubious coherence, and certainly without instance in normal human life. What substance could there possibly be to the idea of things being determinately thus and so, phenomenally speaking, *for a subject* without anything being presented as being any way *to him* at all? In what else other than *how things seem to him* could the determinacy of the phenomenology *for him* reside? Thus, I believe, all phenomenology is a matter of the mode of presentation of certain states of affairs to a person, not anything distinct from and independent of such representation.[8] If I am right about this, then the third kind of

---

[7] This would, of course, embrace the need for a desire-like state directly; but only by making the pain itself representational in nature. Hence it cannot be adopted by the proponent of this line of objection to my argument for (C), in reply to the previous point about the need for some desire to get rid of the pain in giving the subject's reason for acting as she does.

[8] This idea has been a central theme of Naomi Eilan's work, originating with her thesis (1988; see also its recent development in her 1997*a*, 1997*b*, and forthcoming). See also Cassam, 1993, for similar points made in criticism of Kant's notion of purely inner sense.

putative counterexample to (C) is untenable from the start. Even if I am wrong, I cannot see where its proponent might hope to find a genuine case. How could a mental state which does not represent anything to the subject as being any way whatsoever possibly give her a *reason* to believe anything: how could it give her a reason to believe that *p* rather than anything else, that is, how could it make her believing that *p*, as opposed to *q*, say, intelligible in the required way?[9] Again then, in the absence of any serious candidate, and given the prima facie case against, I contend that there are no counterexamples of this third variety.

Let me return, then, to the counterexample sketched in the abstract above, which aims to put pressure on the final move in my argument for (C). The suggestion is that a person's having a reason for believing that *p* might require him to be in a mental state with a representational content which need not be conceptual. This may instead be a *non-conceptual* representational content related more indirectly than by identity to a premise proposition, *q*, from which *p* can somehow be inferred. In order to demonstrate the impossibility of any counterexample along these lines, I follow McDowell's discussion in the Afterword to *Mind and World* (1994*b*, pp. 162–6), in focusing upon what is

---

[9] I suppose that it might be claimed that, if my previous point is mistaken, then a person's simply being in a purely sensational mental state provides her with a reason for thinking that she is. But this would, I think, be a mistake. If her condition were purely sensational, then it would provide a reason for such a belief only in the sense of constituting its truth, and not in the required sense of being a reason, recognizable as such *by her*, for her to embrace its content in judgement. I would be inclined rather to present this case the other way around, as further evidence for my contention that phenomenal consciousness is a matter of mode of presentation. Since being in certain phenomenal states does indeed provide the subject with a reason for believing that she is in them, and only representational mental states could do so, it follows that such states are themselves representational in nature.

I should also explicitly acknowledge here the existence of *non*-reason-giving explanation in common-sense psychology. For example, we might explain that S is irritable because she has a headache, where this constitutes a genuine explanation of a non-rational reaction. My claim in rejecting this third putative source of counterexamples to (C) is simply that non-representational mental states, even if there are such things, could not provide *reasons* for belief (or action): they could not provide the explananda in *rationalizing* psychological explanations.

perhaps the most familiar, and certainly, to my mind, the most carefully worked out, exemplar of the model. This is Christopher Peacocke's (1989*b*, 1992) account of the way in which the non-conceptual contents of perceptual experiences provide reasons for judgements about the way things are in the mind-independent world around the perceiver.

The story starts with what Peacocke calls 'scenario contents'. These are supposed to register the most basic ways in which perceptual experiences represent the world. Roughly, the idea is that the scenario content of an experience is given by saying 'what ways of filling out the space around the [perceiver] . . . with surfaces, solids, textures, light and so forth, are consistent with the correctness or veridicality of the experience' (Peacocke, 1989*b*, pp. 8–9). Properly characterizing a scenario content requires two things. First, the labelling of origin and axes, for example, labelling the origin as the point midway between the perceiver's eyes and the axes as the following three lines through this point: (1) that given by the direction in which his nose is pointing; (2) that joining his two eyes; and (3) that in the direction of gravitational down–up. Second the specification, relative to this frame of reference, of certain ways of locating surfaces and their properties. Now, suppose that a person's experience has such a scenario content. It will be veridical in this respect if and only if 'the volume of the real world around [him at that time]. . ., with an origin and axes in the real world fixed in accordance with the labelling in the scenario . . . falls under one of the ways of locating surfaces and the rest which is in the family of ways in the scenario. The correctness of such a content is explained as a matter of instantiation, rather than as the correctness of some set of propositions comprising the content' (Peacocke, 1989*b*, p. 10).

Note that the scenario content of a perceptual experience is explicitly non-conceptual on this account. For there is no requirement upon fixing its correctness conditions in this way that we should restrict ourselves only to concepts which the subject himself possesses. It may very well be that the fineness of grain required fully to characterize the scenario content of his experience essentially requires the use of many concepts of which he has no grasp. As Peacocke puts it: 'Any apparatus we want to use, however sophisticated, may be employed in fixing the spatial type, however primitive the conceptual resources of the perceiver with whom we are concerned. This applies both to the apparatus used in characterizing distances and directions, and to that employed in characterizing the surfaces, features and the rest' (1989b, p. 10). The scenario content itself is *not* the proposition specifying its correctness condition: this basic kind of experiential content is not itself the kind of thing which could serve as a premise or the conclusion of an argument at all.[10]

So, how is a perceptual experience with a scenario content supposed to provide a reason for the subject to believe that things are determinately thus and so in the world around him? Well, consider for example the set of scenarios whose correctness requires that there be a square surface in front of the perceiver. Select from these those for the correctness of which this surface is required to be of a suitable size and sufficiently close to perpendicular to the line of sight (however exactly the relevant ranges are to be determined here). Then a person whose visual experience has one of these scenario contents thereby, according to Peacocke, has a reason to judge that there is something square in front of him.[11] For, '[i]f the thinker's perceptual systems are functioning properly, so that the non-conceptual representational content of his experience is correct, then when such experiences occur, the object thought about will really be square' (Peacocke, 1992, p. 80).

Putting this in the context of my argument for (C), it is admitted, on Peacocke's account, that the presence of this reason is dependent upon an association between the experience in question and a certain proposition, that there are various lines, sur-

[10] I think that we should already be worried about whether we can really be dealing here with a story on which experience represents the world *to the perceiver* as being determinately thus and so around him. For the perceiver himself may be completely incapable of grasping precisely which way it is that experience is supposed to be representing the world as being. What is left, then, of the idea that it nevertheless genuinely represents things (*to him*) as being *just that way*? See n. 20 below.

[11] The story is in fact a little more complicated than this. Peacocke argues that the subject's perceptual experience must also have 'protopropositional' non-conceptual content giving salience to the appropriate symmetries—namely about the perpendicular bisectors of the sides rather than the bisectors of the angles in this case—if he is automatically to have a reason to believe that there is a square in front of him (see his 1992, ch. 3, esp. sect. 3.3).

faces, and so on, distributed in such and such a way around the perceiver. This serves, along with the geometrical definition of a square, as a premise of a deductive inference to the conclusion that the relevant item in front of him is, roughly, square-shaped. This, in turn, is the content of the belief for which his experience therefore provides him with a reason. Having this reason does indeed require him to be in a mental state, then, with a representational content which is identified by reference to a proposition which serves as the premise of an inference to the content of the belief for which it provides a reason. But the relevant association relation, between the experience and the proposition reference to which identifies its representational content, is *not* that this premise proposition itself constitutes the conceptual content of the experience. The proposition that there are various lines, surfaces, and so on, distributed in such and such a way around the subject is, rather, essential in specifying the correctness conditions for the non-conceptual scenario content of his experience; and it is this proposition, in turn, which entails that the item in front of him is, roughly, square in shape. His experience may have no fully conceptual representational content, though, and certainly need not have that given by the relevant premise proposition itself. For it is possible for a person to have an experience with just that scenario content, who therefore has a reason to form the belief in question, yet who does not have the component concepts of the proposition, those concepts required to state explicitly exactly how the lines, surfaces, and so on, are represented as distributed around him. Yet this experience is still supposed to provide him with a reason to believe that there is something square in front of him, as explained above. Hence, on this account, my argument for (C) must be mistaken. Reasons do not require mental states with *conceptual* contents.

In his Afterword (1994*b*, pp. 162–6) McDowell makes three points against this suggestion that such an experience might genuinely provide a reason *for the subject* to believe that there is something square in front of him. First, he assimilates Peacocke's account to one of another kind of quasi-rational explanation, which more obviously fails in this regard. Second, he explains what would have to be added to this account to make it one on which the subject's own reasons really are being provided by such scenario contents—but argues that the required addition will not generally be available, and certainly cannot be regarded as essential, in cases where perceptual experiences provide reasons for empirical beliefs. Third, he appeals to a 'time-honoured connection between reason and discourse' which 'Peacocke cannot respect' (McDowell, 1994*b*, p. 165). As with much of his book, I find McDowell's discussion here highly suggestive, but crucially incomplete and, so, ultimately unsatisfying. By developing these three points in detail, though, I hope to extract and establish the underlying principle which unifies them, and which I believe refutes Peacocke's account, and, indeed, any other like it in trying to secure for non-conceptual experiences a genuinely reason-giving role in connection with empirical beliefs. This will therefore complete my argument for (C).

First, then (p. 163), McDowell considers an explanation which we might give of the bodily adjustments made by a skilled cyclist rounding a curve in terms of these being of a kind required for her balanced ride in the desired direction. This may well be why she leant over at just that angle: after all, she is a *skilled* cyclist. The fact that just that angle of lean is required to keep her balanced, though, does not give *her* reason for making the movement. She just does it, without reflection and most likely without any reason at all. The claim offered by McDowell at this point is that the same is true in Peacocke's case. At most, he provides an explanation of why saying that there is something square in front of him is appropriate for a perceiver whose experience has the relevant scenario content in the following sense. Things are, with his perceptual system, such that, provided the system is functioning normally, such an utterance will be true. For the non-conceptual content of his experience has been characterized in such a way that the truth of the claim that a given item is square is required for the correct functioning of his perceptual system in its delivery of an experience with the particular scenario (and protopropositional) content in question. This may well, in a sense, be why he makes that claim in these circumstances: after all, he is a highly evolved and skilled respondent to and negotiator of his environment. Nevertheless, the fact that its squareness is required for the correctness of his experience *in this sense* does not give *his* reason for making the claim. Given just what has been said so far, it might rather be that he simply makes the 'appropriate' claim without reflection and without any reason at all.

As yet, this is just an analogy, which puts some pressure on Peacocke either to insist that explanations of unreflective skilled behaviour really do cite agents' own reasons for acting as they do, or to bring out the relevant differences between such cases and the account which he gives of judgements based upon perceptual experiences with scenario contents. In his second point (pp. 164–5), McDowell goes on to explain how to supplement this account in such a way that non-conceptual experiences, as conceived by Peacocke, *would* uncontroversially figure in giving a *subject's* reasons for judging the world to be thus and so around him. Suppose that a person knows that experiences of the kind which he is currently enjoying are normally produced by square things directly in front of him, and that he judges that the thing in front of him is square on this basis. That is to say, he argues as follows: I am having an experience which is such that it is required by the normal functioning of my perceptual systems that there be something square in front of me; therefore (assuming, as is reasonable, though defeasible, the normal functioning of my perceptual systems), the thing in question is square. This is a perfectly acceptable piece of what might be called *instrumental reasoning*, by analogy with a case of reasoning to the obtaining of the state of affairs indicated by an instrument of some kind from the reading on the instrument along with some understanding of its role as a reliable instrument of the relevant kind.[12] Equally, it is evidently not the nor-

---

[12] See 3.4 for my definition of *instrumental reasons*, which are clearly precisely the kinds of reasons provided by Peacocke's perceptual experiences in this case, as elucidated by the instrumental reasoning given in the text. The crucial point is that a person might have an experience of exactly this type, yet have no reason to believe that there is something square in front of him, due to ignorance of the reliable normal connection between such experiences and the existence of something square there. His having a reason, therefore, depends upon both his knowledge of his own experiential condition—the reading on the relevant 'instrument'—*and* his knowledge of the reliability of such experiences as indicators of squareness—the reliability of the instrument as a 'shape-detector'. This addition to Peacocke's account transforms his position into one on which the truth of (R) is given a *second-order* explication (see 4.3 above), structurally very similar to that proposed by the classical foundationalist. It is clear that Peacocke himself would reject any such assimilation.

mal way in which a person arrives at his beliefs about the world on the basis of perception. Indeed, any suggestion that this supplemented account correctly captures the underlying order of epistemic justification for empirical knowledge faces all the familiar difficulties of classical foundationalism and classical coherentism[13]

Unfortunately, the crucial claim upon which any *general* argument against Peacocke's approach here, or anything like it in advancing a counterexample of the present type to the last step in my argument for (C), ultimately depends is left as an entirely implicit hypothesis in McDowell's discussion. He neither explicitly states it nor gives any direct argument for it. It is clear enough what it must be though: that this unsatisfactory instrumental supplementation to Peacocke's account is made necessary, if the account really is to be one of a person's *own* reasons for believing what she does about the world around her, precisely by the fact that the experiences supposedly providing such reasons are held to be non-conceptual. McDowell's third point suggests a line of argument for this claim; but nothing more. He claims that Peacocke 'has to sever the tie between reasons for which a subject thinks as she does and reasons she can give for thinking that way' (p. 165). He clearly has in mind a development of this point in the context of a general requirement upon the possibility of the subject's linguistic articulation of her reasons in response to the question 'Why do you believe that?' The idea must be that any non-conceptualist account is bound to fail to meet this requirement. I am inclined to think that explicit linguistic expression of this kind is inessential to the point; but I do think that McDowell's suggestion can be made into something clear and compelling.

The starting point is the idea that a person's own reasons for believing or doing what she does must, in some sense, be *recognizable* by her as such.[14] This idea has been explicit in my talk of reasons right from the outset (Ch. 2); and it is precisely the idea which I argued above is given misplaced recognition by the

---

[13] See Brewer, 1996, and 4.2–4.3 above.

[14] See Stroud's (1977, pp. 60 ff.) discussion of Hume's attack on the rationality of induction for application of this important point in a different, but clearly related, context.

second-order accounts of the truth of (R) proposed by both classical foundationalists and classical coherentists alike (4.2–4.3). Furthermore, it is, I believe, the crux of the distinction between *quasi*-reason-giving explanations, on the one hand, of the kind paradigmatically illustrated above in the case of unreflective skills like bicycle riding, and explanations which cite *the subject's* reasons for doing what she does, on the other: genuinely reason-giving explanations of the kind which I am concerned with here, explanations which reveal *her own* reasons for believing what she does, or acting in a certain way. In the latter, but not in the former, she recognizes the given reasons as her reasons, and bringing this out is essential to explaining why she believes or does what she does.

It may be objected that this condition that genuine reasons are essentially recognizable as such in some way by the subject is wrong-headed from the start. Indeed, it might be urged in filling out the objection that it is only some misguided respect for this condition which drives philosophers into the dead-end occupied by the classical foundationalist and classical coherentist accounts of the epistemology of perception which I rightly dismissed above (4.2 and 4.3). I think that this objection is mistaken on a number of points.

First, the difficulties of classical foundationalism and coherentism are the result of a conjunction of commitments: (1) to the thesis that a person's reasons are essentially recognizable by her as such; and (2) to the idea that this recognition can only be a matter of her *second-order* knowledge that the mental state providing the reason in question is appropriately related to that for which it is her reason, where this is independent of the first-order state itself in that she might have been in just that state yet not had the second-order knowledge required for its status as a reason for her. Denial of (1) leads to the serious problems which I outlined above (4.1) for any reliabilist approach to the epistemology of perception. Hence the correct response to the difficulties of classical foundationalism and coherentism is absolutely not to reject the requirement that genuine reasons for the subject are essentially recognizable in some way by her as such, but rather to rethink the assumption that only a second-order account along these lines can possibly meet it.

Second, the notion of a reason with which I have been working has been explicitly committed to this requirement right from the start. It is precisely such a notion which was involved in my argument for (R) above—the claim that perceptual experiences provide reasons for empirical beliefs—in that the Switching Argument of 3.1 establishes that the content-determining relations between experiences and beliefs are necessarily reason-giving *in this demanding sense*. For otherwise they could do nothing to contribute to *the subject's own understanding* of the beliefs in question. My explicit focus upon this notion is therefore entirely justified.

Furthermore, and third, the requirement is independently motivated. As I suggested in my provisional clarification of (R) (ch. 2), it is only if a person's reasons are necessarily recognized as such that it is appropriate to cite their status as reasons in genuinely reason-giving causal explanations of what she believes and does. This is a large issue, which I cannot address fully here,[15] but the key line of thought is this. Reason-giving explanations are explanations of certain transitions which a person makes in thought and action (very broadly construed), acquiring new beliefs, say, or performing various actions, transitions which accord with certain norms prescribing how things ought to be done in these areas given the subject's circumstances. In every such case, though, there is always a distinction to be made between a person's simply making such a transition in a way which happens to accord with the relevant norms and her being guided by such norms in what she does (Wittgenstein, 1958, esp. §§ 135–242). Only in the latter case is a genuine reason-giving explanation appropriate, in which the fact that the transition in question is prescribed by these norms is given crucial explanatory relevance. Only then is it appropriate to cite the status of her prior condition as having a reason for making that move in thought or action in a rationalizing explanation of her doing so. Furthermore, it is central to this distinction, between action in accord with a rule and genuine rule-following, that in the latter case she is guided in making the transition by her recognition of her reason *as a reason for doing so*. Coming to believe something *for a reason* in this sense essentially involves some conception of what one is up to in doing so, some sense of why this is the right

---

[15] See Brewer, 1995*b*, for further discussion of this claim.

thing to do.[16] Thus, if a person's reasons are to be cited as *her reasons* for believing or doing what she does, then she necessarily recognizes them as such. In other words, the condition which forms the starting point of the present line of argument does indeed obtain: genuinely reason-giving explanations cite reasons which are necessarily recognized as such in some sense by the subject.

Now, in cases in which the explanans in question involves a conceptual mental state, there is a clear context in which an account can, and must, be given of the subject's recognition of his reason as a reason for doing what he does. This is the case of directed deductive reasoning. Otherwise, there is no such context; and I shall argue that this is what forces the move to the unacceptable, second-order, instrumental supplement offered above in an attempt to transform Peacocke's account into a genuinely reason-giving one. In this, then, he is condemned to follow the discredited classical foundationalists and coherentists, as is anyone else who is sympathetic to the possibility that the reason-giving role of perceptual experiences in the determination of empirical belief content might require the subject's possession only of non-conceptual mental states. Let me take the two types of case in turn.

Recall that a conceptual mental state is one whose content is the content of a possible judgement by the subject. Crucially, then, the state is one being in which necessarily involves *understanding* the propositional content of the corresponding judgement. Now, it is a constraint upon a correct account of understanding that it should explain how understanding makes possible the subject's knowledge of which propositions logically follow from which, in such a way as to open the possibility of extending his knowledge by deductive argument. In other words, understanding a given propositional content is precisely the sort of thing which enables a person to recognize which things follow from it, with a genuine sense of what he is up to in deriving these consequences, and why they are correct.

---

[16] It is precisely this which Dummett's challenge to realism suggests cannot be done, or at least faces serious difficulties, in connection with the characteristically realist—classical, as opposed to intuitionistic—rules of inference. See especially Dummett, 1978 and 1991*b*, chs. 8–15.

Understanding a proposition in this way is a matter of grasping its truth condition, or condition of correct assertion of some other kind, on the basis of the way in which this is systematically determined by the semantic values of its components and their mode of combination, in such a way as to make such recognition of its deductive relations with other conceptually structured propositions possible.[17] Now, I have argued that a person has a reason to believe that *p*, say, only in virtue of his being in some mental state suitably related to a proposition which serves as a premise in a valid inference to some other proposition suitably related to *p*, most likely the proposition that *p* itself. In the conceptual case, the premise proposition is precisely the content of the mental state in question, which provides the subject's reason for believing that *p*. Thus, the subject of such a conceptual mental state is necessarily in a position to recognize his reason as such. For he understands its propositional content; and this essentially involves his being in a position to recognize the validity of the inference upon which his thereby having a reason to believe that *p* depends. Of course, it is no easy matter to give a satisfactory account of understanding which succeeds in explaining this connection between understanding and the capacity to recognize logical validity.[18] Nevertheless, the connection itself is surely uncontroversial; and given this, the context is at least set for an account of a person's recognition of the status of his reasons as such, when these are provided by his conceptual mental states.

The situation is more difficult in the case of supposedly nonconceptual reasons. For here mere possession of the mental state involved in having such a 'reason' is explicitly insufficient for the subject's understanding of the proposition whose association with this state grounds its putative status as his reason for doing what he does. Hence any account of his essential recognition of his reason as such which attempts to exploit the connection between understanding and knowledge of what follows from

---

[17] Again, it is precisely this which Dummett (esp. 1991*b*) maintains is a serious challenge to any *realist* theory of meaning, on which understanding is characterized in terms of knowledge of entirely epistemically unconstrained semantic values and truth conditions.

[18] Dummett's pathbreaking work on this topic (see especially his 1981, ch. 15, and 1991*a*, ch. 4) in my view provides the key.

what along the lines suggested above is inapplicable. The only alternative seems to be that he must have some second-order knowledge of the relation between mental states of the type in question and the truth of the belief (or appropriateness, in some sense, of the action) for which he thereby, and only instrumentally, recognizes his having a reason.

The difficulty here is that although conceptual contents are essentially grasped by their subject in precisely the way which has evident relevance for their inferential powers which are in turn crucial to sustain their status as reasons, non-conceptual contents are not. Thus, in the former case, there is no need for second-order reflection to accommodate the essential recognition of reasons as reasons. In the latter case, though, this is required. Indeed, to categorize a state as non-conceptual just is to deny that it is given to the subject in such a way as to provide for the possibility of this recognition directly. Instead, he must argue about the state as follows: this state is *F*; anything which is *F* is a reason for believing that *p* (or for ϕ-ing); therefore I have reason to believe that *p* (or to ϕ). Only then can he recognize his position as one of having a reason for believing that *p* (or for ϕ-ing); only then, therefore, does he have a genuine reason for doing so.

An obvious initial objection to this account of non-conceptual reasons concerns the subject's knowledge that the state in question is *F*, and that anything which is *F* is a reason for believing that *p* (or for ϕ-ing). For, if it is true, as it must be, that anything which is *F* is a reason for believing that *p* (or for ϕ-ing), then what stands in place of '*F*' will have, at best, to be hideously complex.[19] So it will be extremely implausible to suppose that many, if any, people are even capable of having this knowledge, and hence of having the putative reasons in question.

More directly relevant to my argument for (C), what emerges from all of this is that a non-conceptual mental state can only possibly figure in an account of a person's own reason for believing or doing something if it is conjoined with his second-order knowledge of the appropriate rational relations between the

---

[19] See McDowell, 1979, and Child, 1993 and 1994, ch. 2, for arguments to the conclusion that any such general 'codification' of reasons for believing that *p* (or ϕ-ing) by a predicate '*F*' is in principle impossible.

two—between mental states of that type, which are *F*, and beliefs or actions of the relevant kind. In that case, though, his reason is really provided by his second-order belief that he is in a mental state which is *F*. This is clearly a conceptual state. Hence it follows that all reasons are conceptual. The argument can be put as a *reductio*. Suppose that experiences with non-conceptual contents provide reasons for empirical beliefs. If they are genuinely to be the *subject's* reasons, then these have to be recognized by him as such. Given the non-conceptual nature of the contents of the experiences in question, this is only possible on the second-order instrumental model given above. This model is not the norm, though; it cannot be the most basic case; and in any case it is really one of reasons being provided by the subject's fully conceptual second-order beliefs about his experiences. So such experiences themselves do not after all provide the subject's reasons for his beliefs about the world around him.[20]

I conclude, therefore, that there are no genuine counterexamples of this final kind to my argument for (C), on which mental states with non-conceptual representational contents purportedly provide reasons for empirical beliefs. Thus, thesis (C) is established: reasons require conceptual contents.

5.3 Non-Conceptual Experiential Content Is Unmotivated

Given this conclusion, it is worth raising the question why it might nevertheless appear attractive, or even obligatory, to attempt to capture the reason-giving representational contents of perceptual experiences *non-conceptually*. For a fully satisfying

---

[20] Given the second premise of my argument for (R) above—that if experiences are to be the source of empirical significance, then their relations with beliefs must be reason-giving—it follows from this conclusion that the worries which I raised in n. 10 above are well-founded. Experiences as Peacocke conceives of them are incapable genuinely of providing empirical significance to the purported beliefs about the mind-independent world to which they give rise because they are not in themselves reason-giving with respect to such empirical beliefs. So we do not have here anything recognizable as representation *for the subject* of things being determinately thus and so around him.

defence of (C) involves undermining any motivation there may be for this contrary approach. A large number of considerations are thought to exert pressure in this direction. I cannot possibly deal with all of them in any great detail, but I do want to say just a little about what strike me as some of the more important arguments which have been offered in this connection. I shall focus upon those which highlight various ways in which perceptual experiences differ from judgements, from which it is supposed to follow that the former are therefore non-conceptual in nature, in contrast with the paradigmatically conceptual status of the latter. I want to consider four variants of this line of argument. First, perceptual experience has a fineness of grain which is not matched by the contents of possible judgements by the subject, as the latter are restricted by his limited conceptual repertoire. Second, perceptual indiscriminability is non-transitive, whereas conceptual identity is transitive. Third, experiences are belief-independent, whereas judgements are not. Fourth, perception is shared by both humans and other animals who may not even have the capacity for conceptual judgement at all. I shall also mention a fifth, methodological, motivation for a non-conceptualist approach to the reason-giving representational content of experience, which seems particularly important to Peacocke (1992).[21]

5.3.1 *Fineness of Grain*

First, then, it may be held that perceptual representation has a fineness of grain which far outstrips that of the contents of possible judgements by the subject, which are restricted to those discriminations for which the subject actually has corresponding concepts. Hence, given the definition of conceptual contents as those of possible judgements by the subject, it follows that perceptual experiences represent non-conceptually (Evans, 1982, e.g. p. 229; Peacocke, 1986a, 1989a, 1989b). Two kinds of example serve to illustrate the notion of fineness of grain at work here. First, most people can perceptually discriminate far more

---

[21] Like much of the present chapter, my responses to these lines of argument for a non-conceptualist approach to perceptual experiences are very much in the spirit of McDowell (1994b, especially Lecture III and Afterword, Part II).

shades of red, say, than they have concepts for such shades expressible by words such as 'burgundy', 'scarlet', 'terracotta', or whatever. Second, people can also perceive spatial magnitudes quite accurately without having any concept of the particular magnitudes in question expressible in terms of any appropriate unit of measurement. A person may be able to see, for example, that a certain volume of space in a kitchen is just large enough to contain a cooker, say, without having any concept of that volume expressible in cubic feet, cubic metres, or any other unit of measure of volume. Since there is a determinacy in perceptual representation in such cases which transcends the subject's conceptual repertoire, it follows that this must be captured non-conceptually.

There is an unacceptable assumption behind this line of argument, that concepts necessarily correspond with entirely context-independent classifications of things, in such a way that they can, in principle at least, be grasped by anyone, anywhere, regardless of their current relations with the semantic values in question. This is what sustains the restriction upon the concepts available to capture subjects' perceptual discriminations of colours and volumes, in the examples given above, just to those associated with verbal expressions, like 'scarlet' or 'four cubic feet', which have context-independent norms of application. This restriction unacceptably rules out any appeal to context-dependent demonstrative concepts, though—concepts associated with expressions like 'that shade of red', or 'just that large in volume', grasp of which essentially depends upon the subject's relations with the actual entities which constitute their semantic values. Of course, far more is required to grasp such concepts than simply the ability to mouth such expressions in the presence of the items in question; and part of what the additional requirements must achieve is a certain distance between the subject's conception of the relevant semantic value and the mere obtaining of her confrontation with it which makes this way of thinking of it available to her in the first place.[22] Nevertheless,

[22] The background capacities required fully to grasp perceptual demonstrative concepts of spatial particulars and their mind-independent properties will be of crucial importance in developing my own positive account of the truth of (R) below (see especially 6.1).

with the required cognitive capacities in place, these demonstrative expressions perfectly easily figure in the expression of genuine judgements by the subject, and so contribute to the characterization of fully conceptual states. This is how I would propose to capture the absolutely genuine phenomena which motivate the present line of argument for non-conceptual experiential contents. My reply is that the fineness of grain in perceptual discrimination is matched precisely by the perceptual demonstrative *concepts* which the subject has in virtue of her conscious contact with the items in question. In other words, for any fineness of grain in perceptual content to which my opponent wishes to appeal in making this argument, the subject is capable of making a perceptual demonstrative *judgement*, 'that is thus', with just that fineness of grain. Paradigmatically conceptual judgement therefore matches perception precisely in respect of fineness of grain. So, although the phenomena from which its proponent takes off are real enough, this first argument loses all force in support of the claim that the reason-giving representational contents of perceptual experiences are non-conceptual.

The proponent of non-conceptual experiential content may object that this appeal to irreducibly demonstrative concepts is insufficient on its own to capture the phenomena which motivate him. There are certain shapes and shades of colour in the world, say, and there are indeed essentially experiential demonstrative concepts under which these fall, grasp of which depends upon the subject's actually standing, or having stood, in certain perceptual-attentional relations with the things in question; but there are also determinate ways in which these shapes and shades experientially appear to the subject, which stand in many–one relations to the shapes and shades themselves, and to which his demonstrative concepts in turn stand in many-one relations. Crucially, the way in which a particular colour patch is given to a particular person in experience on a particular occasion, for example, cannot be explained in terms of his exercise on that occasion of various perceptual demonstrative concepts. It is, rather, what makes these demonstrative concepts available to that person: an intermediate level between the worldly phenomena themselves and any demonstrative concepts which the subject applies to them, which has to be characterized *non-*

conceptually and is in turn essential to the correct characterization of perceptual experience.[23]

In reply, I deny that any real need has yet been demonstrated for an intermediate level of just this kind. Suppose that there is a colour patch in the world of a certain specific shade. This, of course, falls under many different demonstrative and non-demonstrative concepts: 'that shade', 'that scarlet', 'red', and so on. There is also, let us say, a person, standing looking at it, whose relations with it, subpersonal information processing, and background conceptual capacities make various essentially experiential demonstrative conceptions available of the colour patch in question. His perceptual experience is to be characterized, in my view, centrally, and to begin with, by reference to the demonstrative concepts which he actually entertains, given the focus of his attention and his present needs and purposes. Its background is then to be characterized by reference to the demonstrative conceptions of the relevant colour patch and other things around him which are possible for him, without any further uptake of information, in virtue of his actual possession of appropriate general concepts to be drawn upon in demonstration, and the subpersonal operation of the information-processing systems subserving his perception.[24]

The non-conceptualist may object further that this account of the matter is unsatisfactory, because it cannot deliver what are intuitively the right answers to questions of inter- (and presumably also intra-) personal sameness and difference of perceptual experience in certain cases. Suppose, for example, that two people are looking at the same patch of colour, one thinking of it as 'that red', the other as 'that scarlet'. The accusation is that the respect in which they may nevertheless experience the colour patch *in just the same way* cannot be accounted for without the intermediate level of non-conceptual content mentioned above. For the mere fact that it happens to be the same colour patch in the world will not do; and yet there appears to be nothing else to which the conceptualist can appeal.

---

[23] This objection, and its development below, are due to Christopher Peacocke.

[24] See 7.4.3 for further elucidation of this conceptualist account of the distinction between the foreground and background in perceptual consciousness. See also n. 26 below.

The accusation is unjust, though. For, provided that there is *some* general concept which both perceivers share, 'shade (of colour)' for example, the possibility, without further uptake of information, for each of them to think of the patch as 'that shade' captures precisely what is required by way of shared background phenomenology, whilst also giving prominence, as is surely right, to the important respect in which each of them also *perceives* the patch slightly differently. The only case in which nothing at all is common to the two subjects' experience, on this view, is that in which they have entirely non-overlapping general concepts of the relevant kinds. It is not at all clear to me that this is really a coherent scenario; but in so far as it may be, this result does not strike me as obviously unacceptable. Indeed, in so far as I can make any sense of the case, phenomenal distinctness seems to be the right verdict. Suppose, as far as this is possible, that two people have totally disjoint sets of general concepts applicable to shapes: one has only abstract theoretical-geometrical concepts; the other has only aesthetic concepts of some kind, embroiled in a strange system of mystical significance, say. If they really have no generic concept of shape in common *at all*, as the (neutral) way in which something fills or articulates space, then it seems to me to be quite reasonable to conclude that the only thing which their shape perception has in common is that it is sometimes the very same shape in the world which they perceive, in their otherwise entirely different ways.

5.3.2 *Non-Transitivity*

Second, the non-transitivity of perceptual indiscriminability along certain dimensions of continuous variation is thought to constitute a conclusive refutation of the conceptualist position (Peacocke, 1986*a*, 1989*a*, 1992, pp. 83 ff.; Cussins, 1990, pp. 406 ff.). The argument can be put like this. Indiscriminability in the domain of colour perception is non-transitive in the following sense. Colour samples A, B, and C can be found such that, for a perfectly normal person, B is indiscriminable in colour from A; and C is indiscriminable in colour from B; yet C is discriminable in colour from A. Now, suppose that colour perception is conceptual in content, in the way I suggest in response to the first line of argument above. It follows that two samples fall under the same demonstrative colour concept if and only if they are indiscriminable in colour. Thus, B falls under the same concept as A; and C falls under the same concept as B; therefore C falls under the same concept as A. Yet C does not fall under the same concept as A. For C is not indiscriminable from A. This is a contradiction. So colour perception cannot be conceptual in this sense.

I agree that colour perception cannot be conceptual *in this sense*, for precisely the reason given; but the burden of proof is upon the non-conceptualist to establish that this is the *only* way in which it might be characterized conceptually. This, though, is impossible, for the following account is a perfectly coherent conceptualist alternative. Given a colour sample, A, let 'that$_A$ shade' be an expression for the demonstrative colour concept grasped in virtue of a normal person's confrontation with A, the way of thinking of its colour which is provided by her experience of A. Now, suppose that something counts as having that$_A$ shade if and only if it is indiscriminable in colour *from A* (see McDowell, 1994*b*, pp. 170 ff.). Note that, for the reasons briefly alluded to above, this must be a concept which can be employed to some extent, and however briefly, in the absence of the sample A itself, although its being available in thought at all depends upon the subject's experience of A; and the extent here determines the retentiveness of the subject's memory for the shade in question. The crucial point in the present context is that it does not follow from any of this that a sample counts as having that$_A$ shade if it is indiscriminable in colour from something, other than A, which counts as having that$_A$ shade for the reason given. Suppose, that is to say, that B counts as that$_A$ shade, because it is indiscriminable in colour from A, and C is indiscriminable in colour from B. Although it follows immediately that C counts as that$_B$ shade, and even though B has that$_A$ shade, it does not follow that C has that$_A$ shade. Thus, the purported contradiction disappears. For, if C is discriminable in colour from A, then there is no difficulty in asserting, as the account requires us to do, that C therefore does not count as that$_A$ shade. Of course, if C is indiscriminable from A, then it does count as that$_A$ shade, for that reason; but, again, there is no contradiction. Either way, then, the account is perfectly consistent. So non-transitivity of this kind is no threat to the conceptualist approach.

5.3.3 *Belief Independence*

Third, it is objected that experiences are belief-independent, in the sense that they have the contents which they do quite independently of whether the subject has any matching belief, whereas judgements are clearly not (Evans, 1982, pp. 123 ff.). The Müller–Lyer illusion provides a familiar example of the phenomenon, for one of the two lines appears longer than the other regardless of whether or not the subject believes that it actually is longer. Indeed, the two lines continue visually to appear different in length even to a subject who knows that they are equal in length, and who understands the way in which the illusion works. A judgement, on the other hand, that two lines are equal or different in length, or whatever, just is the forming of a belief to that effect. So the subject of such a judgement cannot possibly be neutral, or even take an opposite view, on the matter so far as his beliefs are concerned. Thus, again, it may appear that perceptions are sufficiently different from judgements in this respect for it to be untenable to maintain that the former conform to the conceptual paradigm exemplified by the latter.

The obvious reply to this argument, which I think is the correct one, is that the question of belief independence is quite independent of the *type of content* in question, and has rather to do entirely with whether or not the subject actually endorses this content. A proponent of the present line of thought might just as well argue that simply entertaining the thought that all swans are white, say, is a non-conceptual state, since it is possible for a person to do so without actually believing that all swans are white, whilst mulling over whether the evidence is sufficiently conclusive, for example. Yet this is a paradigmatically conceptual state: it has a representational content which is characterizable only in terms of concepts which the subject himself must possess and which is of a form that enables it to serve as a premise or the conclusion of a deductive argument, or of an inference of some other kind. This is the content of a *possible* judgement by the subject, even though it might equally well be the content of some other attitude whilst not actually endorsed in judgement. Just the same goes for the reason-giving contents of perceptual experiences. So this third line of argument for the non-conceptualist position is again unconvincing (see McDowell, 1994*b*, pp. 60–3).

5.3.4 *Animals and Infants*

Fourth, it is often said that certain animals have perceptual experiences just like ours, yet they lack the capacity altogether for conceptual judgement; hence, it may be concluded, the experiences in question cannot be conceptual, since their being so requires the subject's capacity for conceptual judgement. Following McDowell again (1994*b*, pp. 63–5), I would reply that the hypothesis that animals have perceptual experiences with the very same reason-giving contents as ours is not the only way to understand the fact that they have a faculty of perception as we do. He puts it like this: 'We do not need to say that we have what mere animals have, non-conceptual content, and we have something else as well, since we can conceptualize that content and they cannot. Instead we can say that we have what mere animals have, perceptual sensitivity to features of our environment, but we have it in a special [thoroughly conceptual] form' (p. 64).

This immediately highlights a further issue, though. For it is plausible that something similar to what is said about animals of these kinds should also be said about human infants at certain stages of their development, at which they clearly have perception of some kind, even though they lack the sophistication for this to be characterized thoroughly conceptually. Yet if it is correct to characterize the contrast between animals and mature humans in terms of perceptual sensitivity to features of the environment of two quite different forms, as opposed to postulating a shared layer of non-conceptual experiential content which mature humans learn to conceptualize, then a parallel account of human infants raises the question of how perceptual sensitivity of the one form develops smoothly into perceptual sensitivity of the other, thoroughly conceptual, form. This difficulty can easily be exaggerated. For one thing, developmental psychology just is a very difficult area of enquiry; and we should certainly not expect that every significant advance in cognitive development should be in any way obvious, or must easily fit into any simple additive model. Indeed, I cannot myself see straight away why the difficulties in accounting for the crucial transitions between infant and adult perception should automatically be thought to be greater according to my preferred characterization of matters than according to the non-conceptualist's alternative. Furthermore, since it must be acknowledged on all sides of this dispute that creatures who are incapable of conceptual thought *do* develop into those who are capable of such thought—for otherwise infant perception could simply be characterized fully conceptually from the start—there must be some story to be told about what is involved in this transition; and this will be precisely the kind of account to which a theorist might reasonably appeal in making sense of the move from infant to adult perception. In other words, if the objector has some reason to suppose that any transition from pre-conceptual to thoroughly conceptual perceptual sensitivity to features of the environment is incompatible with a *smooth* account of human development, then all that follows is that not every significant cognitive development is *smooth* in this sense. It does not follow that animal and infant perception, on the one hand, and mature human perception, on the other, must each share a common core of non-conceptual experiential content.

This fourth line of argument certainly poses a challenge to the proponent of wholly conceptual experiential content. The concept of conscious perceptual experience has close connections with both the perceptual sensitivity of animals and human infants, and with our own fully conceptualized thought about the world around us. No account of perceptual experience could be complete without respecting both of these connections. Yet they seem to pull in opposite directions. The challenge is to resolve this tension. The non-conceptualist aims to do this by starting with a level of perceptual representational content which is common to adult humans, animals, and infants, and is therefore non-conceptual in nature. He then faces the challenge of connecting this level up with the level of fully conceptualized empirical thought.[25] The conceptualist faces an equal and opposite challenge. For he begins with the level of fully conceptual, although perhaps essentially demonstrative, thought about the world, and must connect this in some way with the non-conceptual perceptual sensitivity of animals and infants. The difficulty of meeting these challenges obviously depends upon the nature of the connections which are sought between the

---

[25] See Campbell, 1997, for a suggestion of how this might be done by appeal to the role of selective perceptual attention.

respective theorists' favoured starting points and what is thereby regarded as the secondary manifestation of perceptual experience. What kind of connection must the non-conceptualist make between non-conceptual perceptual content and conceptual thought; or what kind of connection must the conceptualist make between conceptual thought and non-conceptual perceptual sensitivity? Without a fully worked-out account of the constraints which these connections must meet, it is unreasonable to claim that one version of the challenge can be met, whereas the other cannot. So it is unacceptable to use this line of argument on its own as a motivation for the introduction of non-conceptual perceptual content.[26]

5.3.5 *Non-Circularity*

Finally, and somewhat relatedly, it is objected that unless the most basic perceptual experiences are non-conceptual, there can be no satisfactory theory of concepts. The thought is this. We saw above that empirical concepts have their significance in part through the reason-giving relations between certain perceptual experiences and the beliefs in the contents of which the concepts in question occur. Now, suppose that all such experiences are conceptual. It follows that any attempt to say which concept a particular empirical concept *C* is will be circular in the following sense. The account is bound to characterize *C* by reference to the experiences which provide reasons for beliefs in whose contents it figures; yet these experiences are in turn bound to

---

[26] A related challenge to the conceptualist, which may also be thought to motivate some appeal to non-conceptual experiential content in an account of empirical knowledge, is to make sense of the permanent presence within adult human perceptual experience of a foreground and background of awareness. Indeed, it might be thought that background awareness is of precisely the kind which is common between adult humans and animals and infants, whereas foreground awareness is what connects up more directly with fully conceptual empirical thought (see, again, Campbell, 1997). I discuss the way in which this phenomenon might be handled on the conceptualist view in 7.4.3 below. An initial difficulty for the proposal that the background against which attention selects a foreground in human perceptual consciousness constitutes the level of non-conceptual content common between humans and animals is that it appears to leave no room for an attentionally modulated distinction between the foreground and background in animal perception. Yet it strikes me as extremely implausible to rule out a priori any such thing.

presuppose a grasp of certain empirical concepts, most likely C itself, but if not, the circularity is simply enlarged rather than avoided. For the experiences in question are conceptual, by hypothesis, and therefore require their subject's possession of the concepts in terms of which their contents are characterized.

The reply, obvious enough again, is to resist the implicit requirement upon a satisfactory theory of concepts, that it have the reductive, non-circular, shape which is threatened here by the conceptual status of perceptual experiences (McDowell, 1994*b*, pp. 166–70). Why must we accept that a theory of concepts has to be of this form? Indeed, given what has been said so far, there are good reasons to suppose that any account meeting this requirement is bound to fail as an account of concepts which are really apt to figure in genuine empirical contents. For, recall, such contents are in part determined by their reason-giving relations with perceptual experiences. Yet reasons require conceptual contents. Hence, it is impossible to give a satisfactory account of empirical concepts by appeal only to their relations with experiences whose reason-giving contents are required to be non-conceptual by the reductive demands of non-circularity. In the present context, though, this is just to admit that any need there may be for a non-circular account of concepts in this sense is in serious tension with my thesis (C). The real question concerns what independent motivation there may be for this requirement of non-circularity.

This is where the relation comes out with the previous argument based on the need for an intelligible account of the development of human cognition. For if the only available account of what it is to grasp empirical concepts presupposes subjects' possession of such concepts, then it appears impossible in principle to give any adequate explanation of what is involved in the developmental transition from pre-conceptual infancy to mature conceptual thought. Carefully put, I think that this point presents a genuine, although not insurmountable, difficulty, and puts significant pressure on the confidence which I expressed in responding to the fourth non-conceptualist argument as I did above.

Very roughly indeed, an account of concept possession meeting the non-circularity requirement consists of, or entails, a series of claims of the following form:

Being in non-conceptual state N_i is constitutive of being in conceptual state C_i.

Given such an account, then, it is possible to give a complete explanation of what is involved in acquiring the capacity for conceptual thought. It is simply a matter of developing sufficient complexity, of a kind which presupposes no concept mastery, and is therefore perfectly intelligible on the part of a pre-conceptual infant exposed to suitable training and learning opportunities, to get into the appropriate N_i states.

Given the impossibility of any such account, on the other hand, this type of explanation cannot be given. So the conceptualist is left with the task of providing an alternative, or at least of arguing that some alternative could in principle be provided. Yet it is far from clear to what he should appeal in attempting to do so. The burden of proof is very delicate here. Crudely, there are three ways in which the assessment of this situation might be approached. First, it might be held that we can lay down a priori an exhaustive list of all the possible forms which a satisfactory theory of concept acquisition could take. The issue then is whether any of these is even in principle available to the conceptualist. Second, it might be held that such a list is available to us by careful reflection upon our explanatory practices, but is currently only implicit in the range of accounts to which we presently appeal in making various parallel transitions and relations in the natural world intelligible to ourselves. Third, it might be argued that any list of acceptable modes of explanation of this kind is always bound to be open-ended, and subject to revision and expansion in the light of new types of explanation, which are widely accepted as genuinely illuminating, although they do not obviously fit the models to which any existing accounts conform.

The decision between these approaches is itself a highly contentious matter. The conceptualist is surely in a strong position on the third, though. For, in that case, he can draw continually upon the detailed progress of developmental psychology in piecing together a plausible story about human cognitive development, about the key steps and transitions which take place as light dawns gradually, for a growing child, upon the whole of conceptual thought: how and when the major developments occur, what provides the ideal conditions for them, what other capacities they presuppose and themselves bring with them, and so on. It would take a rash philosopher indeed to insist at this stage that every such story is bound to be incompatible with the conceptualist's rejection of the particular kind of non-circularity requirement currently in question. The second approach also leaves the conceptualist with a good deal of room to move. For the correct taxonomy of all the relevant modes of explanation which are already in play in our thinking about the world is hardly obvious. So the question whether the conceptualist might avail himself of one, or a combination, of these in making human cognitive development intelligible consistently with his rejection of the non-circularity requirement is far from straightforward, and even further from being straightforwardly answerable in the negative. The first approach seems to me to be the least defensible of the three; and even then, I am entirely unpersuaded that it constitutes a conclusive victory for the non-conceptualist. For I cannot see which defensible principles could possibly be advanced from which it follows that only the above model of explanation and others like it in being inconsistent with the conceptualist's rejection of the particular non-circularity requirement which is in question here are ever satisfactory in any area of human investigation.

Thus, it seems to me that none of the arguments which I have considered in defence of a non-conceptualist account of the reason-giving representational contents of perceptual experiences is in the end compelling. This completes my case for (C): reasons require conceptual contents. Putting this together with my earlier thesis (R), which dominated discussion in Part I, yields the following conclusion. Conscious perceptual experiences have conceptual representational contents which provide a person's reasons for his empirical beliefs about how things are in the mind-independent world around him. In the chapters which follow, I shall be exploring in more detail the nature of these conceptual contents, how exactly they are made available by experiences, and what is involved in their thereby providing reasons *of an especially fundamental kind* for the subject's empirical beliefs. So far, my focus has been upon the essential role of perceptual experiences in a person's very possession of empirical beliefs. My claim in what follows is that pursuing this investigation further brings out the crucial role of such experiences in his acquisition of empirical *knowledge*. The epistemology in this area is therefore best approached through close attention to its philosophical logic. As I have already suggested, the more traditional enterprise of taking the latter for granted, and aiming for an independent attack on the former is, in my view, entirely misguided.

6

The Rational Role of Perceptual Experiences

My question now is this: how exactly *do* perceptual experiences provide reasons for empirical beliefs? So far, all I have offered is that they do so in virtue of their possession of certain conceptual representational contents. But any such suggestion faces the following dilemma. Conceptual contents may be endorsed, in the form of beliefs, or simply entertained in some way, unendorsed in belief. There are two reasons why the reason-giving representational contents of perceptual experiences cannot be endorsed in belief. First, as I have already noted (5.3.3), experiences are belief-independent: they have the contents which they do independently of whether the subject endorses those contents in belief or not. Second, identifying reason-giving experiential states with beliefs threatens to reduce the account to a version of the coherentism which I rejected earlier (4.3), on which such beliefs' role in providing reasons turns entirely on the subject's possession of further, independent, second-order beliefs to the effect that the first-order beliefs are reliably formed. Yet thinking of the reason-giving contents of perceptual experiences as entertained in some way unendorsed in belief is equally problematic. For simply entertaining a content in this way in general gives a person no reason whatsoever to endorse it in belief, or to endorse anything else for that matter, except perhaps the self-ascriptive thought that he is entertaining the content in question.[1] What is required, then, is an account of the peculiar nature

---

[1] The obvious exceptions to this claim are contents which are knowable a priori. Although I shall myself eventually argue that the resemblance between perceptual experiential demonstrative contents and these a priori contents is extremely close in precisely this respect, this parallel is hardly the most natural starting place for an account of empirical knowledge.

of perceptual experiential contents which avoids this dilemma, and therefore elucidates the sense in which they provide peculiarly basic, but nevertheless perfectly genuine, although perhaps defeasible, reasons for empirical beliefs. This requires a closer focus upon their essentially experiential demonstrative nature, in contradistinction to beliefs, or idly entertained, unendorsed thoughts, generally.

This is the point in his own account at which McDowell appeals to the widely remarked, although never to my mind properly elucidated, *passivity* of perceptual experience (1994*b*, esp. Lecture I, pp. 10–13): ' [E]xperience is passive. In experience one is *saddled* with content' (p. 10, my emphasis). What exactly does this mean, though? And how is it supposed to help? It cannot simply be the claim that experiences are thoughts which just occur to a person quite out of the blue. For belief-independent such occurrences, as we have seen that experiences would have to be, would simply be a subset of the thoughts he entertains unendorsed in belief generally, none of which actually give him a reason for anything. The idea, I think, is rather that *which particular* contents a person's experiences have is in an important sense quite outside his control. Given the way things are in the mind-independent world, the subject's location, direction of gaze and attentional set—which question he is directing at which part of his environment to be answered by perception—then the particular conceptual content delivered by his perceptual experience is something over which he has no control: it just comes to him. Things just strike him as thus and so, in the relevant respect, around him: that (there) is thus. Very roughly, then, the concepts figuring in experiential contents do not simply pop up from nowhere; nor are they the product of the subject's active reflection or directed reasoning about some matter or other. Rather, they are provided directly by his attentional relations with the particular things around him, by the way in which he is interrogating his environment in perception.[2] The suggestion

---

[2] This idea of perception as 'interrogation of the environment' is due to Rowland Stout (in conversation). It is taken up by Naomi Eilan (1997*b*), drawing on work by John Campbell (forthcoming), in her account of the mixture of activity and passivity in perceptual experience. I am grateful to all three of them for helping me to see, a little better at least, how to develop my own views here.

which I want to pursue now is that a proper account of what is involved in his *grasp* of such perceptual experiential contents, as revelatory of the way things are with persisting objects and their properties in the mind-independent world around him, illuminates the source of a person's epistemic, albeit defeasible, right to endorse those very contents in belief. This, I propose, is where to find the fundamental role of conscious experience in the acquisition of empirical knowledge.

Recall from my argument for (C) in Chapter 5 above, that the whole point of insisting upon the conceptual nature of reason-giving experiential contents is to ensure that their determinate truth-conditions are given to the subject in precisely the way required for him to recognize their status as providing reasons for his empirical beliefs. Thus, the thesis which I shall be advancing in response to the dilemma threatened above is this. Perceptual experiences are essential to a person's grasp of certain demonstrative contents, whose reference to particular mind-independent objects and properties is achieved in such a way that his simply entertaining these contents gives him a reason to endorse them in belief. The perceptual demonstrative contents in question are expressible, in the first instance, only as 'That thing (there) is thus'. Given the relevant facts about the way things are in the world around the perceiver, the direction and focus of his attention, and so on, which contents these are is, as I say, beyond his control. In what follows, I want to press the following questions. What exactly is involved in his *understanding*, that is to say, his actually being the subject who is entertaining, these perceptual demonstrative contents? What does his knowledge of their objective truth-conditions consist in? More specifically, to begin with, what is involved in his grasp of the embedded singular demonstrative Idea of the particular mind-independent object in question?

6.1 *Objective Demonstratives*

I argued in Chapter 2 that this Idea cannot be purely descriptive. Indeed, I argued that reference to spatial particulars is, in the most basic cases, *essentially* experiential: the subject's actually standing in certain perceptual-attentional relations with the particular object in question is a necessary condition upon his grasping this very Idea of that thing. So the question to ask now is exactly what a person's perceptual experiences contribute to his Idea of the relevant worldly object on a given occasion. A plausible answer here, at least in certain central cases, and especially where vision is the prominent modality, is that perceptual experience displays the *spatial location* of the object, which contributes to the subject's knowledge of which particular object is in question. Indeed, I shall explain in detail how it is that I think that this is the correct answer in such cases, which I treat as illustrative of the structure of my positive account, which is to be generalized only when all the pieces are in place with respect to this illustrative example. This, then, is what experiences contribute to determinate reference to spatial particulars in such cases: they display the location of the relevant object in such a way as to provide the subject with identifying knowledge of which particular object is in question.

This is possible, because there is a fundamental interdependence between making a numerical distinction between qualitatively identical spatial particulars and assigning them different locations at a given time: for every time t, every mind-independent spatial object which exists at t has a location at t, it has just one such location at t, and no two numerically distinct objects (of the same sort) have the same location at t. So a key to reference to spatial particulars is knowledge of their location. In the cases under consideration, this is what constitutes the subject's knowledge of *which* object is in question. It provides him with a genuine Idea of that particular thing, employed in the content in question and in any other content entertaining which involves thinking of that thing in the same way.

As I have effectively already established, if this location is given only in terms of certain spatial relations to other objects and places identified purely by description, then the possibility of massive reduplication returns to undermine the purported uniqueness of location and hence of determinate reference to any particular occupant. For, on the assumption that a person is normally in a position to know that she is referring to a particular place when she is, then the argument which I gave in 2.2 above, and refined in 2.3, against purely descriptive reference to mind-independent particulars, goes through with only minimal revision in the case of particular spatial locations. For, consider a person, S, with a perceptually based belief about a particular place, *l*; and suppose that S actually knows that she is referring to *l*. Given what has just been said, stipulating this situation is legitimate. Now, assume, for *reductio*, that S's Idea of *l* is purely descriptive. That is, her conception of which place *l* is is exhausted by a wholly general description, 'the *F*', which purports to identify *l* by reference to its own occupants and its spatial relations with other places and things, all identified purely descriptively. Thus, her entertaining the Idea is quite independent of any experience of the place in question. Now, however detailed and extensive this description of *l* may be, it is bound to be an epistemic possibility for S that '*F*' is multiply satisfied, in the following sense. It is logically consistent with all that S knows that '*F*' is satisfied by more than one place. For she cannot knowledgeably rule out the possibility of a massive qualitative reduplication elsewhere in the universe of the relevant sector of her environment.[3] So there is a possible world in which '*F*' is multiply satisfied and everything which S actually knows is true. Thus, there is a possible world in which '*F*' is multiply satisfied and S refers as she does to *l*; for that she does so is something which she knows. This is a contradiction. For in that case, 'the *F*' *fails* to refer. Hence S's Idea of *l* cannot be purely descriptive after all. It must involve some kind of demonstrative component, with respect to which her experience is *essential* to her grasp of which place is in question.[4] Genuine perceptual reference to particular places is therefore essentially experiential. What is required, therefore, for genuine reference to a particular mind-independent thing, is knowledge of what would make true an identification of that object with one whose location is given in experience.

This immediately raises the question of exactly how particular places *are* displayed in experience. The crucial point here is

---

[3] See ch. 2, n. 14, for a demonstration of the underlying equivalence here, between 'it is epistemically possible for S that *p*', and 'S is not in a position knowledgeably to rule out that *p*'.

[4] See 2.3 for extended discussion of various objections to this line of argument in the case of reference to particular objects. Parallel objections arise in the present case of reference to particular places; and I would offer parallel replies to them.

that perception presents its objects as determinately located *relative to the perceiver*. A person experiences mind-independent things as distributed *around and in relation to him*. Certainly, he does not figure as one object among many absolutely on a par with those he perceives in the normal way; for he is not presented *in that way* as one among them: surveying the perceptually displayed scene, he is not normally among the many possible objects of perceptual attention, as he would be, say, when looking in a mirror, or feeling the configuration of his legs. Nevertheless, the locations of what he does perceive in this way—the possible objects of this perceptual-attentional selection—are displayed in relation to him and his own place amongst them in the following sense. It is the actual spatial relations between the things he perceives *and himself* which determine whether or not he perceives them as being where they actually are.

Where must we look, for example, to discover whether my perception that there is a cat just *there* (in front) on the mat is veridical? Not on any old mat; nor on the mat with all, or most, of the qualitative features which I am able to report on the basis of my experience, since, however detailed the description, there may be more than one such mat; but on the mat directly *in front of me*. So my perception involves *some* representation of myself as located thus and so in relation to its standard objects—the cat and the mat in this case. Correlatively, it is therefore in relation to myself that the perceived cat is presented as determinately located.

Given my Strawson Argument from the possibility of massive reduplication, the point applies quite generally, however much additional qualitative information is provided, including spatial relations with other descriptively identified objects. In other words, indeterminacy equally affects the purported identification 'on the mat below the window between the red chair and the blue sofa', for example, and every other such attempt. Perceptually presented locations are therefore uniquely determined only *egocentrically*, as up/down, left/right, in front/behind, *where these determinations are essentially subject-relative*. For the place perceptually presented as to the right a little up and in front, say, is that to *the perceiver's* right, a little above and in front of *him*. Hence perceptual reference to particular places is essentially subject-relative, in the sense that displayed locations are identified relative to the subject making the reference himself.

This identification may be given indirectly, as it would be by appeal to a suitably demonstratively anchored description, such as 'in the box under that table'. This possibility obviously rests upon that of a person's more direct identification of a particular location relative to his own, though—in this case, that exploited in his demonstrative reference to *that table*. In general, I claim, perceptual demonstrative contents of the kind which I am concerned with are precisely those which display the locations of the relevant objects directly in just this way. Perceptual reference and egocentric location come together, then, at least in the central cases which I am currently considering, in which determinacy of reference is secured by exploiting the interrelation between the numerical identity and spatial location of mind-independent particulars at a time. This is (at least part of) the essential contribution made by a person's perceptual experiences at a given time to his understanding of certain demonstrative contents making reference to particular mind-independent things around him at that time.[5]

Now, if such a perceptual demonstrative content is to refer to a particular *mind-independent* thing, in this way, then the subject's Idea of its location must be an Idea of a location *in a world of places and things which are quite independent of his actual experiences of them*. For his Idea of its location contributes essentially to his Idea of its identity. He must therefore understand that the very same location might have been spatially related in a quite different way with him: that thing *there* might equally have been perceived from any number of different points of view.[6] Yet how is this condition to be met, since I also insist

---

[5] There is of course a debate at this point about precisely what the relations of priority are, if any, between identifications, of various kinds, of objects and their locations in this basic case, in which the things and places in question are displayed in experience (Strawson, 1959, ch. 1; Wiggins, 1963; Woods, 1963; Evans, 1982, ch. 6; Campbell, 1993*b*). I am confident, though, that what I have to say here is independent of the detailed differences of view on these matters.

[6] What if the thing in question is a part of the subject's body? Things get very complicated in this case. First, bodily awareness is likely to be involved in a peculiar way. Although I am sympathetic to the idea that perceptual systems are normally both exteroceptive and proprioceptive (J. J. Gibson, 1979), the

that, in order to avoid reference failure due to the possibility of massive reduplication, the location in question must be presented in experience, and therefore given *relative to the subject himself*, and to his own actual place amongst the objects in question?

There are two lines of response to this problem. First, it might be denied that a person's recognition that the same thing, at the same place, might have been perceived from a different point of view really is a necessary condition upon perceptual demonstrative reference to mind-independent spatial particulars. Second, it might be argued that the apparent inconsistency between the claim that this condition must indeed be met and my insistence that determinate reference to particular places and things is ultimately subject-relative, or egocentric in some sense, is only illusory. I take it for granted that a third possible suggestion, to resist the essentially experiential-perspectival nature of spatial reference—to both places and things—is simply ruled out by my discussion of the Strawson Argument from the possibility massive reduplication both in Chapter 2 and in its obvious extension to locations above. I consider each of the two genuine responses in turn.

If the singular Ideas involved in perceptual demonstrative contents refer to mind-independent things, then it certainly follows that these are Ideas of things whose locations are in fact independent of the subject's experiences of them. It does not follow, though, according to the first line of response above, that any person entertaining such an Idea must therefore *recognize* the independence of the location of the relevant mind-independent thing from his actual experiences of it in any way. He need have no understanding whatsoever, then, that that thing there might equally have been perceived from any number of

object of exteroception is not normally *itself* an object of proprioception, as it is in the case of a person's visual or tactual perception of his own body, say. Second, and relatedly, a person's body parts are normally experienced *as his own* (Brewer, 1995a). Nevertheless, if the body part in question is anaesthetised and experienced only as 'that hand', as opposed to 'my hand', then the condition in the text applies. At least, in cases in which it is the hand's displayed location which informs the subject's perceptual reference to that particular hand, then he must grasp that that location might have been displayed as differently located to him: that hand might have been further out to the right, or directly in front of him.

different points of view. The claim that he must, the response will continue, can only be sustained by appeal to an absurd principle along the following lines. If a person refers to an object, *o*, which is *F*, on the basis of a perceptual demonstrative Idea, *I*, then in grasping *I* he necessarily recognizes that its object is *F*. In its present application, this principle simply obliterates the difference between its *being* a metaphysical possibility that *o* be perceived from any number of different points of view, on the one hand, and the subject's *appreciating* this possibility, on the other.

The principle as it stands is indeed absurd, not least because it entails a person's omniscience about the objects to which he refers in thought and belief. Furthermore, it is absolutely right to insist in general upon a sharp distinction between the fact that a certain metaphysical possibility obtains, on the one hand, and its being recognized to obtain by anyone, on the other. The untenable universal principle above is *not* required by my argument, though. The crucial point is rather that it is *only* on the basis of his grasp of its location—displayed relative to him in experience—that the subject has an Idea of *that object* at all, in the cases under consideration. Unlike its other properties, its location is not something which he can remain completely ignorant about, having already identified the relevant object in thought. For his Idea of its location contributes essentially to his identification of which object is in question. Hence, which object *is* in question—which object his Idea is an Idea of—is determined in part by his Idea of its location. Thus, if he has no understanding whatsoever of the independence of this location from his actual experiential point of view upon it, then it is wrong to claim that he has an Idea of a mind-independent spatial thing at all. This is not the sort of thing which *could* be determined as the object of his Idea in that case. His appreciation in some sense of the relevant metaphysical possibilities is essential to their obtaining *with respect to the objects and places which are thereby determined as the semantic values* of the Ideas which he entertains of them. So the condition is quite genuine. A person's Idea of the relevant location must be an Idea of a location which might have been spatially related in a quite different way to him, in the sense that he must actually grasp that that thing *there* might equally have been perceived—still just where it is, there—

from any number of different points of view. The first line of response is therefore unacceptable.

Can anything really be made of the second suggestion either: to argue that meeting this condition is after all consistent with the requirement that determinate reference to particular locations is ultimately subject-relative in some sense? For if the location of a perceived particular is necessarily given in relation to the perceiver's own, then how can his perceptual demonstrative Idea involve any genuine understanding at all that that thing there, in just that place, might equally have been displayed as quite differently spatially related to him, from another point of view?

To see how this might be done, it is crucial to get clear about a distinction which is due to John Campbell (1994, p. 119; 1998).[7] There is both a *monadic* and a *relational* use of egocentric spatial terms such as 'to the left'/'to the right', 'above'/'below', 'in front'/'behind' and so on. Whenever a person uses these terms to give the location of something, its location is thereby specified in relation to something else: they are in that sense essentially *relational*. A person can have more or less *understanding* in his use of them of their relational nature, though. Representing sentences in which such terms occur as applications of the relation 'xRy', to begin with—'x is to the right of y', as it might be—then the issue is over the appropriate range of the notional variable 'y'. There is a primitive use of such sentences in which this is effectively tied to the thinker himself, in his actual location at just that time, in such a way that he has no comprehension of what it would be for the object or place represented as standing in that 'relation' to him then to be differently spatially related to *something else at some other time*. So he is not really *thinking relationally* at all. Although it is *a*'s spatial relations *with him then* which determine its truth or falsity, his thought is more properly regimented as '$R'a$': 'a is to the right and a little in front', say, as opposed to 'a is to the right and a little in front *of me now*'. For it is a minimal necessary condition upon discerning the genuinely relational structure in this thinking which

---

[7] I am also indebted at this point to Naomi Eilan for some very helpful suggestions.

motivates articulating his thought as 'aRi', where 'i' is a singular term referring to himself or his own present location, that he has some conception of what it would be for 'aSj', 'aTk', and so on, to be true, for some appropriate range of alternative spatial relations, 'S', 'T', and so on and singular terms 'j', 'k', and so on.[8] The primitive use of egocentric terms, in which the subject has no such conception at all, is what Campbell calls *monadic*; the associated concepts, or Ideas, of spatial 'relations' and particular locations are monadic spatial concepts, or Ideas.

There are different types of genuinely relational uses of such terms, different types of relational spatial concepts and Ideas, which vary, amongst other things, according to the generality introduced by the range of the variable 'y': that is, the range of appropriate alternative singular terms to 'i'—'j', 'k', and so on above—which are such that the subject's grasp of the thought 'aRi' commits him to knowledge of what it would be for 'aSj', 'aTk', and so on, to be true. Two significantly different types of relational egocentric thinking would be, first, that in which 'y' ranges only over alternative possible points of view of the same thinking subject; and, second, that in which its range explicitly allows for generality across different thinkers. For present purposes, though, the basic distinction between monadic and relational egocentric spatial concepts, or Ideas, is sufficient.

I have argued that determinate reference to particular locations is ultimately egocentric in some sense. That is to say, the embedded experience-based Idea of a particular place in the subject's environment must identify this place in some way relative to himself, or his own present location. Our current problem is to explain how this requirement is consistent with his meeting the further condition upon perceptual demonstrative reference to particular *mind-independent things*, in cases where this exploits the subject's grasp of their location, that he should recognize that the very thing in question, just there, where it actually is, might equally have been perceived from any number of different points of view.[9] Now, suppose that his egocentric

---

[8] This is of course an application to the current case of Evans's Generality Constraint (1982, esp. sect. 4.3). The requirement is derived from Strawson (1959, esp. ch. 3).

[9] From the theorist's point of view, the appearance of an inconsistency here

perceptual identification of the location in question is purely monadic. So his conception of which place is in question is exhausted by its actual present spatial relations with him. Thus, he is incapable of any recognition that the thing in question, *at just that location*, might equally have been displayed as differently located—relative to him. For there is no degree of freedom in his thinking, along which to register the changes in his own position required to make sense of these alternative perspectives. He therefore fails genuinely to refer to any mind-independent spatial particular. His thought is not really thought about *mind-independent* reality at all. Put slightly differently, the difficulty here is that the perceptual demonstrative content in question is bound by a kind of idealism about space, on which there is nothing more to where things are than where they presently appear to be. Given that his knowledge of their location is supposed to contribute to his knowledge of which the particular objects are about which he is supposedly thinking at any time, it follows that he can equally have no conception of these as existing independently of his particular experiences of them. His experience therefore fails altogether to display to him the way things are in a *mind-independent* world around him.

Thus, if it is to refer to a particular mind-independent thing in the world around him on the basis of his grasp of where that thing is in relation to him, then a person's perceptual demonstrative, 'That thing (there) is thus', must comprise a singular Idea, 'that thing', which exploits a genuinely *relational* egocentric

---

is evidently illusory. For it is due to a simple confusion of scope: the first of the following two claims does not entail the second. (1) Necessarily, some spatial relation of the perceived particular to the perceiver fixes the perceived particular's location. (2) Some spatial relation of the perceived particular to the perceiver is such that necessarily it fixes the perceived particular's location. Claim (1) captures the necessary perspective dependence of location identification. Only (2) is inconsistent with the idea that the particular location of a given object might vary, either over time or across possible worlds, in its spatial relations with the subject in question. The issue, though, is how the initial appearance of inconsistency is resolved *for the subject himself*. He must be able to make sense of the possibility that that thing, there, whose identity is given by its location in relation to him, might nevertheless be presented as differently located relative to him. My proposal will be that only *relational* egocentric spatial representation makes the crucial scope distinction available to the subject, on the basis of which he can then make sense of this possibility quite easily.

identification of the location of the thing in question.[10] How exactly does this help? Well, a person whose perceptual demonstrative contents are relational, in this sense, can immerse himself in his present perspective, so to speak, and entertain the corresponding purely monadic spatial contents, 'That thing—there$_m$—is thus', say. These capture how things *appear* (spatially) to him—from that perspective, wholly immersed in it, and suspending any reflection upon it or its contribution to his experience. Yet in arriving at the appropriate monadic content on any particular occasion *on the basis of his prior understanding of the corresponding relational content*, in this way, he grasps its grounding in the prior relational facts. In other words, this is to appreciate the joint dependence of how things currently appear to him (spatially) upon the way particular mind-independent things are actually distributed in the world around him,

[10] It may be objected that this move from the failure of the most basic monadic egocentric thinking to meet the present challenge to reconcile subject relativity and mind independence, on the one hand, to the need for fully relational egocentric spatial thinking, on the other, is too quick. For there are clearly many animals who continually and systematically update their monadic representations of certain key locations in their environment in response to monitoring their own movements through this environment, and successfully control their spatial behaviour in connection with such locations accordingly. (See Gallistel, 1990, for an excellent survey of the various modes of spatial learning in animals.) Here, it might be argued, there is monadic egocentricity, yet with sufficient sensitivity on the creature's part to the fact that what is presently in front and a little to the left, for example, was previously a long way in front and just right of straight ahead, and will soon be over to the left and a little behind, to justify regarding it as representation of mind-independent places in the environment through which the animal moves. A great deal could be said about this kind of case. I admit that there is *a kind of* objectivity in such a creature's representation of the places around it. For this certainly transcends a simple identification of the place in question with a particular monadic egocentric relation. Nevertheless, this sensitivity comes out only in the creature's modulation of its spatial behaviour over time in response to its own movement, and not at the level of reflective thought about the identities over time of certain particular objects and their places in the world. See my comparison of my own position below (6.3.1) with those of Evans (1982, ch. 6) and especially Peacocke (1983, ch. 3) for more on this distinction, and its importance. Yet I contend that only objectivity at this level of reflective thought serves to constitute the Ideas of objects and places involved as Ideas of persisting mind-independent objects and their changing places in the subject's environment. For only this contributes to a subjective conception on his part associated with such Ideas which uniquely determines particular mind-independent objects and places as their semantic values.

and his present location amongst them—his current perceptual *point of view* upon them. Equally, he is therefore in a position to make sense of the possibility that the thing in question, *at just that location*, might have been displayed as differently located—relative to him—from elsewhere. Indeed, he may even be capable to some extent of simulating the monadic contents which would be associated with his taking up different points of view upon the same range of particular things, in the particular places which they occupy. That is to say, he has certain of the materials essential to the capacity to construct, in imagination, the systematically varying monadic contents which he would arrive at by immersing himself in various alternative, possible but non-actual, perspectives upon the same mind-independent things, just where they are around him. (For example, that thing there$_{r1}$, although there$_{m1}$ from here$_{r0}$ would be there$_{m2}$ from there$_{r2}$, where subscripts 'r0'–'r2' and 'm1'–'m2' index different relational and monadic egocentric spatial Ideas respectively.)[11] Crucially, though, in appreciating the dependence of his monadic perspective on the world upon a more fundamental egocentrically relational conception of where the relevant object is in his environment, he is capable of grasping that that thing, just there, where it actually is, might equally have been perceived from any number of different points of view. He is therefore able to meet this crucial condition upon genuine perceptual demonstrative reference to mind-independent things consistently with the requirement that the location exploited by his Idea of the particular thing in question should be specified egocentrically, in relation to his own.

So far, I have been focusing exclusively upon those cases of perceptual demonstrative reference in which the subject's Idea of the particular object in question is informed by his grasp of its

---

[11] I do not mean to claim here that the subject must explicitly operate with a *theory* about the way in which spatial appearances vary with changes in his point of view. Rather, he has the potential, at least, to trip to and fro between a fixed relational conception of where a certain thing is relative to him, and both his actual, immersed monadic impression of its location, and various non-actual possible alternatives to it had he perceived that thing from a different point of view, simulated in imagination. His skill in this regard may not be at all well developed, but relational egocentric spatial thinking is the essential ground for any such imaginative routine in which he is actually capable of engaging.

spatial location. Although I believe that this is a central class of cases, it is by no means exhaustive; and a parallel problem arises in any other case to the difficulty which I have just been discussing in these spatial cases of reconciling the essentially perspectival nature of spatial perception with the mind-independence of its objects. For in every case, an explanation will be required of how *essentially experiential* reference can nevertheless be reference to *mind-independent* particulars. Suppose that the contribution of experience to securing determinate reference to a particular mind-independent thing in the case under consideration is its displaying the relevant object's characteristic feature ϕ. In the central cases which I have been discussing up until now, ϕ is the target object's spatial location. In other cases, it might be the timbre of sound produced, for example, in auditory reference to a particular member of an unseen wind quintet; or it might be shape, in the visual tracking of a single letter 'B' amongst a host of 'D''s, or whatever. The Strawson Argument which I set out in Chapter 2, and applied to the case of spatial location above, applies again here, to establish, on the one hand, that this experiential contribution to determinate reference is to make available to the perceiver an *essentially experiential* demonstrative Idea of the object in question, such as 'that ϕ-thing'. The mind-independent reference of this Idea, on the other hand, requires that her grasp of the characteristic ϕ in question should not be exhausted by the way in which it is actually presented in her experience, the ϕ-appearance, as it were. As in the spatial case, the apparent tension between these two points is to be resolved by the subject's grasp of the actual experiential appearance of ϕ, from immersed within her present perspective and suspending any reflection upon it or its contribution to her experience, as the joint upshot of the mind-independent ϕ of the object in question and the relevant features of her particular perceptual perspective upon it.

Something very similar also sustains the mind-independent significance of the predicative component of these perceptual demonstrative contents. Experiential demonstratives, like 'that ϕ-thing is thus', refer to mind-independent particulars—as we have just seen—of which they predicate, not just subjective appearances, but mind-independent properties, which are the categorical grounds of the relevant objects' powers to produce certain appearances in appropriately placed perceivers. A given such content presents a particular thing as mind-independently, categorically, *thus*. A person whose experience enables her to grasp this content can immerse herself in her own perspective, so to speak, and entertain the corresponding appearance—from there and in those circumstances—that that thing appears thus. In arriving at the appropriate appearance *on the basis of her prior understanding of the corresponding perceptual demonstrative presentation of the way things mind-independently are*, in this way, she grasps its grounding in the prior categorical facts. In other words, this is to appreciate the joint dependence of how things currently appear to her (with respect to the properties she perceives them to have) upon the way particular mind-independent things actually are in themselves, and her current point of view upon them and other relevant circumstances. Equally, she is therefore in a position to make sense of the possibility that a particular thing, just as it is, might have appeared differently—in the immersed sense, parallel to monadic spatial contents—from a different point of view or in alternative circumstances. Indeed, she may even be capable to some extent of simulating the appearances, in this immersed sense, associated with her taking up different points of view on the same things, with the same properties, in different circumstances. That is to say, she has certain of the materials essential to the capacity to construct, in imagination, the systematically varying appearances of those things' being just the way they are from various alternative, possible but non-actual, perspectives and in various alternative, possible but non-actual, circumstances. (For example, that thing's being $thus_{c1}$, although appearing $thus_{a1}$ as circumstances are$_{c0}$ would appear $thus_{a2}$ if circumstances were such and such$_{c2}$, where subscripts 'co'–'c2' and 'a1'–'a2' index different categorical ground and appearance predications respectively.) Crucially, though, as I say, although her conception of this may be essentially experiential in nature, she nevertheless predicates a genuinely mind-independent, categorical property in thinking of that thing as *thus*, in virtue of her understanding of its actual experiential appearance, from immersed within her present perspective, as the joint upshot of the way it is in itself—$thus_c$—and the relevant features of her perceptual circumstances. This comes out in her grasp of the possibility of a range of different immersed appearances of the same thing's being just thus_c in alternative such circumstances.

I shall explain shortly why I think that it is precisely this resolution of the apparent tension between the essentially experiential nature of perceptual reference and predication, on the one hand, and the mind-independence of its objects and properties, on the other, which provides a person with her most basic reasons to endorse the perceptual demonstrative contents in question in belief. Since it plays such a crucial role in my positive account of perceptual knowledge, though, it is worth dwelling a little longer upon the abstract structure of my proposal here. Perceptual demonstrative thinking is essentially experiential, in the sense that its subject's grasp of its determinate contents depends upon her possession of certain conscious experiences; yet these contents are fully objective, in the sense that they present a world of objects and properties which are quite independent of any particular experiences of them, and they present such things *as mind-independent* in this way. This combination is possible only in virtue of the subject's understanding, crucial to her grasp of any particular such perceptual demonstrative content, of the possibility of alternative experiential snapshots of the very same phenomena under alternative circumstances, from different points of view, and under different perceptual circumstances. This is *what makes it the case* that her essentially experiential demonstrative thinking nevertheless has objective content.[12]

Naomi Eilan (1997*a*) draws an illuminating contrast between this approach and Descartes's (1986) account of perceptual knowledge. The issue is how to explain the possibility of knowledge of what is *objectively* true from within the *subjective* perspective of conscious experience. Clearly, if the subjectivity of consciousness and the objectivity of empirical truth are defined by direct opposition with each other, then there will be no such

[12] I am drawing substantially upon Campbell (1993*a*) here. This general approach to the question of how a subjective experiential perspective gets to be a perspective upon a mind-independent objective world is Kantian in origin, and is set out in Strawson's pathbreaking and influential account of the transcendental deduction (1966, 2.II). It has been taken up more recently by Evans (1980, 1982, ch. 7), Cassam (1989, 1997), Peacocke (1983, ch. 3, 1992, ch. 3), myself (Brewer, 1992), and Eilan (1997*a*), as well as by Campbell (1984–5, 1993*a*).

possibility. Descartes's response is, first, to characterize subjectivity in terms of what is evident and incorrigible to the subject. That is, the subjective is that realm about which, necessarily, the subject has a belief if and only if it is true. As Eilan puts it, 'On this account, conscious states are subjective precisely in the sense that all truths about their intrinsic conscious properties are believed by their owner, and everything the owner believes about them is true' (1997a, p. 240). Descartes then goes on, second, to characterize objectivity in terms of what Bernard Williams (1978) calls the 'absolute conception'. Objective facts are those which figure in an entirely context-independent representation *from no point of view*, stripped of all the 'idiosyncrasies' of any particular personal perspective. The contents of objective reality are therefore those things whose identity we can grasp independently of any experiential perspective upon them.[13] Descartes's account of perceptual knowledge, as outlined in Chapter 1 above, is then presented as one on which evident and incorrigible first-person, present-tense propositions about the subject's own mental states provide the deductive foundations for an absolute conception of the physical world constituted entirely by the various modes of extension.

My own proposal, precisely in line with Eilan's recommendations (1997a), adopts the mirror image of the Cartesian strategy. What is characteristic of the subjective perspective of conscious perceptual experience, on my account, is its provision of essentially perspective-dependent demonstrative contents, grasp of which requires actual perceptual attention to their objects in the environment. Here subjectivity is defined in contradistinction to Descartes's objectivity of the absolute conception; it is not regarded as a realm of evidentness and incorrigibility. The objectivity of the mind-independent world, on the other hand, consists in the fact that its layout and nature is not exhausted by any particular experience of it. It is there to be revealed in experi-

---

[13] This Cartesian criterion for membership of mind-independent reality, reality as it is in itself, or 'what is there anyway' (Williams, 1978), has been extremely influential in excluding all sorts of things from this precious realm. The argument is almost universally acknowledged with respect to secondary qualities as-we-perceive-them, for example. The upshot of my Strawson Argument (Ch. 2), though, is that the criterion must be rejected; for it unacceptably excludes particular spatio-temporal objects as elements of the mind-independent world (see Campbell, 1993a).

ence from various different points of view and in various different circumstances, provided, of course, that the appropriate enabling conditions obtain. It is therefore defined in contradistinction to Descartes's evident and incorrigible subjective realm: not every truth about the world is believed by anyone, and mistakes about it are possible by anyone. Furthermore, there is no commitment to anything like the absolute conception as a criterion of objective truth. Indeed, as I argued in Chapter 2, there is no such thing as absolute, perspective-independent empirical thought at all. The most basic empirical beliefs have essentially experiential perceptual demonstrative contents. Objective knowledge is possible from within the subjective perspective of consciousness, on this account, then, precisely because such perceptual demonstratives are nevertheless recognizable as drawing upon just one among many possible experiential perspectives upon the same world of objects and properties, whose layout and nature might equally not have been displayed in any such experiences. This is what sustains their reference to and predication of genuinely mind-independent spatial particulars and their properties.

It is worth highlighting in this context that perceptual demonstrative Ideas and concepts, as conceived here, are *unitary*, in the sense of 3.4 above, in that the associated subjective conception constitutive of their possession and application uniquely determines their semantic value. For a person's grasp of such Ideas and concepts depends upon his being subject to certain conscious experiences—these provide him with his subjective conception of which worldly objects and properties are in question—which are in turn constituted by his standing in appropriate perceptual-attentional relations *with these very semantic values*. This is what enables such experiences to provide the subject with reasons, recognizable as such from his own point of view, for certain beliefs about precisely these objects and properties, as opposed to any others.[14]

---

[14] These themes will be taken up again in more detail in my discussion below (8.2) of a version of Russell's Principle of Acquaintance, that 'every proposition which we can understand must be composed wholly of constituents with which we are acquainted' (1917, p. 159), which I think is entailed by my account of perceptual knowledge.

I should also make absolutely explicit before moving on that the perceptual demonstrative contents which I am concerned with here are, as they must be if they are to provide genuine reasons for empirical beliefs (see Ch. 5, esp. 5.1), fully conceptual contents. Although the subject's possession of the component demonstrative Ideas and concepts depends upon his actually standing, or having stood, in certain essentially experiential perceptual-attentional relations with the objects and properties in question, his possession of these Ideas and concepts is absolutely crucial to his having perceptual experiences with the whole contents themselves. Furthermore, contents of the form 'That is thus' are perfectly capable of constituting a premise or the conclusion of inferences of various kinds. Perceptual experiences therefore have representational contents which are characterizable only in terms of concepts which the subject himself must possess and which are of a form which enable them to serve as a premise or the conclusion of a deductive argument, or of an inference of some other kind (e.g. inductive or abductive). So they are, as I say, conceptual mental states, with fully conceptual, albeit essentially experiential-demonstrative, contents.

6.2 Epistemic Openness

To return to my main line of argument, then, with respect both to the singular and the predicative components of perceptual demonstrative contents, the genuine mind-independence of their reference resides in the subject's recognition of what they present as the categorical ground of the corresponding immersed monadic contents and appearances from his present point of view in the present circumstances, and, equally, of the various alternative monadic contents and appearances associated with possible but non-actual points of view and circumstances, some of which he may be able to grasp in imaginative simulation. Hence, a perceiving subject of such contents necessarily recognizes that the way things currently appear to him is the joint upshot of the way things are anyway, in the mind-independent world around him, and his current point of view upon them and other relevant circumstances of perception. He is necessarily alive to the possibility of alternative presentations of *that very thing's being just thus*, from different points of view or in different circumstances.[15] It is this, I claim, which provides him with a reason to endorse those very contents in belief. For, simply in virtue of entertaining perceptual demonstrative contents of this kind, he recognizes that it is that thing, there in relation to him, say, if determinacy of singular reference is secured by grasp of spatial location, and mind-independently thus, which is currently displayed—from where he is and in those circumstances—as apparently thus monadically there: it is that thing there$_r$'s being thus$_c$ which is currently displayed, from here and in these circumstances, as thus$_a$ there$_m$. That is to say, he understands that his current apprehension that things are thus and so is in part due to the very fact that they are. His grasping the content that that is thus is in part due to the fact that that *is* thus. He therefore recognizes the relevant content *as* his apprehension of the facts, his *epistemic openness* to the way things mind-independently are out there.[16]

So, his experiences contribute essentially to his grasp of certain perceptual demonstrative contents. These contents refer to particular mind-independent things in the world around him, of which they predicate determinate mind-independent properties. In doing so, they give him a reason to endorse those very contents in belief. Simply in virtue of grasping the content that that φ-thing is thus, he has a reason to believe that that thing is indeed

[15] See Strawson, 1974, for an influential preliminary development of this idea in connection with a contrast between Hume's and Kant's conceptions of perceptual experience. On Strawson's account, it is precisely in virtue of fulfilling this condition that the latter constitutes a conception of experience as the presentation to the subject of a mind-independent world of objects and properties whose existence and nature is independent of the subject's awareness of them in such experience.

[16] Notice, then, that the way in which perceptual experiences are belief-independent, that is, the way in which they have their demonstrative contents independently of whether or not the subject endorses those contents in belief, is absolutely not to be assimilated to the way in which his entertaining the non-demonstrative content that *p*, say, is belief-independent when he is raising to himself the question whether or not *p*. Rather, perception brings certain determinate, but essentially demonstrative, contents to mind in such a way that these present themselves to the subject as answers to certain questions about how things are in the world around him. For his grasping them, as the objective contents which they are, involves his recognition of them as his apprehension of the relevant empirical facts.

thus; for he necessarily recognizes that his entertaining that content is a response to that thing's actually being thus, given his
location and present circumstances.

Once acquired in this way, such beliefs in turn provide
reasons for further beliefs about the mind-independent world
around the perceiver. Equally, though, like all conceptual contents, the perceptual demonstratives in question are themselves
always open to rational reflection and rejection. The subject's
reason to endorse them in belief may be undermined by any
reasons he might have to disbelieve the contents in question. In
that case, he must weigh up all the evidence either way, and come
to a rational judgement on the matter. Nevertheless, perceptual
experiences enable a person to grasp certain perceptual demonstrative contents concerning the empirical world around him;
and in doing so they provide reasons for empirical beliefs with
those very contents, and so, indirectly, further reasons for further, appropriately related, empirical beliefs. This is how condition (R), above (Chs. 2 ff.), upon the very possibility of beliefs
about a mind-independent spatial world is met: we can now see
how perceptual experiences do indeed provide reasons for
empirical beliefs. The position can be put as follows: a correct
account of the sense in which perceptual experiences are experiences
of mind-independent spatial particulars and their properties—
that is to say, a correct account of the reference of the perceptual
demonstrative contents of experiences to mind-independent particulars and their properties—is itself an account of the way in
which such experiences provide reasons for the perceiver's
beliefs about the way things are in the world around him.

Notice that this has the required form of a *first-order* elucidation of (R), as characterized in 4.3 above, in contrast with the
rejected second-order approach common to both classical foundationalism and coherentism. For the truth of (R) emerges
directly from a correct account of a person's possession of certain basic perceptual demonstrative beliefs about the mind-
independent world around him, from a proper account of what
is involved in his grasping their determinate empirical contents,
rather than from any independent requirement upon his second-
order reflection upon his acquisition or possession of such
beliefs. Notice also that the parallel here with certain traditional
conceptions of a priori knowledge is quite striking, as intimated

earlier (Ch. 6, n. 1). Although the characterization of a priori knowledge is itself a highly controversial matter, one familiar idea is that certain basic contents are knowable a priori in the sense that, perhaps in certain favourable circumstances and only for appropriate subjects, understanding them is sufficient for knowledge of their truth. In this sense, the perceptual demonstrative contents with which I have been concerned in this chapter are knowable a priori, or at least they are a priori reasonable. For a person's grasp of their reference to spatial particulars and their mind-independent properties in his environment provides him with a reason to endorse them in belief: they are presented to him as his epistemic access to the objective facts. Having pointed up this analogy with the a priori, though, it is important to realize at the same time that such contents are about as far from being a priori as they possibly could be on another familiar conception of what this involves. For it is clearly false that their epistemic status is in any way independent of experience. Perceptual experiences are precisely what provide the subject's reasons for believing them. The initial oddity of this cross-categorization of perceptual demonstrative beliefs by two perfectly familiar criteria of a-priority is immediately resolved by recognizing that the perceptual experiences which provide reasons for them are essential for understanding them. This is how it is that a person's understanding of them can be sufficient for their positive epistemic status, even though this epistemic status is essentially experiential in source.

Returning to my discussion in Chapter 1, of the historical development of philosophical accounts of perceptual knowledge from Descartes to Kant, it is worth emphasizing the way in which the present account is broadly Kantian in spirit. As I characterized Kant's approach there, his starting point is the insistence, *pace* Hume, that a correct account of the nature of a person's perceptual experiences essentially draws upon the concepts involved in characterizing the objective spatial world around him. We cannot even begin to characterize perceptual experiences other than as the presentation of such a world to the subject. Furthermore, I claimed, his view is that acknowledging this fact is crucial to understanding the way in which such experiences provide the subject with genuine reasons for the empirical beliefs to which they give rise about the way things are out there. It follows from the point about how we have to characterize perceptual experiences that we cannot give a satisfactory account of them other than as *reasons*, albeit defeasibly so, for empirical beliefs. This is exactly the approach which I have adopted myself to these issues. For, on my account, what makes perceptual demonstrative contents the subject's epistemic openness to the way things are in the world around him, and evidently so—what makes it the case that such contents provide genuine reasons for his endorsement of them in belief, that is— is precisely their comprising demonstrative Ideas and concepts which make reference to particular mind-independent things and their objective properties. The epistemically crucial role for perceptual experiences, then, is absolutely not their furnishing themselves a peculiar realm of reference—impressions, sense-data, the experiential 'given', or whatever—with respect to which the subject is supposed to be in some epistemologically foundationally privileged position. It is rather their ineliminable role in making reference to the mind-independent world possible in thought at all.

6.3 Clarifications

Before going on further to clarify, defend, and develop my position in the following two chapters, it is worth concluding the present discussion, first, with a brief comparison between my own views and those of Evans (1982, ch. 6) and Peacocke (1983, ch. 3); and, second, with a comment upon the cross-modality of perceptual demonstrative reference on my view.

6.3.1 Evans and Peacocke

Evans's answer to the question how reference to mind-independent places and things is possible upon the basis of perceptual experience depends upon the subject's capacity to impose his objective cognitive map upon the egocentric system of relations given in experience, 'to locate his egocentric space in the framework of a cognitive map' (1982, p. 163). There is some controversy about how exactly this requirement is to be interpreted, and it seems to me that Evans himself is at least unclear, if not undecided.[17] For the most illuminating comparison with my own position, and contrast with Peacocke's, though, I offer Brewer's Evans, in the spirit of Kripke's Wittgenstein (Kripke, 1982, p. 5). On this account, what enables egocentric information, conceived purely monadically, to sustain an adequate Idea of a particular position in *public* space around the subject, or to contribute, in the way outlined above, to the subject's adequate Idea of a particular mind-independent object at that place, is his knowledge of what it would be for a certain identification to be true: the identification of the egocentrically presented position or object in question with one represented, at the *fundamental level of thought* about places and things (1982, sect. 4.4), on his wholly detached cognitive map of the relevant part of the world, which is *absolute* in the sense defined earlier of being an entirely context-independent representation of this sector of reality from no point of view within it. Of course, the precise content of this condition turns crucially upon what is thought to be involved in knowledge of what it would be for such an identification to be true. For my purposes, though, the two most important points are these. First, the condition concerns the subject's thought about the identity of the place or object in question. Second, objectivity of reference is supposed to be secured by appeal to the subject's possession of an absolute conception of (some sector of) the spatial world.

Peacocke's account in *Sense and Content* (1983, ch. 3) can be seen as rejecting both of these points. It aims to capture the conditions necessary for an organism to have contentful states making reference to particular mind-independent objects and places in terms of the systematic sensitivity displayed by its actions to changes in the purely sensational properties of its perceptual experiences in response to its own varying spatial relations with the objects and places in question. The basic idea is that a creature is capable of attitudes towards spatial particulars only if, keeping its relevant intentions, needs and desires fixed, its spatial actions in relation to these things, or dispositions to actions in relation to them, vary appropriately with its own movements in relation to the relevant objects as these in turn are registered

---

[17] See McDowell, 1990, and Peacocke, 1991, for a dispute both about the interpretation of Evans and the truth in this area.

by the corresponding changes in its experiences of the objects in question. A precise specification of this condition obviously involves a lot more work, and depends upon a certain amount of Peacocke's own controversial apparatus of the time. The important points for my present purposes, though, are these. First, the condition concerns the subject's dispositions to action in relation to the things in her environment, rather than her reflective thoughts about the identities of the various objects and places around her. Second, Peacocke's account nowhere makes reference to the subject's possession of any absolute map of the world, from no point of view within it. His condition can therefore be met without appeal to the subject's capacity in any way to transcend her position of immersion in and engagement with the world around her.

My own account shares with Evans the concern with the subject's thoughts about the identities of the various objects and places around her, as opposed simply to the complex sensitivity of her actions to her changing relations with them. It shares with Peacocke the rejection of any requirement for an absolute conception of the spatial world. In common with the latter's appeal to *perspectival sensitivity* (Peacocke, 1983, pp. 66 ff.), I focus on the structure within a person's *context-dependent* responses to her environment. The difference, as I say, is that I am concerned with this structure at the level of thought, whereas Peacocke is concerned with its structure in connection with intentional action. Since the Strawson Argument establishes that there cannot be a non-demonstrative, wholly context-independent representation of spatial particulars, Brewer's Evans's account is clearly out of place in demanding one for a person's thought about the world around her. Evans is right, though, in my view, in insisting that the question to which objects and properties a person makes reference in her thoughts and beliefs is to be answered by appeal to her own conception of their nature, and of what their identity consists in. (This is of course a further recurrence of the idea that the most basic, perceptual demonstrative, empirical Ideas and concepts are *unitary*.) Correlatively, then, Peacocke is wrong, I think, in assuming—in so far as this is a correct interpretation of his view—that the impossibility of an absolute conception of the spatial world requires an account of reference to mind-independent particulars given only in terms of the complexity in a person's responses to the world *in action*. For there is an intermediary position, which respects the Strawson Argument by invoking only context-dependent *demonstrative* reference (or reference which ultimately depends upon such), and which also respects the condition that what, if anything, a person succeeds in thinking about is determined by the conception which she herself has of the objects of her beliefs, and of what their identity actually consists in. According to this position, objective reference depends upon the subject's grasping the mind-independence of the objects and properties in question at the level of her perspective-dependent thoughts about their identity, which in turn control and co-ordinate her intentional action, in so far as this is appropriate, in connection with these objects in the world around her.

This is precisely my own proposal. The condition upon a person's reference to persisting mind-independent objects and properties in her perceptual demonstrative beliefs, meeting which at the same time provides the subject with reasons for such beliefs, has at least the following two components: first, the capacity to keep track of the particular item in question over continuous changes in its appearance with respect to precisely those features on the basis of which she grasps its identity, where this keeping track is a matter of recognizing its numerical identity over time, rather than simply retaining orientation towards something or other with one of its salient qualities; second, the capacity to make sense of informative identities with respect to such items in response to experientially discontinuous demonstrative identifications of them.

Let me elucidate each of these points in turn, in the first place in the context of my paradigm case of a person's reference to a particular mind-independent thing on the basis of her grasp of its relational egocentric location. The first condition involves simply her ability correctly to take for granted, in the stability and evolution of her beliefs, the numerical identity of that thing there$_r$ throughout its continually observed changing monadic presentations as there$_{m1}$, there$_{m2}$, there$_{m3}$, and so on, and also throughout its own observed changing location, as it moves itself, from there$_{r1}$ to there$_{r2}$, say.[18] Thus, she might change her

---

[18] This is surely the condition which Evans has in mind when he talks of the

mind about the value of a particular work of art on seeing a poor maker's mark stamped on it as she moves around or peers behind it, or as she feels that what appeared visually to be high-quality material is actually second-rate. Here she recognizes that the very same thing which she used to think was very valuable is in fact worth very little. She realizes that she made a mistake, by keeping track of the numerical identity of the relevant object over the change in her view of its value. Or she might retain her belief that a particular thing is a car of a certain type, as she watches it go by her window, even though at one point it appears from a very unfamiliar angle, from which she may not have recognized it. In this case, her continuing to believe that the thing in question is a Mini, say, even whilst it presents an unusual visual appearance, is due to her taking it to be the very same object as that which she previously saw clearly to be a Mini. Similarly, she might retain this same belief as her spatial tracking of the car changes from sight, on the basis of which she can tell that it is a Mini, to hearing, on the basis of which she would otherwise have been less sure, and back to sight again, as the car passes behind a visual obstacle. The second condition involves her ability to make sense of the identity of that thing (there) with a previously identified object, by appeal to some account of a second intersection between its continuous spatio-temporal route through the world and her own. 'Oh, I see', she might say. 'It used to be there, but John has moved it.' Or, on returning home for the family Christmas, 'Gosh, so that same box of chocolates has been there since last Christmas'; and so on.

Similar examples might be given of each of these two conditions being met for both non-spatial demonstrative identification of particulars and demonstrative predication. So, a person might revise her view about the ability of the particular oboist in a given wind quintet as she listens to them play, where the oboist is identified by the timbre of his sound, precisely as this oboe sound gradually breaks up and goes very harsh; or she might retain her conviction that the horn player is a pupil of Barry Tuckwell, even as his sound momentarily changes in such

importance to demonstrative identification of places and things of the subject's ability to *keep track* of the particular item in question over periods of time (1982, ch. 6, esp. pp. 164, 174–6).

a way that she might have been disinclined to come to that view on hearing just that momentary fragment of the performance; or she might discover, to her surprise, but none the less perfect comprehension, that that trumpeter, whom she previously heard in a poor student recording, is the very player playing so beautifully in front of her now. Similarly, a person might revise her view about the appropriateness of a certain shape of window in a given building as she moves to see the windows from a different position, from which the ugliness of their proportions becomes clear; she might remain wholly convinced of the equality in length of a certain line with another, even as various further marks are added and taken away from each of them which briefly produce certain illusions; or she might come to recognize that two familiar rooms are painted precisely the same shade as she adjusts to the lighting conditions in one of them for the first time.

What is being expressed in all of these cases is the subject's grasp, essential to her recognition of the objects and properties in question *as mind-independent* in the relevant sense, and therefore also essential to her successful reference *to mind-independent objects and properties* at all, of the possibility of any number of different presentations of the very same things, from different points of view and in different circumstances. In other words, she is demonstrating her comprehension, in her grasp of what it is that she is thinking about, of her evident openness to the way such things mind-independently are given her actual point of view upon them and other relevant circumstances of perception. So she understands her situation as one of being presented with these independent facts, from that point of view and in those circumstances. Thus, she has a reason to endorse the relevant perceptual demonstrative contents delivered by perception in her beliefs about the world around her.

6.3.2 *Cross-Modality*

So far, I have been stressing the importance, both for the mind-independence of the perceived world and for the reason-giving role of perceptual experiences with respect to empirical beliefs, of a person's operating with a conception of the natures of the things which she perceives as rendering these susceptible to any number of alternative perceptual presentations, from different points of view and in different circumstances. I want to end this chapter by making it explicit that this will normally also involve the possibility of exploiting more than one sensory modality in connection with the very same things. Again, singular reference upon the basis of grasp of egocentric spatial location provides the most helpful illustration. Both with respect to tracking a single object over time, and with respect to grasp of informative identities concerning spatial particulars, more than one modality may well be involved. To return to the examples which I gave earlier, a person's change of mind about the value of a piece of art which she is investigating may occur when tactual perception of its second-rate material overturns her view based upon previous or present visual perception. She tracks the very same place, relationally conceived as there$_r$, as this is presented monadically as there$_{m1}$, in vision, and there$_{m2}$ in touch, respectively. In the same way, her belief that a car is of a certain type may be sustained by her tracking its movement first by sight, then hearing, then sight again, as it passes behind a visual obstacle. Similarly, she might come to realize that the pie which she smelled earlier in the kitchen is the very one which she now sees in front of her on the table and is about to eat, when she is told that John carried it through from the kitchen into the dining room whilst she was getting the chocolates from the sitting room.

This all highlights the fact that egocentric locations are relationally identified on the basis of a single system of spatial representation common to each of the sensory modalities. That is, the identity or distinctness of visually and tactually presented locations, say, is evident without any need for reflection or calculation: they are in this sense *perceived* as the same place, or different places. Similarly with respect to spatial perception in the other modalities.[19] And this fact is exploited in a person's grasp of the identity of a given object of demonstrative reference across presentations in the various different sensory modalities, as he keeps track of it by keeping track of its spatial location. Indeed, I would say that the relation between spatial perception across the sensory modalities is more intimate than just this. For

---

[19] See Brewer, 1993, for a parallel point about the integration of spatial vision and action.

it is not simply that a number of distinct channels, as it were, conveniently all happen to share the same language, when speaking of spatial relations. Rather, the egocentric spatial significance of each particular sensory modality is ineliminably bound up with the integration of that modality with the others. Following Michael Ayers, consider, as a single example among many, the possibility of a total inversion of the visual field by prismatic spectacles.

Since everything seen is (until the brain adjusts) seen as inverted, the frame of reference for the apparent inversion must lie outside the deliverances of sight, in the sensory field as a whole. That is to say, the frame must be supplied by the other senses . . . in so far as they are integrated with vision. (Ayers, 1991, pp. 187–8)

He sums up the overall position as follows.

It is wrong to think of the senses as in general the source of disparate streams of information or content, each discrete from the deliverances of the other senses which it is left to some superior intellectual faculty to relate to one another in constructing knowledge of objects in space. The common objects of the different senses are presented as such, and as spatially and causally related to us. (1991, pp. 153–4)

In short, perception as a whole unites to present a single world around a single subject.[20] In the tracking and understanding of informative identities which structure a person's grasp of the identities of the objects of the demonstrative contents delivered by his perceptual-attentional relations with the things around him, all the sensory modalities contribute together and draw upon each other. In this sense, his perceptual demonstrative identifications of these things are cross-modal.

With respect to singular reference which exploits features of objects other than their spatial location, and also with respect to perceptual-demonstrative predication, the story is obviously a

[20] For further discussion of this idea of a single, cross-modally integrated egocentric spatial frame of reference for perception and action, see Evans, 1985b; Ayers, 1991, ch. 21; Peacocke, 1992, ch. 3; Brewer, 1993; Eilan, 1993 and forthcoming; Driver, 1994 and 1996; and Campbell, forthcoming (a). Its antecedents can be found in the phenomenological tradition. See especially Bell, 1990, ch. 4, on Husserl and Merleau-Ponty, 1962. For discussion of the nature and importance of bodily awareness in this connection, see O'Shaughnessy, 1980, pt. II, and Bermúdez, Marcel, and Eilan, 1995.

little more complicated. If the feature involved in a singular demonstrative Idea 'that φ-thing' is perceptible in only one modality, then tracking an object by that feature clearly cannot be cross-modal in the sense in which I am interested here. Nevertheless, there is room in such a case for the subject's recognition of informative identities concerning the object in question, as when, for example, she learns that that (oboe-timbre) player from the unseen wind quintet is that person (there), seen for the first time as the players come onto the stage, having played behind the scenes as background music in a play. There is obviously no possibility of either cross-modal tracking or informative cross-modal identity in connection with predication of a property which is accessible only to one modality. If the property in question is perceptible by more than one modality, though, certain possibilities of cross-modality do open up, although many of these may well turn out to be parasitic upon cross-modal identifications of particular objects with that property. For example, a child who very much wants a particular type of sweet in a lucky dip—a Toblerone rather than a packet of Smarties or a Mars bar, of each of which there are quite a few to be found, let us say—may just conceivably track its characteristic shape as the sweets are dropped from sight into a tub, and as she feels around for her prize. Similarly a person might tactually identify a given item as having just the same shape as something which she knows only by sight, whilst suspending all judgement upon their numerical identity. Thus, there is rich cross-modality in almost every aspect of a person's perceptual demonstrative perspective upon the world.

7

The Epistemological Outlook

7.1 Foundationalism and Coherentism

How exactly does my own position stand in relation to the standard opposition between foundationalist and coherentist theories of perceptual knowledge? In considering this question, I hope also to be able to spell out precisely the sense in which I have succeeded in capturing my own 'undeniable datum' (Ch. 2) that perception is a *basic* source of knowledge about the mind-independent spatial world. This will in turn return me to the claim which I made in discussing classical foundationalist and coherentist accounts above (4.2–4.4), that their choice of a second-order elucidation of the truth of (R) is unacceptable, and that the correct story here must be a first-order one. First though, to the standard opposition.

Foundationalism is the view that a person's knowledge is divided into a mutually exclusive and jointly exhaustive 'foundation' and 'superstructure' meeting the following conditions. The foundation is the set of things known, whose status as known is independent of reason-giving relations with any other knowledge; the superstructure is the set of everything else known, whose status as known is therefore dependent in some way upon reason-giving relations with other knowledge; and membership of the superstructure ultimately depends, either directly or indirectly— if a branching tree of such relations is involved—upon reason-giving relations with one or more members of the foundation. *Coherentism* denies any such bipartite structure, insisting that the status as knowledge of everything which a person knows depends upon reason-giving relations with other knowledge. Where does my own position belong relative to this taxonomy?

It clearly has some foundationalist affinities. For I claim that certain pieces of knowledge—that that φ-thing is thus, when these are the contents of perceptual experiences in appropriate circumstances—have their status as such simply in virtue of what is involved in the subject's grasping those very contents, as concerned with the way particular mind-independent things objectively are. Entertaining such contents, which is made possible in part by his standing in various perceptual-attentional relations with the particular things in question, provides him with a reason to endorse them in belief, a reason which, in those circumstances, is sufficient for their status as knowledge. In this sense, they constitute basic, *non-inferential* knowledge. On the other hand, there are clearly coherentist affinities, too. For the subject's grasp of these very contents is absolutely not innocent of substantive commitments and requirements on my view. In so far as the beliefs in question really are empirical beliefs about mind-independent particulars to the effect that they are determinately, objectively, thus and so, their perceptual demonstrative contents necessarily fit into a whole system of related such contents between which the subject moves as he keeps track of the objects and properties in question and reidentifies them in future experience. This 'cognitive dynamics' (Kaplan, 1989; Evans, 1982, see esp. p. 235; Cassam, 1992 and 1997, esp. ch. 5) constitutes his sensitivity to the perceptibility of these things from other points of view and in other circumstances, and so also his grasp of his evident openness in experience to the way such things mind-independently are, given his actual point of view upon them and other relevant circumstances of perception. Furthermore, their place in this complex system of cognitive dynamics equally contributes to the status as knowledge of these systematically related perceptual demonstrative beliefs. Thus, there is a sense in which his knowledge that that ϕ-thing is thus owes its status as such to his possession of related knowledge about the world around him.

A person's understanding of the perceptual demonstrative contents delivered by his perceptual experiences, then, as the objective contents which they are, depends upon their place in a system of related such contents constituting his capacity to keep track of the worldly objects and properties in question over changes in his point of view and other perceptual circumstances, and their own changes and movement through the world. Nevertheless, with respect to each of the perceptual demonstrative contents in this cognitive dynamic system, his understanding of it, that is, his actually being the subject of perceptual experience with that content, is sufficient to provide him with a reason to endorse it in belief, which, in the right circumstances, is sufficient in turn to constitute such a belief as a piece of knowledge.

This latter, foundationalist, element in my account comes out very clearly in the obvious contrast between normal perceptual knowledge and what I call *instrumental knowledge*, by analogy with the way in which knowledge of the reading on a certain instrument can inform a person about otherwise epistemically inaccessible features of his environment.[1] In such a case, in which a person learns—comes to *know*, that is—that the current running through an electric circuit is 5 amps by reading the dial of an ammeter, say, he might equally have arrived at the very same belief, in just that way, yet not have *known* that the current is 5 amps, because, and only because, he did not know that the instrument is indeed an accurate measure of current: his belief might have been an epistemically indefensible lucky guess. This is characteristic of *instrumental knowledge*, in which a person acquires knowledge that p on the basis of his prior knowledge that q and independent knowledge that the fact that q is a reliable indicator that p, in such a way that he might equally have come to believe that p, yet his belief that p might have failed to qualify as knowledge, even given his knowledge that q, because, and only because, he did not know that the fact that q is a reliable indicator that p. Perceptual knowledge, on my account, is absolutely *not* instrumental in this sense.[2] For its epistemic status is intrinsic to the subject's very understanding of the belief in question, and does not wait upon any further, independent knowledge that this belief is acquired in a reliable manner, knowledge of a kind which he might have lacked and yet still acquired the perceptual demonstrative belief whose status as knowledge is in question. This, I claim, is the sense in which perception is a *basic* source of knowledge. The knowledge which it supplies is non-inferential and entirely non-instrumental.

[1] See the related definition of *instrumental reasons* in 3.4 above.
[2] Classical foundationalism (4.2) is the archetypal instrumentalist account of perceptual knowledge. I also argued above (4.3) that a very natural reading of Sellars's coherentism characterizes perceptual knowledge instrumentally too.

All of this also accords very well of course with my insistence upon a first-order elucidation of the truth of (R). For in resisting altogether an instrumentalist account of perceptual knowledge, and yet at the same time respecting the requirement that a person's reasons be recognized as such by him if they are really to be his reasons for believing what he does, my account is indeed first order in the relevant sense. A person's recognition of the reasons which are provided by his perceptual experiences for his perceptual demonstrative beliefs, as the reasons which they are for him to believe such things, is, on my account, integral to his very understanding of the contents in question, so integral to his possession of empirical beliefs with such contents, and absolutely not derived from any independent reflection upon the general reliability of the method by which such beliefs are acquired. Thus, the truth of (R) emerges directly from the account which I am offering of what is involved in a person's possession of certain beliefs about the mind-independent world around him, of what is involved in his grasping their determinate empirical contents, rather than from any independent requirement upon his second-order reflection upon his possession of such beliefs.

There is a further foundationalist element in my view here. Not only is it important to realize that perceptual knowledge is non-instrumental in nature; but, having done so, it is also clear that instrumental knowledge depends upon this non-instrumental perceptual knowledge in the following sense. Instrumental knowledge essentially involves prior knowledge of the condition of some 'instrument' or other—direct perceptual knowledge of some fact q—from which the relevant fact which is instrumentally known—that p—can be inferred, on the basis of knowledge of the instrument's reliability—that is, knowledge that the fact that q is a reliable indicator that p. In this sense, non-inferential, perceptual knowledge provides foundations of a certain kind for instrumental knowledge, which is inferred from it on the basis of knowledge of the reliable correlations between various empirical facts.

Nevertheless, the counterbalancing coherentist elements of the view are equally striking. For consider the question exactly *what* can be known directly—that is, non-instrumentally and non-inferentially, in the way described above—in perception. In other words: what *range* of objects and properties (broadly construed) are the possible referents of perceptual demonstrative reference and predication? My view here is that this is very significantly variable, both between different subjects and within a given subject, as it were, over time, in a way which introduces a significant contribution from the coherentist side of the standard opposition. For the determination of semantic values for the singular and predicational components of perceptual demonstrative contents is, as I have been stressing all along, crucially sensitive both to the subject's capacity to track the relevant objects and properties across changes in his point of view, the sensory modality involved, and various further circumstances of perception, and also to his capacity to make sense of informative identities concerning such items. That the appropriate semantic values are mind-independent objects and properties at all depends upon sufficient structure in such capacities to provide him with a conception of his position in grasping the relevant perceptual demonstrative contents as an epistemic openness to the way such things are in themselves out there, which is in turn required if his experiences are to provide the reasons which they must for his empirical beliefs; but far more structure is required in these capacities for tracking and re-identification uniquely to determine *which* mind-independent objects and properties are actually in question. This involves some sensitivity to the kinds of changes which an object can and cannot survive and yet remain the very same thing, and a similar sensitivity to the boundaries between objects' possession of the relevant property and their loss of it. The cognitive dynamic system of related contents to which a given perceptual content necessarily belongs can therefore become quite rich. As it does so, the range of objects and properties capable of constituting the semantic values of perceptual demonstrative reference and predication for the subject in question clearly grows significantly; and with this increase in conceptual-recognitional sophistication, the range of facts which he can come to know to obtain directly on the basis of perception grows significantly too.[3]

---

[3] As I explain in more detail below (8.1), this increase in sophistication drives, and is in turn driven by, a person's acquisition of the shared language terms

Given the way in which my position combines both foundationalist and coherentist components, it is worth considering the
question how I respond to the traditional regress argument
offered in support of foundationalism over coherentism.[4]
Indeed, addressing this question is another way of bringing out
the two sides to the account which give it its affinities with both
of the standard opponents. There is, in a sense, an end to the
regress of justifications for various empirical beliefs held by a
particular person at a given time. This is in line with the foundationalist's recommended response to the argument. For the
subject's reasons for these beliefs will eventually advert to something which she has learnt directly on the basis of her perception
of the world around her, in the way in which I have described.
Such direct perceptual knowledge is non-inferential and non-
instrumental: its status as knowledge does not depend upon its
contents' standing in reason-giving relations with further knowledge which is in any sense epistemologically prior. There are
epistemologically essential conditions upon her grasp of these
contents, though. And these entail her possession of a system of
empirical knowledge of which any particular perceptual belief
of this kind is a part. Nevertheless, the other pieces of knowledge
constituting this system do not sustain the epistemological status
of the target perceptual belief by providing reasons for it, from
which it is in any way inferred. Nor is this status maintained by
appeal to anything remotely like the classical foundationalist's
experiential 'given', so comprehensively undermined by Sellars
(1963; and see 4.2 above).

In a sense, then, direct perceptual knowledge owes its status
as such to its membership of a system of interrelated empirical
contents, with respect to each of which the subject has a reason
to endorse it in belief when she finds herself entertaining it in the
course of her perceptual investigation of the world around her.
Thus, although there is certainly a foundationalist flavour to my
response to the regress objection, I must also face a familiar

which mark the complex categorizations and classifications which articulate the
public world around him.
    [4] See Dancy and Sosa, 1993, pp. 209–12, for a useful introduction to this
extremely influential line of argument. The literature engaging with the regress
argument is far too vast to be referenced properly here; but the bibliography on
p. 212 of Dancy and Sosa, 1993, provides reasonable initial direction.

difficulty for coherentism which is closely related to the problem which the original objection is intended to expose. For what reason does a person have, on my account, for bothering with the whole cognitive dynamic system of related empirical contents of which the target perceptual demonstrative content is a component? My answer is that her entertaining these, or at least her capacity to do so, in earnest under various actual changes in her point of view, circumstances of perception and so on, and perhaps also in imagination under various simulations of such changes, is a necessary condition upon her understanding the initial content in question, a necessary condition, that is, upon her being the subject of a perceptual experience with that content, and, indeed, a necessary condition upon her having any empirical beliefs susceptible to assessment for their epistemic status at all. This is another reappearance of the central thesis (R) of Part I, that perceptual experiences provide reasons for empirical beliefs. Either the subject has genuine empirical beliefs, *for which she has reasons provided by her perceptual experiences in the way in which I have described*; or she is not a subject of empirical belief at all, in which case questions about the reasons for her adoption of this or that world view simply do not arise. So, I claim, my response to the traditional regress argument faces neither the difficulties of classical foundationalist attempts to halt the regress with some mythical 'given' nor those of classical coherentist attempts to embrace the regress by appeal to certain beliefs' place in a free-floating, yet purportedly mutually supportive, coherent set.

Another way of seeing how my response to the regress argument works is this. Perceptual demonstrative contents are delivered by experience *unendorsed in belief*. That is, experience simply provides a person with the resources to *grasp* certain contents of the form 'That is thus'. (This is the belief-independence of perceptual experiences again.) *As unendorsed contents*, though, there is no question of the subject's *reasons* for them. They are not the kind of condition of a person for which it is appropriate to seek after her reasons at all. Certainly, which such contents are delivered by experience is determined not just by how the world is, but also, and crucially, by the direction and focus of her attention to the relevant portion of the world around her; and this, in turn, is highly sensitive to her current projects, both practical and theoretical, as it were, both in connection with achieving certain goals in action, and discovering for any other reason how things stand with respect to various worldly phenomena. So, given how the world is, the subject has reasons of this kind, instrumental to her larger aims, for it to be those contents which come to mind, rather than any others presenting different aspects of how things are out there. No further reasons of any other kind are required, though, for the perceptual demonstrative contents themselves. They are not yet in the arena of *epistemic* appraisal. For they are not yet something to which the subject is in any way committed. Nevertheless, once grasped in this way, these unendorsed contents do provide reasons of a genuinely epistemic kind for their own endorsement in belief. For, as I have explained, the requirements upon a person's understanding of them as objective contents, making reference to mind-independent particulars and the ways these things are in themselves out there, have the consequence that she recognizes these as her epistemic openness to mind-independent reality, given her actual point of view upon it and other relevant circumstances of perception.[5]

This interesting blend of foundationalist and coherentist elements in my view is therefore independently motivated, internally consistent, and further supported by the resources which it generates for avoiding certain familiar obstacles to pure accounts of either of these kinds.

7.2 *Imagination*

I have made a certain amount so far of the possibility of a person's engaging in the imaginative simulation of immersed, monadic egocentric presentations or other appearances, of certain mind-independent things from various different points of

---

[5] Of course, the move from unendorsed understanding of these perceptual demonstrative contents to endorsement of them in belief will normally be almost instantaneous, and only rarely involve anything like a considered decision on the subject's part. They are importantly distinct stages of the story, though. The first is something for which the subject need have no epistemically relevant reasons, which in turn provides her with reasons of a genuinely epistemic kind for the second.

view and in different circumstances of perception. Does this not pose a difficulty for my view, though? For simply imagining that things are thus and so in the world around him provides a person with no reason whatsoever to believe that they are. Yet it is not clear why everything I have said about the reason-giving role of perceptual experiences should not apply equally in this case. So, it seems, my account cannot be sufficient for a person really to have a genuine reason to believe anything.

This objection raises a large number of difficult and interesting issues about the similarities and differences between imagination and perception. My response will be rather piecemeal: to say just enough about those issues which strike me as most relevant in this context to establish that it presents no serious threat to my view.

To begin with, it is extremely important to recall the precise setting in which my talk of imaginative simulation arose (6.1). The question was what requirements there are upon a person's understanding of perceptual demonstrative contents as genuinely objective—that is, concerning particular spatial things to the effect that they are mind-independently thus and so. The upshot of the Strawson Argument always stands in the background here. Such contents are essentially experiential in the sense that the subject's actual perceptual-attentional relations with the particular things in question, and their relevant perceptible features, are essential to his grasp of them. Furthermore, I claimed, if they are to be genuinely objective, in the required sense, then he must also recognize the possibility of alternative perceptual-attentional relations with the very same things, just as they are; and it is some of these which he may be in a position imaginatively to simulate. So the whole exercise of imagination depends upon the subject's being in perceptual demonstrative contact with a particular thing's being just so in his environment. The imagination is therefore of nothing other than what is in fact the case. It is rather a matter of how what is the case might alternatively have been apprehended by the subject in experience. Of course, I do not mean to suggest that this imaginative simulation is infallible. It might well happen that a person imaginatively entertains a monadic/appearance content which in some ways diverges from what he actually arrives at whilst immersing himself in his perception from the alternative point of view in question. Nevertheless, this is anchored to the actual facts in explicitly being an imaginative immersion—albeit in certain respects an inaccurate one—into an alternative perspective *upon the very same facts* as those which are presented by the relational/categorical content of his actual experience: in particular, that that thing (there$_r$) is thus$_c$. So the current objector, in making his claim that 'simply imagining that things are thus and so in the world around him provides a person with no reason whatsoever to believe that they are' must be moving beyond this kind of case to a mode of imagination which is not similarly tied essentially to the facts.

There are, of course, such imaginative projects, in which we all engage; but I am convinced that they all differ from genuine perceptual demonstration in ways which undermine the present line of objection. For the clear absence of reasons for belief in such imaginative cases is, I contend, correctly to be explained by reference to these differences with the genuine perceptual case, and therefore does nothing to undermine my account of the way in which genuine perceptual experiences provide reasons for empirical beliefs. I consider the very important residual case of absolutely convincing perceptual error, which is as much like genuine perception as possible, in 7.3 below. I complete the current section, though, with a brief discussion of three important ways in which the imaginative projects which are at issue here differ from standard perception.

First, there are dimensions of informational richness and cross-modal integration which distinguish imagination of the relevant kind from perception. For perceptual demonstration involves the selection of one among the many objects from which the subject's perceptual systems are picking up information at that time, as the object of reference. That is, it involves actually attending to one among many possible alternative objects of such selective attention (Campbell, 1997; Martin, 1997). Similarly, it involves the selection of one among the many properties from which his perceptual systems are likewise picking up information, which are also alternative possible targets of attention. Imagination, on the other hand, is often lacking in precisely this informational richness. Imagining the lamp on my desk, for example, is not normally a matter of selecting this particular object for attention, as against a range of alternatives constituting the background of imaginative awareness. Furthermore, a visual image, say, will most likely be flatly contradicted by perceptual experience in other sensory modalities.[6] Closing my eyes and imagining a peaceful country view *may* draw my attention away from the traffic noise, but I am still aware of the latter in the background; and particular car noises bursting through and dragging my attention back to the racket give me strong reasons to reject any idea that I am lying in a beautiful quiet valley. As attention ranges around in perception, on the other hand, both within and across sensory modalities, there is normally nothing but mutual support.

Second, perceptual demonstrative contents refer to the particular worldly things which they do in virtue of the subject's perceptual-attentional relations with precisely those things; and this in turn determines the subject matter of his subsequent beliefs derived from such experiences. An image succeeds in being *of a particular thing*, if it does so, only because this particularity is derived from the subject's attendant beliefs and imaginative intentions, rather than from the world. More generally, the determinacy of perceptual demonstrative content is the direct product of the determinacy of the world and the subject's selective attention to certain of its constituent objects and their properties. The determinacy of imagination, on the other hand, is derived from the subject's prior beliefs, desires, intentions, and so on.

This second point is related to the first. Perceptual demonstration involves the selection of certain objects and properties from many others in the subject's environment from which his perceptual systems are picking up information. Empirical belief content is in this way derived from the world. Imagination, on the other hand, involves filling out an imagined world with various objects and properties chosen from those of which the subject has a prior grasp as relevant to the imaginative project in question. Perception is a matter of world-driven belief, whereas imagination consists of the construction of a belief-driven 'world'.

---

[6] See my discussion above (6.3.2) of the integrated, cross-modal nature of a normal perceptual perspective, for the materials for an account of how such direct contradiction is possible between different sensory modalities.

Third, and again relatedly, imagination is often *voluntary* simulation, or pretence perception. As such, it is experience explicitly within the scope of a counterfactual hypothesis, introspectibly quite distinct from the impact of the world upon the 'passive' perceiver.[7] Furthermore, if I am engaged in this kind of introspectibly distinguishable active simulation, then I shall not be inclined to endorse as actually the case, the way things appear in imagination. (At least, I shall not be inclined to do so in the normal way, although, as I have already suggested, there may well be epistemologically acceptable uses of such imaginative simulation, in coming to know, for example, how things appear from another person's point of view, or how something might look from a different position.) Thus, in the relevant cases, there will be no actual belief of mine whose status as knowledge is up for assessment.

Informationally rich, cross-modally integrated, 'passive' imagination, introspectibly indistinguishable from genuine perception, whose content is endorsed in judgement, is effectively perceptual error or illusion. I turn now to consider this residual case, which is perhaps the most pressing problem of this kind for my own position.

7.3 Error and Scepticism

Even if it is granted that perceptual experiences bring about a person's entertaining certain demonstrative contents, his very grasp of which involves some conception of these as a presentation from his particular point of view and in his circumstances of the way things mind-independently are around him, what reason does he thereby have to take this to be the way things *really* are? After all, perceptual error is always a possibility. So nothing involved in his apprehending the perceptual

---

[7] I mean 'passive' here only in the following sense in which perception itself is not a voluntary action. Given the way in which a person attentionally interrogates his environment in perception (see Ch. 6, above), which of course is within his voluntary control, and sensitive to his needs, goals, and current practical and theoretical reasoning, the particular perceptual demonstrative contents which he thereby grasps are quite outside his control: entertaining one of these, rather than another, is not a voluntary action. See Ayers, 1970, for a helpful discussion of the passivity of perception.

demonstrative contents in question can possibly be sufficient for
him to have a genuine reason to believe that things are indeed,
really, thus and so out there.

This is, of course, a version of the traditional argument from
error for scepticism. The point is that for every true perceptual
demonstrative content which a person entertains, there is a possible illusory condition which he might have been in, which is
subjectively indistinguishable from it. How, then, can his simply
being in the non-illusory perceptual condition, entertaining the
specific demonstrative content in question—that that thing is
thus—possibly constitute his having an epistemic right, a genuine reason of the kind which I am concerned with, to believe
that that thing really is thus, regardless of the complexity which
I claim is involved in his grasping the content in question?

The key to answering this objection lies, to my mind, in getting absolutely clear about what is involved in the possibility of
an illusory yet subjectively indistinguishable alternative to entertaining a true perceptual demonstrative content. In short, my
claim will be that when the various different readings which this
might be given are clearly distinguished, then either there is no
such possibility (or at least it is question-begging of the sceptic
simply to assume that there is), or it simply does not follow from
the fact that there is such a possibility that a person entertaining
a true perceptual demonstrative content in the way in which I
describe does not thereby have a genuinely epistemic reason to
endorse it in belief.

More precisely, the original objection can be put like this:

(1) Every true perceptual demonstrative content which a
person entertains has a subjectively indistinguishable yet
illusory possible correlate.

(2) A perceptual condition with a subjectively indistinguishable yet illusory possible correlate does not provide a
reason for belief.

∴ (3) No true perceptual demonstrative content provides a
reason for belief.

The argument is clearly valid. My strategy in reply is to distinguish readings of the notion of a perceptual condition's having
a *subjectively indistinguishable yet illusory possible correlate* in

such a way that it becomes clear that on every such reading, either premise (1) or premise (2) is false. In other words, although there are readings on which each of the premises is indeed true, there is no reading on which both are true. So the objection fails.

First, I consider a related line of response, which I think is correct as far as it goes, but does not get to the bottom of the objection.[8] The suggestion, to begin with, is that the correct notion of subjective indistinguishability is identity with respect to the correct taxonomy of psychological states. That is, two psychological states are subjectively indistinguishable if and only if they are of the very same type according to the theoretically properly motivated categorization of psychological states into such types. The claim, then, is that no true perceptual demonstrative content has a subjectively indistinguishable yet illusory possible correlate. For actual perceptual-attentional relations with the object and property constituting the semantic values of its singular and predicational components respectively is essential for the availability of that very content to be entertained at all; and its being that world-dependent content in turn enters essentially into its correct psychological taxonomy (Hinton, 1973; Snowdon, 1980–1, 1990; Evans, 1982, esp. ch. 6; McDowell, 1984 and 1986; Child, 1994, esp. ch. 5). So there *is* no illusory correlate of exactly this type. In the absence of the object in question, and its possession of the property in virtue of which the content is in fact true, that very content is simply unavailable; and so there can be no condition of the subject of the very same psychological type as his actually veridical perception that that thing is thus. The idea of a subjectively indistinguishable yet illusory correlate of a true perceptual demonstrative content is therefore incoherent on this account. Hence the first premise of the objection from error is false.

Now, it is clear that, on this interpretation of subjective indistinguishability, the objection fails: premise (1) is indeed false. Furthermore, I agree that this notion of subjective indistinguishability is appropriate in the present context. For two related reasons, though, I believe that the current line of reply is quite unsatisfactory as it stands. First, nothing has yet been done

---

[8] I associate this response very strongly with McDowell (esp. 1982).

to motivate the preferred—that is, according to this reply, necessarily uninstantiated—notion of a subjectively indistinguishable
yet illusory possible counterpart to a true perceptual demonstrative content, as appropriate to the assessment of the objection under consideration. Second, nothing has yet been done to
capture the extraordinary intuitive force of premise (1) in
precisely this context of a sceptical argument from error. The
relation between these two points is that subjective indistinguishability is itself at bottom an *epistemological* notion; and it
is simply unclear from the present reply so far why it should be
thought to be remotely relevant to answering the sceptical objection that demonstrative contents are world-dependent in the
way outlined, given the evident possibility of convincing perceptual error of the kind exploited by (1). Nothing has so far
been done to respect at least *a* sense in which premise (1) is intuitively highly compelling.

What do I mean by the claim that subjective indistinguishability, as it enters into the sceptical argument above, is an epistemological notion? Well, just that it has to do with a person's
not being in a position to *tell* his actual condition apart from a
counterfactual alternative in various senses. Subjective indistinguishability is failure to distinguish subjective states simply on
the basis of being in them; and being able to distinguish one
thing from another, or not, is an epistemological matter. In that
light, there are three ways which I can think of to capture the
first premise of the sceptical objection, that every true perceptual
demonstrative content which a person entertains has a subjectively indistinguishable yet illusory possible correlate. Each is
derived from (1) above by giving a different interpretation to the
subject's failure to tell apart true and illusory perceptual contents, when it is said that these are subjectively indistinguishable.

(1a)   A person entertaining a true perceptual demonstrative
       content—that is thus—is not thereby in a position
       knowledgeably to rule out the possibility that that is not
       thus.

(1b)   A person entertaining a true perceptual demonstrative
       content—that is thus—is not thereby in a position
       knowledgeably to rule out the possibility that his cur-
       rent experiential content is false.

(1c) A person entertaining a true perceptual demonstrative content—that is thus—is not thereby in a position indubitably to rule out the possibility that this content is false.[9]

Reading this first premise as either (1a) or (1b) is question-begging in the present context. For both simply *assume*, contrary to my central thesis, that a person entertaining a true perceptual demonstrative content—that is thus—is *not* thereby in a position to know that that is thus. That (1a) assumes this is obvious. For if the subject is in a position to know that this fact obtains— that that is thus—then he is clearly in a position knowledgeably to rule out the possibility that it does not. Similarly, though, if he is in a position to know that that is thus, then, given his surely unproblematic knowledge that the experiential content which he is currently entertaining is indeed *that that is thus*, he is in a position to infer that his current experiential content is true, and therefore knowledgeably to rule out the possibility that it is false. Hence (1b) also makes the question-begging assumption. Neither (1a) nor (1b) is an acceptable first premise of an *objection* to my position, then, since both simply assume that this position is untenable.

So we are left with reading (1c) of the first premise of the sceptical objection. I gladly admit that this is true. In what remains of this section, I argue that it does not follow from (1c) that perceptual experiences cannot provide genuine reasons for empirical beliefs in the way in which I suggest. In other words, with the possibility of subjectively indistinguishable yet illusory possible correlates of true perceptual demonstrative contents understood according to (1c), premise (2) of the original objection is false. The crux of my defence is that, on the proposed account of perceptual demonstratives, a person's simply grasping such contents essentially involves his recognizing their status as a presentation of the way things are in the mind-independent world around him: such contents evidently (to him) make the world epistemically accessible to him. Hence, when he is right

---

[9] A person is in a position indubitably to rule out the possibility that the content p is false if and only if, on considered reflection, the belief that p is not false is indubitable for her. The belief that q is indubitable for a person S at time t if and only if S cannot possibly doubt that q at t.

about the world, as he necessarily is if the content in question is of the perceptual demonstrative form which he takes it to be (given the world-dependent view of such contents) he automatically recognizes the content in question as providing the reason for his endorsing this content in belief which it thereby does indeed provide.

As I have already said (6.1), such reasons are open to rational reflection and rejection in the sense that further background beliefs may make it unreasonable for him to endorse the content in question, if he believes, with reason, that he may well be hallucinating, for example, or that it would be extremely unlikely to come across anything which is thus in his present environment. Furthermore, his possession of such a reason at all is defeasible in the following sense. It is not *indubitable* for him whether or not he has one. A subjectively indistinguishable correlate, in sense (1c), of a true perceptual demonstrative content *appears* in this sense to give him equal right to endorse the content in question in belief. In such a case, though, since the content in question is entirely illusory, he is both wrong about the world and about his apparent epistemic openness to how things are out there. Thus his apparent reason for belief is entirely undermined. In the veridical case, his reason depends upon his rightly recognizing his openness to the world. In the illusory case, he can have no such genuine recognition, hence any epistemic right to belief is merely apparent.

Notice here that I am insisting implicitly upon a distinction which goes against a strong grain in the epistemological tradition, and which I now want to make fully explicit. There is an absolutely crucial distinction, in my view, between having a fully adequate reason to believe that p and having a sceptic-proof guarantee for the truth of p. This has, I think, been obscured by a very strong tendency to identify the articulation of reasons for beliefs with the refutation of scepticism about the subject matter of such beliefs. It is generally assumed, or even stated, that a complete articulation of a person's reason to believe that p must constitute, or provide, a refutation of scepticism about the truth of p, and, by generalization, a refutation of scepticism about other related contents, on the sceptic's own terms. Indeed, the issue of providing such reasons is often approached precisely through the question of what can be said against scepticism of the relevant variety, as if the identification were axiomatic. In the area of perceptual knowledge, this identification comes out in the idea that a person has a perceptually based reason for his empirical belief that p if and only if his perceptual experience puts him in a position to derive the truth of p from premises which the sceptic must accept, by arguments which the sceptic must accept also. Since the sceptic will raise doubts about anything which can possibly be doubted, this amounts to the requirement that the subject must be in a position to derive the truth of p from premises which cannot possibly be doubted by arguments which cannot possibly be doubted either. Thus, in its strongest form, we have the requirement that the subject should be in a position to derive the truth of p from premises which are indubitable for him, by deductive argument alone.

It is absolutely obvious, though, that this requirement cannot be met. For a person's perceptual beliefs about the mind-independent world are not indubitable in the relevant sense. That is, completely convincing perceptual error is always a genuine possibility, relative to what a person cannot possibly doubt on any particular occasion, given the perceptual experiences which he then has. In other words, it is logically consistent with the truth of everything which is indubitable for him then that the empirical beliefs in question are false. Yet this entails that any deductive argument which he might be in a position to offer, from indubitable premises to the truth of these beliefs, is bound to be invalid. For its *counterexample set*, consisting of its premises and the negation of its conclusion, is logically consistent; and this is precisely what it is for a deductive argument to be invalid. The sceptic who operates on these terms is therefore bound to win. Given the identification between having reasons and being in a position to refute this kind of sceptic, then, it follows that nobody ever has adequate reasons for any of his empirical beliefs—from perception, at least, and it is far from clear where else these might be thought to come from.

Now, one reaction to this situation is simply to succumb to scepticism, at least of the relevant variety. That is, it may seem obligatory to admit that nobody ever has reasons of the demanding kind which I am interested in for his perceptual beliefs, but then possible to go on to insist that this is not a problem, since many such beliefs are *true*, and indeed reliably formed, and also that they enable us to get around perfectly well in the world in which we find ourselves, and achieve, at least in principle, all that is really of any importance to us by way of success and flourishing. If my argument so far is on the right lines, though, then this rather Humean reaction is absolutely not an option. For it simply assumes that empirical beliefs are perfectly possible in the absence of any provision of reasons for them by perceptual experiences. Yet this is precisely the combination which is ruled out by my argument for (R) in Part 1 above. In particular, it is inconsistent with the crucial claim, (H), established in the course of that argument, that the hypothesis that perceptual experiences do not provide reasons for empirical beliefs rules out the possibility of beliefs about a mind-independent spatial world (Chs. 2 ff.). So, regardless of one's intuitive sympathy, or not, for the sceptical claim that perception provides us with no genuine reasons for our empirical beliefs, this first reaction to the impossibility of a head-on refutation of scepticism on the sceptic's own terms is untenable. The price of this submission to scepticism is the intolerable consequence that nobody has any beliefs about a mind-independent spatial world, which I simply deny.[10]

A second, initially more plausible, reaction is to retain the identification between giving reasons and refuting sceptics, but relax some of the relevant sceptics' demands. This could be done both by admitting as premises things which are not indubitable for the subject, but to which he is supposed to be epistemically entitled by something other than the impossibility of doubt, and by allowing other forms of argument in the move from these premises to the truth of certain empirical beliefs. In the presence of the initial identification, though, this relaxation is entirely unmotivated. At least, it can be motivated only by a *prior* conviction that people do actually have perceptually based reasons for their empirical beliefs, which is undermined by the strong reading of the identification given above. For what else could the motivation possibly be for retaining the identification whilst admitting as refutations of the relevant sceptics arguments whose premises and rules of inference are explicitly recognized to be subject to irrefutable sceptical challenge?

[10] See my discussion of assumption (W) in Ch. 2.

The correct response, in my view, is therefore to reject the identification altogether, and to make the distinction which I have been insisting upon between epistemically adequate perceptually based reasons for empirical beliefs, on the one hand—something which normal people normally have—and a refutation of the external-world sceptic on his own terms, on the other—something which I admit that nobody ever is or could be in a position to give. Indeed, the difficulty with the identification to which I am objecting should not be thought to be simply that it leads to an uncomfortable choice between a hollow victory for the sceptic who denies that a person ever has adequate perceptually based reasons for any of his empirical beliefs, and who therefore has to accept that nobody really has any such beliefs, on the one hand, and a wholly unmotivated fix which is designed only to avoid this scenario, on the other. For, in its application to perceptual knowledge as outlined above, this identification leads to internal incoherence on two counts. Recall that the upshot of this application is the condition that a person has reasons for his empirical belief that *p* if and only if he is in a position to derive the truth of *p* from indubitable premises by deductive argument alone: the premises and intermediate conclusions of this argument then *constitute* his reasons. The first difficulty for this approach is that, as I argued above in discussing classical foundationalism (4.2), the whole idea of an indubitable epistemological 'given', of non-inferential knowledge of the way things perceptually appear to a person which is supposed to be constituted simply by his being appeared to in that way, is completely unacceptable. So the sceptic's insistence, which is endorsed by the proponent of the objectionable identification of giving reasons and refuting the sceptic, that a person's foundational reasons for his perceptual beliefs—the premises of his anti-sceptical argument—should be precisely of this form, is equally unacceptable. Even if, *per impossibile*, a valid deductive argument could be given from indubitable premises to certain empirical truths, this should not in the end convince the consistent proponent of the basic identification. This is the second difficulty. For, as Descartes himself is quite clear in the First Meditation (1986, p. 14), even given indubitably known premises, a deductive conclusion is itself not indubitably immune to sceptical challenge. For it is surely at least conceivable that a malicious demon might ensure that I go astray whenever I make *what I then take to be* a watertight logical inference. Once one agrees to engage with the sceptic head-on, in this way, the credentials of deductive inference are themselves open to question; and the whole project therefore collapses.

Perception and deduction are both dubitable, in that it is logically consistent with what is indubitable for a person who acquires knowledge by these means that the thing which he thereby knows is false. So such a person's possession of the reasons which he has on the basis of deduction or perception for this piece of knowledge can only be defeasible in the sense given above: it is not *indubitable* for him whether or not he has the reasons in question. Equivalently, no head-on refutation of the corresponding mode of scepticism can possibly be given on the sceptic's own terms. Nor is one required, though. For possession of epistemically adequate reasons is *not* to be identified with possession of such a sceptic-proof guarantee. Thus, in the case of perceptual knowledge, as I account for it, a person's reasons for his empirical beliefs survive this version of the sceptical argument from error: although premise (1c) is true, the corresponding reading of premise (2) is false. Hence the sceptical objection is no threat to my position on any of the readings of the notion of a subjectively indistinguishable yet illusory possible correlate of a true perceptual demonstrative content which I can make out.

7.4 *Further Objections*

7.4.1 *The Foundationalist's Dilemma*

In section 4.2 of Chapter 4 above, I argue that classical foundationalism faces a dilemma. 'Given' introspective knowledge either depends upon the perceiver's possession of concepts of determinate appearances or it does not. If it does, then she might be mistaken in judging her experience to fall under one such concept rather than another. Hence she needs some further reason to believe her current introspective judgement is true, over and above a blind inclination to make it, if this is to constitute knowledge on the proposed account. Yet this is inconsistent with the claim that the 'given' is epistemologically foundational: in need of no justification from anything else. If introspection is supposed to be independent of her possession of appearance concepts, on the other hand, then it is difficult to see how this can possibly constitute genuine knowledge of a particular experiential state that it is determinately thus and so rather than some other way. Yet it must constitute factual knowledge of this kind if it is to serve as a premise in the inferential justification of her knowledge of how things are in the world around her. How, it might be objected, does my own conception of the reason-giving role of perceptual experiences avoid a parallel dilemma? For I too maintain that these provide non-inferential reasons for genuine beliefs. The only difference seems to be that these concern a mind-independent spatial world rather than some internal world of sensory appearances.

It is true that both views claim that perceptual experiences put a person in a position to know certain things directly, without inference from knowledge of anything else; but their rationale for this is crucially different. According to classical foundationalism, a person's knowledge of how she is being *appeared to* in such experiences, at least, is in need of no justification whatsoever, because there are no possible errors for such a justification to rule out. There could only possibly be such a non-inferential reason, on this account, for something which is, as her beliefs about appearances are supposed to be, indubitable for the subject, because classical foundationalism is firmly committed to, indeed largely motivated by, the identification of giving reasons with refuting the sceptic which I rejected in the previous section. It is precisely the claim that non-inferential knowledge of appearances must be indubitable which creates the problem, though. For the insistence upon indubitability is what is inconsistent with the idea that there is substantial factual knowledge here at all.

On my account, on the other hand, it is not that perception involves the presence of very special kinds of objects, appearances, about the existence and nature of which the subject cannot possibly be in any doubt, and from her foundational knowledge of which she somehow infers the existence and nature of the everyday objects around her, about which she can be mistaken. Indeed, as I argued above, any such inference is bound to be deductively invalid. The position is rather that perception involves a person's entertaining certain essentially experiential perceptual demonstrative contents, her very grasp of which constitutes her recognition of them as a presentation to her of how things mind-independently are around her, given her point of view and other relevant circumstances of perception. In this way, perception presents a person in a very special way with the mind-independent world itself. She has no need to infer the way things are out there from the way things appear to her along with a general rule that this is a reliable way of acquiring beliefs on such matters. For in grasping any particular perceptual demonstrative content of the form 'That is thus', she recognizes this as her epistemic openness to that's being thus out there.

Thus, returning to the supposed dilemma, a person's grasp of these perceptual demonstrative contents does indeed involve an exercise on her part of certain empirical concepts, albeit essentially experiential demonstrative concepts. This, in turn, makes room for the possibility of doubt of various kinds: as I said above, perceptual belief is not indubitable. But this does nothing to undermine the provision of genuine reasons for empirical beliefs , for reason giving is, on my account, explicitly distinguished from attempting a refutation, on behalf of the subject in question, of the external-world sceptic who is bent upon raising doubts wherever these are possible. The source of the status of perceptual demonstratives *as reasons* for endorsing those very contents in belief comes rather from elsewhere, from the fact that the subject recognizes their presentation to her of the way things are in the world around her from her point of view and in her perceptual circumstances.

7.4.2 A Second-Order Account?

Perhaps this will provoke a further objection, though. For my account may now appear to exhibit a damaging structural similarity to the classical foundationalism which I rightly rejected above (4.2). Does it not effectively offer the following *inference* in response to the acknowledged need to explicate the role of a person's perceptual experiences in the provision of reasons for his empirical beliefs?

(1) I am entertaining the content that that is thus.

(2) This is my epistemic openness to the mind-independent facts.

∴ (3) That is thus.

Yet if my suggestion does amount to anything like this, then it is surely susceptible to analogous objections to those which I gave against the classical foundationalist account. First, there are all the difficulties raised by the apparently foundational epistemic status of the first premise. Second, the success of any such inference in delivering knowledge of its conclusion depends upon independent knowledge of the second premise; and this faces all the familiar problems of circularity. For knowledge that certain contents are a reliable guide to the way things actually are with certain external objects surely requires *prior* knowledge of the relevant mind-independent states of affairs.

I think that this objection rests upon an important misunderstanding of the position. My strategy is not to offer a minor alternative to the classical foundationalist's inference from knowledge of appearances to knowledge of the world. It is rather to insist that perceptual demonstrative contents evidently constitute a direct presentation to the subject of the mind-independent world itself, given the relevant perceptual circumstances. The non-inferential reason-giving status of such contents has absolutely nothing to do with their potential role in some anti-sceptical argument of the form offered above. Again, I resist any identification of these two projects. The fact is that a person grasping such perceptual demonstrative contents, as the objective contents which they are, automatically recognizes them *as* his epistemic openness to the objective spatial reality to which they refer. He therefore has a reason to endorse these very contents in belief. All of this, of course, depends upon the place of such contents in a rich and complex cognitive dynamic system constituting his capacity to keep track of the relevant mind-independent objects and properties, and to make sense of informative identities between them; but it does nothing at all, so far as I can see, to reintroduce the classical foundationalist's inferential structure into the reason-giving relations involved.

7.4.3 *The Foreground and Background of Perceptual Consciousness*

A final objection which I want to consider is this. Surely far more is, in some sense, 'experienced' by a person in perception than is the subject matter of any perceptual demonstrative content which is in the market to be endorsed by him in belief. Yet my account of the role of perceptual experiences in providing reasons for empirical beliefs focuses exclusively on such conceptual perceptual demonstrative contents. Put slightly differently, how can my account possibly make sense of the intuitive distinction between the foreground and the background of perceptual consciousness, between what is currently occupying the subject's attention, on the one hand, for the purposes of acquiring new knowledge about particular things in the world around him, or controlling and coordinating his actions in connection with such things, and the rest of the perceived environment, on the other hand, against which this particular focus of attention is set?

In responding to this point, albeit extremely briefly, I am drawing heavily upon the work of John Campbell (1997 and forthcoming (*a*)) and Naomi Eilan (1995). To begin with, I entirely agree that there is more information available in perception than is conceptualized in perceptual demonstrative contents. This is the information which is being processed automatically by the early operations of the subject's perceptual systems, but is not attentionally selected for further processing and use by the subject in his deliberation—both theoretical and practical—and in the control and co-ordination of his action. Furthermore, this information is not just available in this sub-personal sense of systematically affecting various areas in the subject's brain; but it is also available *for the subject*, although not demonstratively conceptualized, in the sense that it is a *possible* focus for his selective attention, without further ado, either actively directed in the service of some ongoing project, or passively drawn by acquiring some other kind of salience. Thus, the central notion in understanding perceptual experience is therefore the attentional selection of information which is thereby conceptualized in perceptual demonstrative contents. More information is available than just this, though, both in the subpersonal-level sense of being processed automatically by the early operations of the subject's perceptual systems, and also in the personal-level sense of being the possible focus of deliberate attention without the need for any further uptake of information.

Furthermore, it is precisely that information which *is* conceptualized in this way in perceptual demonstrative contents which is the relevant focus of my enquiry into the way in which perceptual experiences provide reasons for empirical beliefs. For it is only such conceptual contents which are capable of standing in the required reason-giving relations. Thus, the evident existence of an attentional background in perception is no threat to my treatment of this topic; and, indeed, I would say that this is only properly to be understood in terms of the perceptual demonstrative contents which I regard here as central.

8

Developments and Consequences

8.1 Non-Demonstrative Perceptual Knowledge

So far, my account of the way in which perceptual experiences provide reasons for empirical beliefs has focused exclusively upon purely demonstrative contents, of the form 'That (φ-thing) is thus'. Yet most of what a person believes about the world around her, indeed, most of her empirical knowledge, is not of this form, but rather involves at least some non-demonstrative material. I argued in Chapter 2 above that a person's beliefs about the mind-independent spatial things around her is ultimately based upon her capacity for perceptual demonstrative reference to such things; but she will almost certainly also think about them in other terms, and it would be completely wrong-headed to attempt to *reduce* the contents of all of her empirical beliefs and knowledge to perceptual demonstratives of the form which I have been considering up until now. Numerous empirical beliefs *ineliminably* employ more detached linguistic categories in their contents, by which the objects and properties in question are identified: 'Tony is furious', 'The triangle is red', 'That is the Tristan chord', 'Your brow is hot', and so on. Many of these are clearly cases of knowledge, which I call *categorial knowledge*. My question now is how exactly such categorial beliefs and knowledge are related to the perceptual demonstrative contents which I have argued are delivered directly by perception, for subjects with the required capacities to keep track of the objects and properties around them and to make sense of certain informative identities between them. How are these basic perceptual demonstrative judgements related to the more linguistically articulated and categorized judgements which a person more standardly makes on the basis of perception, and which constitute the normal expression of her perceptual knowledge about the world around her? Perhaps rather surprisingly,

I shall approach this issue through a discussion of the development of an agent's practical skills: the extension, with teaching and practice, of the things over which she has direct intentional control, the things which she can *just do*.

To say that φ-ing is something which a person can just do, in this sense, or is something over which she has *direct intentional control*, is to say that she is able, in appropriate circumstances, intentionally to φ in such a way that there is no other description 'ψ-ing' of her action such that she intentionally (φ-s by ψ-ing). Acquiring a skill, as I am conceiving of it here, is a matter of extending the range of such things. Consider, for example, a person learning to serve at tennis. To begin with, the range of things within her direct intentional control includes only things like a clumsy racket swing and a very variable ball throw. With practice, coaching, and studying experts, she extends this to include far more precisely swinging the racket, like that; and throwing the ball to the right height at the right distance in front of her. Then she learns intentionally to serve by launching the ball and initiating the swing when it reaches her eye level, say. Next, as the two components become habitually integrated, she most likely forgets this simple recipe and the whole serve is something which she becomes able just to do, at will, as we say. For she has learnt that that (doing it) is how to do it. It may then become further refined, as she learns first intentionally to serve an outswinger by moving her elbow in such and such a way at such and such a point in the serve, and then as this too becomes a single integrated skill, within her direct intentional control. She can now just launch an outswinging serve, in order to wrong-foot her opponent, perhaps, where there is no further description of her action, as her ψ-ing (where any candidate here is likely here to be a complex of sequentially ordered components), such that she serves an outswinger only because she intentionally (serves an outswinger by ψ-ing).

This is an incredibly crude sketch, and the story is obviously continually evolving as a person progresses from her most basic intentional skills, like waving or kissing, through writing a letter 'b', say, to playing a perfectly balanced mezzo forte C minor chord on the piano, and so on. Nevertheless, I think that two slightly different patterns can be discerned in the development of such skills, although most actual cases will no doubt involve elements of both. On the one hand, the agent may be explicitly advised to ψ in order to achieve her goal of φ-ing, or may discover by trial and error that ψ-ing is the most reliable way of φ-ing. In this case she will initially intentionally (φ by ψ-ing). At that stage, this is the only way in which she can φ intentionally. Then, as this skill becomes ingrained, with practice, she may well forget or ignore this recipe, turn her attention instead to the further ends which she can achieve by φ-ing, which she can then *just do*, and shape her larger-scale performance accordingly. On the other hand, she may simply practice, over and over again, without ever formulating any explicit means or aid to φ-ing, but simply witnessing her trajectory towards or away from successful φ-ing. She intentionally (φ-s by trying to φ). Eventually, as she gets the hang of it, so to speak, she attains direct intentional control over her φ-ing itself. In both cases, the important upshot of the learning process is her acquisition of the knowledge that that (said whilst doing so) is how to φ, or a way of φ-ing. This is what both patterns of development provide, by giving her inductive support for her knowledge that she has indeed acquired the integrated skill; and it is precisely this knowledge, that that (doing it) is how to φ, which is required for φ-ing to become something which she can just do. It puts her in a position to φ intentionally, just like that, without having intentionally to (φ by ψ-ing) for any other description 'ψ-ing' of the φ-ing in question.

The transition from perspectival and exclusively demonstrative to increasingly detached, non-demonstrative, linguistically articulated and categorized, perceptual knowledge—categorial knowledge, that is—is structurally very similar, I think. Here again, two models can be discerned, although, as with the acquisition of practical skills, most actual cases are likely to be composite. First, a person might learn by trying it out and seeking the feedback of others, or might explicitly be told, that such and such features are good indicators that the particular thing with them is *a*, or that anything with those features is, or is very likely to be, *F*. At that stage, he acquires the capacity reliably to judge that *a* is thus or that that thing is *F* (or even that *a* is *F*) on the basis of his perception, but the only reasons which he can give for this judgement, indeed, the only reasons which *he actually has*, are inferential. In the first case: that is $A_1, \ldots A_n$ and thus, being $A_1, \ldots A_n$ is a reliable indicator of being *a*; therefore, probably, *a* is thus. In the second case: that is $F_1, \ldots F_n$; being $F_1, \ldots F_n$ is a reliable indicator of being F; therefore, probably, that is F. (In the third case, perhaps, some conjunction of the two.) At this stage, all he has is instrumental knowledge employing 'a' and 'F'. Later, he may well forget each particular such recipe for identifying a, or recognizing that something is F. Yet he may go on reliably judging that a is thus, or that such and such a thing is F, when he perceives them, turning his attention instead to the significance of these judgements for his other interests; and he may do so in the knowledge that he can indeed simply tell such things. He knows that that is a and that being thus is being F, or a way of being F. For he now has inductive support for his knowledge that he has indeed acquired the relevant epistemic skill, although he may be completely incapable explicitly of reconstructing all of the features which he previously took as inferential evidence for such claims. Thus, he is in a position knowledgeably to judge that a is thus, or that that is F (or that a is F) *directly*, that is, non-inferentially and non-instrumentally, on the basis of his experience: he just sees that a is thus, or that that is F, say. Alternatively, and this is the second model of epistemic skill acquisition, he may simply acquire the knack of spotting a when he sees it, or recognizing something's being F, on the basis of trial and error, with some feedback as to the correctness or incorrectness of what are initially his guesses on the matter. As he gets more and more expert at this, and realizes that he is doing so, he again acquires inductive support for the belief that he has the relevant epistemic skills, that he can indeed tell a when he sees it, and tell when something is F. He therefore learns, that is, acquires the knowledge, that that is a, and that being thus is being F, or a way of being F. Thus, again, he is in a position knowledgeably to judge that a is thus, or that that is F (or that a is F) *directly*, that is, non-inferentially and non-instrumentally, on the basis of his experience, just like that.

In both cases, the important upshot of the learning process is his acquisition of the knowledge that that (said whilst perceptually attending to it) is a, and that being thus (again said whilst perceptually attending to something's F-ness) is being F, or is one way of being F. This is what both patterns of development provide, by giving him inductive support for what is thereby his knowledge that he has the relevant epistemic skill: he knows that he is good at spotting *a*—that is *a*—and that he can tell that something is *F*—being thus, thus, thus, . . . are (ways of) being *F*—when he sees it, or hears it, or whatever. And this is precisely what is required for the facts, that *a* is thus, and that that thing is *F*, to become things which he can just perceive to obtain, without having to infer them from, on the one hand, the fact that something which is $A_1, \ldots A_n$ is thus, along with the fact that being $A_1, \ldots A_n$ is a reliable indicator of being *a*; or, on the other hand, the fact that that is $F_1, \ldots F_n$, along with the fact that being $F_1, \ldots F_n$ is a reliable indicator of being *F*. Thus, conjoining the two skills, he simply, knowledgeably, perceives that *a* is *F*. His reasons for this judgement are that that is *a* and that being thus is (a way of) being *F*—he can simply tell such things. Furthermore, he is entertaining the perceptual demonstrative judgement that that is thus, which provides him with a reason to endorse that very content in belief. So, he has reason to believe that *a* is *F*. He knows this without inference from any 'evidence', in the sense of prior knowledge, which he also knows to be a reliable indicator of this fact.

It may be objected that there is some tension here between my use of the model of active skill acquisition for an account of the development of categorial perceptual knowledge, on the one hand, and my objection, in the course of arguing for the thesis that reasons require conceptual contents, to the idea that the 'reasons' which a theorist may discern for a skilled cyclist's leaning at a certain angle whilst taking a given bend are genuinely reasons *for the subject* (Ch. 5, esp. 5.2), on the other. This would be a mistake in my view. For the cyclist's leaning at just that angle is not, in the case envisaged, supposed to be something which she does intentionally. It is something which she needs to do in order to do what she does do intentionally, namely to remain in control of the bike around the bend, or simply to take that bend on her bike. The acquisition of practical skills, which I take as my model here for epistemic skill acquisition, is explicitly the extension of what a person can *intentionally* just do, in the sense outlined above. The difference is precisely that, although in the former case, of the cyclist, the subject herself has no reason to lean just as she does, a person who just φ's, *intentionally*, does have such a reason. For intentional action just is action for a reason, where the reason in question is necessarily the subject's own reason: the reason for which she acts as she does. Similarly, a person's non-inferential knowledge that *a* is *F*, as characterized above, is not just a matter of his being drilled by training and practice to say something when and only when it is true, or to form a belief that *a* is *F* just when *a* is indeed *F* in his vicinity. For he has learnt that that is *a* and that being thus is (a way of) being *F*, by learning that he can just recognize such things. Thus it is not that there are simply the theorist's reasons for his (the subject's) believing that *a* is *F*, namely that *a* is indeed *F*, right there in front of him, but the subject himself has reasons for this belief: that is thus, that is *a*, and being thus is (a way of) being *F*. So, there is absolutely no tension between the present model of categorial perceptual knowledge and my earlier comments about actions under non-intentional descriptions.

To take stock of the present position, I shall consider a particular example in which my two models of epistemic skill acquisition combine to expand what a person can directly come to know on the basis of perception. I shall end this section by drawing together the various elements from the account of perceptual knowledge which I have been developing.

Consider someone becoming familiar with the great works of classical music over a period of many years, and eventually acquiring the capacity reliably, and *knowledgeably*, to recognize that a piece is by Bach, Mozart, Beethoven, Brahms, Strauss, Sibelius, or Stravinsky, say, whether or not she has ever heard that particular piece before. Initially, another's ability to do this appears quite mysterious to her. All orchestral music sounds the same to her, in the sense that any differences which she perceives between particular pieces seem quite on a par, regardless of whether they obtain between pieces by the same or different composers. Later, perhaps, she learns to rule out certain individuals as candidate composers for pieces with various coarse-grained global features: for example, 'It's not by Brahms, as it's too angular'; 'It's not by Bach, as the orchestra is too large'; 'It's not by Mozart, as it's too dissonant'; and so on. Then she may learn fairly reliably to recognize Russian music, for example, and reason from there that particular pieces are by Rachmaninov or Stravinsky on the basis of further characteristic features: a long slow clarinet tune, or playful staccato wind writing. Next, she may begin to feel sufficiently confident occasionally to plump for a given composer straight off: 'I have a hunch it may be Strauss, I'm not sure, and I don't know why'; 'It could well be Sibelius: that harmony sounds a bit like the Seventh Symphony and the orchestration seems right'; and so on. Through getting confirmation or disconfirmation for such guesses she may increase in confidence and accuracy until finally she can reliably judge composers spontaneously, *fully aware that she is very likely to be right,* yet without necessarily relying in making any particular such judgement upon any 'evidence' in the relevant sense of prior knowledge which she knows to be a reliable indicator of the composer in question. She can just hear that it must be Beethoven—'It simply couldn't be anyone else'. She has learnt that music like that is by Beethoven; she knows that because she has inductive support for the claim that she can simply hear such things.

Thus, some evolving combination of a patchwork of forgotten, rough-and-ready recipes, on the one hand, and increasingly confident corrected guesswork, on the other, eventually establish her knowledge that being thus is being by X. Hence her true belief that a given piece is by Mozart, say, is an expression of her knowledge on the matter. Furthermore, this knowledge is direct, and non-inferential in the relevant sense. For it is certainly not the result of any explicit inference on her part: there need be no further judgement 'That music is M', such that her knowledge that the piece is by Mozart is inferred from this along with some linking principle to the effect that music which is M is likely to be by Mozart. She may well be quite at a loss to come up with any such evidential feature 'M'. She simply judges that it is by Mozart, and knows that she can tell Mozart when she hears it: music like that just is by Mozart. Even if, when challenged, she is able to mention certain features of the piece which support her judgement, these may be quite irrelevant to her having the reason which she had for making it in the first place, which was that it just sounded like Mozart.

So, what is the picture of perceptual knowledge which emerges from all of this? Put another way, what kinds of reasons does a person have for the empirical beliefs which he forms on the basis of his perceptual experiences? I think that there are the following three theoretically interestingly different categories of such reasons, or types of empirical knowledge.

First, there is the direct, purely perspectival, perceptual demonstrative knowledge with which I began. This is expressed by judgements of the form 'That is thus', predicating massively fine-grained, essentially demonstratively identified features of determinate material particulars in the perceiver's environment. The identification of such particulars, as the mind-independent things which they are, and of the mind-independent properties predicated of them, and also the subject's having the reason which he has for endorsing the content in belief, depend crucially upon the fact that the relevant, essentially experiential, demonstrative Ideas and concepts form part of a system of demonstrative thinking about the objects and properties in question, which constitutes his capacity to keep track of such things and make sense of informative identities holding between them. This manifests his grasp of such perceptual demonstrative contents—that that is thus—as the joint upshot of how things objectively are and his being suitably placed, in suitable conditions, to appreciate the fact, and therefore as his epistemic openness to the way things mind-independently are, given his point of view and other relevant circumstances of perception. The reason for his belief, in such cases, is provided simply by his entertaining, with understanding, the appropriate objective perceptual demonstrative content.

Second, there is direct, non-inferential, but linguistically articulated categorial perceptual knowledge. This is the result of building upon the first type of empirical knowledge with a recognized skill for the appropriate non-demonstrative categorization of objects and properties in the way which I outlined above. Here, the subject's reasons for his judgement, that *a* is *F*, say, are provided by his being in a position to entertain the perceptual demonstrative content 'That is thus' in the context of his knowledge that that is *a* and that being thus is (a way of) being *F*. I outlined two models for his acquisition of this bridging knowledge, between pure demonstratives and more detached linguistic categories, each of which involves his gaining inductive support for his resultant knowledge that he has the relevant epistemic skill of simply being able to recognize their presence in his environment, which in turn provides reasons for this knowledgeable identification of the object and property in question. Although there is therefore a dependence of such empirical knowledge upon that of the first, purely demonstrative, variety, this dependence should not be thought of inferentially. For the subject's belief that *a* is *F* is not the product of any explicit inference on his part: it is not the product of his perceptual knowledge of some distinct, more basic, 'evidential' fact (or facts) that *p*, whose obtaining he has independent knowledge is a reliable indicator that *a* is *F*.

Third, and finally, there is instrumental, or inferential, perceptual knowledge, in which the perceiver's reasons for belief essentially have this composite form. He knows that *q* in this way, say, if he has direct perceptual knowledge that *p*, of one of the first two forms, along with independent and independently acquired knowledge that the fact that *p* is a good indicator that *q*. I call this knowledge *instrumental*, since its paradigm instances are those in which a person uses the condition of some kind of instrument which he can perceive directly to inform him about otherwise epistemically inaccessible matters. As I have said before, a representative case would be that in which a person derives knowledge of the current running through an electrical circuit from a direct perception of the reading on an ammeter, along with his knowledge that that instrument is a reliable indicator of electrical current.

A key difference between cases of this third kind, on the one hand, and the first and second types of perceptual knowledge, on the other, is that all of the direct, non-inferential cases involve *unitary* Ideas and concepts, in the sense in which I defined these above (3.4), as Ideas, or concepts, with respect to which the subjective conception involved in a person's possession and application of these Ideas and concepts uniquely determines their semantic value. Indeed, the development of epistemic skills which I have been outlining in this section, by which a person moves beyond purely demonstrative perceptual knowledge to more detached and linguistically articulated categorial contents, is precisely a matter of his acquiring competence with an ever wider range of such unitary Ideas and concepts. I established this result for the first category of purely perceptual demonstrative perceptual knowledge in Chapter 6 above (6.1). The argument is similar in connection with the second type of perceptual knowledge distinguished above. For here, again, a person's possession of such knowledge, that *a* is *F*, say, depends, as I have explained, upon his knowledge of contents of the form 'That is *a*' and 'Being thus is (a way of) being *F*'. Now, grasp of such contents both depends upon his essentially experiential attention to *a* and to its *F*-ness, respectively, and also contributes to his subjective conception of which thing *a* is and of what being *F* involves, respectively. Then, since the former condition involves his standing in appropriate relations with precisely the semantic values of the Ideas and concepts in question, to whose associated subjective conceptions these contents in turn contribute, it follows that these subjective conceptions uniquely determine the relevant semantic values: they could not be just those subjective conceptions and yet different semantic values be involved. For possession of the subjective conceptions involves the capacity demonstratively to identify just these semantic values, which in turn requires actually standing in certain perceptual-attentional relations *with them*.

8.2 *Russell's Principle of Acquaintance*

In this section I want to bring out the way in which I think that my own account, as presented so far, lends support to a version of Russell's Principle of Acquaintance (1917, p. 159). The core claim that I am interested in is the claim that there are substantive epistemic constraints upon genuine singular reference.[1] More precisely, the idea is that a person's capacity determinately to refer to a particular object, *a*, say, depends upon her being in position to express direct, non-inferential knowledge about that object. The knowledge in question here is knowledge that *a* is *F*, say, with respect to which there need be no further content, *p*, say, such that her knowledge that *a* is *F* is inferred from her knowledge that *p* and her knowledge that the fact that *p* is a good indicator that *a* is *F*. A person is *in a position to express* such knowledge, either if she currently has a non-inferential reason, on the basis of her own perceptual experience or perhaps the testimony of others around her, for a belief about *a*, or if she has previously been in just such a position and has retained

---

[1] In fact I think that Russell was right to extend the claim to predication also; but I shall focus here only upon singular reference.

knowledge about *a* of this kind in memory. As I shall explain, I think that Russell's Principle of Acquaintance is a version of precisely this thesis. In his hands, though, it leads to a vicious restriction upon the objects of genuine singular reference, to sense-data alone, and perhaps the self (although I shall ignore this latter possibility in what follows). For he conjoins it with a strong empiricist assumption that the only objects of non-inferential knowledge of the relevant kind are such mind-dependent things as sense-data. A standard reaction to Russell's argument is as follows: first, to retain his conception of the limits of what a person is ever in a position non-inferentially to know about, that is, her own mental condition; second, to reject Russell's referentially restrictive conclusion that we can only ever refer to mind-dependent sense-data; and, third, therefore, to deduce that the thesis which I am interested in, asserting substantive epistemic constraints upon reference, is false. I shall argue that this reaction is a mistake. Indeed, it involves the very same mistake, I believe, as that involved in supposing that the content-determining relations between perceptual experiences and empirical beliefs might be non-reason-giving. I shall therefore recommend the obvious alternative reaction: we should, first, endorse the thesis that a person's capacity determinately to refer to a particular object depends upon her being in position to express direct, non-inferential knowledge about that object; second, reject Russell's restriction merely to sense-data, of the objects to which genuine reference is possible; and, third, therefore, conclude that direct, non-inferential knowledge is possible with respect to the middle-sized mind-independent physical objects around us. This is precisely the possibility which I have been elucidating in Part II of this book, and placing it in this context of the debate with Russell helps to locate it more firmly on the map of philosophical options in this area.

Structurally, then, the position is this:

Russell's Argument

(A) Reference is possible only to objects about which a person is in a position to express non-inferential knowledge.

(E) The only objects about which a person is ever in a position to express non-inferential knowledge are sense-data.

∴   (I) The only objects to which reference is possible are sense-data.

The Standard Reaction

   (E) The only objects about which a person is ever in a position to express non-inferential knowledge are sense-data.

   (I') Reference is possible to mind-independent physical objects.

∴   (A') Reference is possible to objects other than those about which a person is in a position to express non-inferential knowledge.

My Alternative Reaction

   (I') Reference is possible to mind-independent physical objects.

   (A) Reference is possible only to objects about which a person is in a position to express non-inferential knowledge.

∴   (E') A person is sometimes in a position to express non-inferential knowledge about mind-independent physical objects.

Notice here that (A'), (E'), and (I') are the negations of (A), (E), and (I) respectively.

I shall consider each of these three lines of argument in turn.

8.2.1 *Russell's Argument*

Russell's Principle of Acquaintance states that 'every proposition which we can understand must be composed wholly of constituents with which we are acquainted' (1917, p. 159). This is, I think, a version of the thesis I am interested in, (A) above. For, first, Russell's conception of singular reference is one on which the objects of such reference figure as constituents of the propositions in which the reference is made; and, second, his notion of acquaintance is precisely as that relation between a thinker and a thing which puts the former in a position to express non-inferential knowledge about the latter. Thus, Russell's principle entails (A), which in turn gives rise to his famous account (1905) of the way in which a person can nevertheless think, *by description only*, of things about which he is not in a position to express non-inferential knowledge. The basic thought here, with which I am also in complete sympathy, is that a person can have beliefs which are made true or false by the condition of objects with which he is not acquainted—that is, on my account, about which he is not in a position to express non-inferential knowledge— only by thinking of these things descriptively in relation to things with which he is so acquainted.

In Russell's own hands, of course, this outlook, and the Principle of Acquaintance in particular, have radical consequences. For he makes the standard empiricist assumption that the only particulars to which we stand in this direct epistemic relation of acquaintance are our sense-data—along perhaps with ourselves, which, as I have said, I shall ignore—since sense-data are those things whose essence is constituted by the way in which they appear to us, and immediate, non-inferential knowledge is supposed, on his account, to require the infallibility, or something like it, to which only a conception of sense-data along these lines (supposedly)[2] gives rise. The upshot is a view on which the only objects of genuine singular reference are sense-data so-conceived. These are the real referents of our demonstratives, 'this', and 'that'; and only these demonstratives are genuine referring expressions, what Russell calls 'logically proper names' (e.g. 1905).

There is a lot going on here; and I want to abstract from most of the detail. Three key elements contribute to the basic argument. First, logically proper names are conceived as those expressions whose contribution to the thoughts expressed by sentences in which they occur is correctly captured by their association with a particular object as their reference, in such a way that, were that object not to exist, there could be no proposition expressed by any atomic sentence containing the expression in question.[3] Second, it is claimed that this reference relation is

---

[2] See my critique of this idea in its role at the heart of classical foundationalism at 4.2 above.

[3] I endorse this conception of Russellian singular terms (see Evans, 1982, pp. 12 and 42 ff.) as the paradigms of genuinely referring expressions. I also embrace the growing anti-Russellian consensus that Frege's (1993) distinction between

essentially epistemically constrained: a given object serves as the reference of any such candidate expression only if, in using the expression with understanding, a person is in a position to express non-inferential knowledge about that object. Third, a strong empiricist restriction is placed upon the range of objects about which a person is ever in such a position to express non-inferential knowledge: these include only his sense-data, whose nature is defined by the way in which they appear to him. Russell's thesis that 'this' and 'that', whose reference is restricted to the subject's sense-data, are the only logically proper names is the conclusion.[4]

8.2.2 *The Standard Reaction*

A standard reaction to this argument is effectively to endorse the first and third of these elements, and then to argue against the second by rejecting Russell's conclusion. Logically proper names, or 'singular terms', are indeed those expressions whose semantic values (see Dummett, 1978; and Evans, 1982, pp. 8 ff.) are particular objects in the world. Furthermore, the only objects of direct, non-inferential knowledge are sense-data: mind-dependent items constituted by the way in which they appear to the subject. For direct, non-inferential knowledge requires the

---

their sense and reference can, and indeed must, be made for such expressions (see e.g. McDowell, 1977 and 1984; Evans, 1982, ch. 1, and 1985c).

[4] Evans (1982, pp. 44 ff.) and McDowell (1986) rightly bring out the following Cartesian motivation for this restriction. No proposition can be expressed by an atomic sentence containing a logically proper name with no reference. Hence the possibility opens up of a person sincerely taking himself to be expressing a thought in uttering such a sentence, when in fact no such thought is available. Russell finds this failure of first-person authority intolerable. So he denies the possibility altogether by restricting the range of reference of logically proper names to entities about whose existence the thinker *cannot* be mistaken. This line of thought is closely related to that which I outlined in the text above. Russell's obsession with infallibility is the villain of both. My version of his argument turns on the idea that it is a necessary condition on the direct, non-inferential knowledge required for singular reference that the subject is infallible about the existence and nature of the object in question. Evans's and McDowell's Cartesian argument rests on rejecting any possibility of a person's being mistaken about whether there is really a thought of precisely the kind which he takes himself to be thinking. See 3.5 for further ways in which this Russellian misinterpretation of genuine epistemic requirements upon direct reference as requirements of *infallibility* causes error and confusion.

infallibility, or something like it, to which only a conception of sense-data along these lines (supposedly) gives rise. Yet it is evident that we can and frequently do refer to mind-independent things in the objective world around us. Hence the idea of any substantive epistemic constraint upon genuine singular reference must be a mistake.

According to this standard reaction, what Russell wrongly supposes are restrictive epistemic conditions upon genuine singular reference are really just harmless causal constraints. Very crudely, a singular expression refers to whatever happens causally to explain the occurrence of its mental-experiential correlate in the appropriate reference-fixing way. As I intimated above, though, this is precisely the picture which I presented (in 3.1 above) as a putative counterexample to my thesis that the content-determining relations between perceptual experiences and empirical beliefs must be reason-giving relations, only to be rejected by the Switching Argument. Thus, this attempt to combine the empiricist restriction upon the objects of non-inferential knowledge, (E) above, with the common-sense rejection of Russell's idealist (I) is unsuccessful. So the standard reaction's argument against my reading of the Principle of Acquaintance, (A), is also unsuccessful.

8.2.3 *My Alternative Reaction*

The Principle of Acquaintance, as encapsulated in thesis (A) above, that genuine singular reference is possible only to objects about which the subject is in a position to express non-inferential knowledge, is, in my view extremely important and true. As I understand its central notion of a person's being in a position to express non-inferential knowledge, its application to the most basic cases of singular reference to mind-independent spatial particulars is a direct consequence of my arguments in Part 1 for the thesis (R), that perceptual experiences provide reasons for empirical beliefs. For I argued in Chapter 2 that the most basic such reference is achieved by essentially experiential perceptual demonstrative contents; and then I argued in Chapter 3 that the relations between the perceptual experiences making such contents available and the beliefs whose empirical contents they thereby determine are necessarily reason-giving relations. Thus, it follows that reference to mind-independent things in beliefs of these most basic kinds essentially involves having experiential reasons for such beliefs. That is to say, in making reference to spatial particulars in this way, a person is automatically in a position to express non-inferential knowledge about the particular things in question. For instantiating this relation of being in a position to express non-inferential knowledge about a particular object, *a*, is a matter either of having a non-inferential reason of the kind which I have argued is provided by perceptual experiences for a belief about *a* (Ch. 6, esp. 6.2), or of having retained in memory knowledge about *a* based upon such a reason. So I claim that (A) certainly applies at least in connection with these most basic cases of singular reference.

Furthermore, I think that considerations from a rather different area lend strong support to the claim that (A) applies far more widely. Recall, first, Evans's comments about a person's use of the proper name 'Louis' in the course of his discussion of the causal theory of names (1985*a*):

A group of people are having a conversation in a pub, about a certain Louis of whom *S* has never heard before. *S* becomes interested and asks: 'What did Louis do then?' There seems to be no question but that *S* denotes a particular man and asks about him. Or on some subsequent occasion *S* may use the name to offer a new thought to one of the participants: 'Louis was quite right to do that.' Again he clearly denotes whoever was the subject of the conversation in the pub. This is difficult to reconcile with the Description Theory [on which there is supposed to be associated with each name as used by a group of speakers who believe and intend that they are using the name with the same denotation a description or set of descriptions cullable from their beliefs which an item has to satisfy to be the bearer of that name] since the scraps of information which he picked up during the conversation might involve some distortion and fit someone else much better. Of course he has the description 'the man they were talking about' but the theory has no explanation for the impossibility of its being outweighed.

The Causal Theory [on which it is sufficient for someone to denote *x* on a particular occasion with a name, that this use of the name on that occasion be a causal consequence of his exposure to other speakers using the expression to denote *x*] can secure the right answer in such a case but I think deeper reflection will reveal that it too involves a refusal to recognize the [Wittgensteinian] insight about contextual definition [that for an item to be the object of some psychological state of yours may be simply for you to be placed in a context which relates you to that thing]. . . . For the theory has the following consequence: that at any future time, no matter how remote or forgotten the conversation, no matter how alien the subject matter and confused the speaker, *S* will denote one particular Frenchman—Perhaps Louis XIII—so long as there is a causal connection between his use at that time and the long distant conversation. (1985a, pp. 6-7)

Evans has two important points here: first, that possession of a uniquely identifying definite description is unnecessary for successful singular reference; second, that the mere existence of a causal chain of reference-preserving links back to the object in question, as these are conceived, for example, by Kripke (1980) and other proponents of the so-called causal theory of reference', is insufficient. Our intuitions about the Louis case surely confirm both of these points. My hypothesis is that these intuitions are organized and controlled precisely by the existence of epistemic constraints upon genuine singular reference. What makes *S*'s context in the pub conversation sufficient for him to denote Louis XIII, say, is that he is there, at that time and in the context of that conversation, in a position to express non-inferential *knowledge* about that man. His grasp of what is being said by those around him, and his understanding engagement in the discussion generally, give him various non-inferential reasons to believe certain things about the person in question.[5] Equally, I contend, what denies his later uses of any such significance, in the circumstances which Evans describes, is that this is no longer the case. He no longer has any reason to believe anything about anyone called Louis—at least, his

[5] I realize that I have said nothing about how exactly testimony might provide non-inferential reasons for belief about the objects of discussion in certain circumstances. I believe that it does; and I would expect the correct account of this possibility to emerge from an investigation into the way in which what might be called *testimonial demonstratives*—as, for example, when S says '*That man* was a villain' in the context of Evans's case of the pub conversation about Louis XIII—succeed in referring to persisting mind-independent objects, very much in accord with the way in which I have derived an account of the way in which perceptual experiences provide non-inferential reasons for empirical beliefs from reflection upon perceptual demonstrative reference to mind-independent things. See 2.3 above for a little more on this notion of a testimonial demonstrative; and see Evans, 1982, chs. 5 and 9; Fricker, 1987; Coady, 1992; and McDowell, 1994a, for important work on the epistemology of testimony.

involvement in the pub conversation no longer provides him
with any such reasons in connection with the particular Louis in
question.

I am reasonably confident that this line of argument can be
generalized. Here all that I can offer is a brief sketch of how this
might be done. Assume that there is some genuine illumination
to be had about the relation of singular reference holding
between certain referring expressions, as they are used in a given
linguistic community, and the things which they denote, through
reflection upon the practice of the radical interpreter in formulating a truth theory for the language in which such expressions
occur (see Davidson, 1984, esp. essays 3, 9, 10, 11, 14, 15, and 16;
Evans and McDowell, 1976, intro.; McDowell, 1977, 1978*b*). As
McDowell often insists (e.g. 1977, 1978*b*), thinking in this way
enables one to give a perfectly adequate account of the relations
between thinkers and things which are required if the former are
to refer to the latter in thought and talk, whilst resisting any supposed need reductively to formulate this account in terms of certain specific causal relations, or relations of any other kind,
conceivable quite independently of their role in the intelligible
engagement of a rational agent with the world around him. He
puts the point like this:

It is not true that we condemn a truth-theory to floating in a void, if we
reject the alleged obligation to fasten it directly to the causal realities
of language-use by way of its axioms [that is, to give a reductive causal
theory of reference]. On my account, those truth-theories that can serve
as theories of sense are already anchored to the facts of language-use
at the level of their theorems: the anchoring being effected by the
requirement that assignments of truth-conditions are to be usable in
specifications of content of intelligible speech-acts. Since the theorems
must be derivable within the theory, the requirement bears indirectly
on the theory's deductive apparatus, including assignments of denotation; and the deductive apparatus needs no attachment to the extra-
theoretical facts over and above what that affords. Thus we can acquire
such understanding as we need of the deductive apparatus (in particular, of the denoting relation) by reversing the order of the theory's
deductive direction, starting from our understanding of the requirement of serviceability in interpretation imposed on its consequences.
We grasp what it is for a name to denote something by grasping the role
played by the statement that it does in derivations of acceptable assignments of truth-conditions to sentences—assignments, that is, which

would pull their weight in making sense of speakers of the language that we are concerned with. (1977, pp. 183–4.)

So, the idea is that the relations between a person's use of a referring expression and the thing to which he refers in using it, in virtue of which the former does indeed denote the latter, are precisely those relations which prompt an ideal radical interpreter, in her attempts to make best overall sense of what he says and does, to regard him as talking about the latter in using the former. Furthermore, my contention is that this process of making sense of what people are thinking and talking about is constrained precisely by considerations of what they are in a position to express knowledge about, most importantly, what they are in a position to express non-inferential knowledge about, in the sense in which I have defined this notion. That is, I claim that the relevant process of radical interpretation is governed by the question of which things in the world around them the subjects to be interpreted have reasons (especially non-inferential reasons) to have beliefs about, given the relations in which they stand to such things in using the linguistic expressions which they use in the ways in which they do. In other words, there are, amongst the factors determining the interpreter's assignment of a particular thing as the reference of a given singular term in use in a certain linguistic community, significant *epistemic* constraints of precisely the kind which my reading of Russell's Principle of Acquaintance, (A), requires. The sort of engagement between the language users and the particular object in question which is required if this assignment is really to make best sense of what they say and do is precisely that involved in their being in a position to express knowledge, most importantly non-inferential knowledge, about just that object in their use of the term. This is the first premise of my recommended alternative reaction to Russell's argument: reference is possible only to objects about which a person is in a position to express non-inferential knowledge. Put another way, the claim is that a person succeeds in singling out a determinate particular in thought, in each of the wide variety of modes of reference by which this is possible, only in virtue of his standing in some relation with that thing which puts him in a position to express non-inferential knowledge about it. These epistemic constraints upon reference are what, in McDowell's terms, anchor the correct semantic theory for a given language to actual facts of its use.

In the context of a certain attractive conception of the relation between the sense and reference of a singular term, along the lines proposed by Evans (1982, pp. 20 ff.; 1985c, esp. pp. 301 ff.), this thesis provides a new way of articulating the idea that its sense constitutes a 'mode of *presentation*' of its reference. Evans's idea is that the sense of a given singular term is to be elucidated, and distinguished from the senses of any other singular terms with the same reference, by giving an explanation of what it is that makes it the case that a person using the term in question is thinking determinately about the particular object which serves as its reference rather than about any other thing, what it is about his thinking which makes *that thing* its object. My present contention is that whatever the correct account here is, it must suffice for the subject's expression of direct, non-inferential knowledge about that thing. Conjoining the two ideas leads to the suggestion that the sense of a singular term is such that grasping it constitutes a capacity for the expression of such knowledge about its reference, the possession of a non-inferential reason for some belief about that thing, or the retention in memory of knowledge based upon such an encounter with it in perception or through testimony. This, I think, gives substance to the metaphor of the sense of a singular term as a mode of presentation of its reference; and grasp of a genuine singular term essentially involves *acquaintance* with its object in just this sense.

Coming finally to the second premise of the line of thought which articulates my reaction to Russell's argument, I claim that, in common with the standard response which I outlined above, we must surely reject Russell's own conclusion, that the only objects to which genuine singular reference is possible are mind-dependent sense-data. Indeed, rejection of this conclusion is entailed by my own initial assumption, (W), that we have beliefs about a mind-independent spatial world (Ch. 2). For the reading of this which I explicitly adopt is that, in believing what we do, we make genuine reference to the mind-independent things around us. Thus, as I put the position at the outset:

(I') Reference is possible to mind-independent physical objects.

(A) Reference is possible only to objects about which a person is in a position to express non-inferential knowledge.

∴ (E′) A person is sometimes in a position to express non-inferential knowledge about mind-independent physical objects.

Of course, this argument presents a serious challenge: to give a satisfactory account of a person's direct, non-inferential knowledge about mind-independent things. Indeed, the difficulty of meeting this challenge very likely plays a significant role in motivating the standard reaction to Russell's argument. I hope, in what has gone before, though, at least to have given some encouraging indication of how this challenge can, and must, be met. Thus, I strongly recommend my alternative reaction.

8.3 *Externalism and A Priori Knowledge*

In this final section, I want to return to my brief comments in 4.2.6 above, on the classical foundationalist's attempt to appeal to some kind of transcendental argument in defence of his mind-to-world linking principle, (L), that a person knows, or is in a position to know, in being subject to certain perceptual experiences, that being appeared to in such and such a way is a reliable indicator that things are thus and so in the mind-independent world around her. The example which I considered there is this:

(T1) I am thinking that there are physical entities.

(T2) S can think thoughts involving the concept of physical entities only if S bears causal-perceptual relations to physical entities.

∴ (T3) I bear causal-perceptual relations to physical entities.

I objected that the classical foundationalist proposing this defence of (L) faces a dilemma. Either a person's perceptual experiences of physical entities—that is, on this view, the introspectively given appearances to which such things give rise—*themselves* provide her with reasons to believe that there are *physical entities* in her environment—that is, they put her in a position to acquire knowledge about such things—or they do not. If they do, then the transcendental argument is completely unnecessary. If they do not, then she is not capable of grasping genuine empirical beliefs at all, and therefore has no determinate understanding of the expression 'physical entities' as this occurs in her purported conclusion: she is in no position to claim that her experiences reliably indicate the presence of—real—*physical entities*, as opposed to anything else.

Developing this line of response in the light of my discussion of Russell's Principle of Acquaintance, I believe, provides a novel and satisfying response to a very closely related issue, which is nevertheless independent of the specific dialectical focus of the classical foundationalist theory of empirical knowledge.[6] This concerns the possibility of combining a so-called 'externalist' theory of empirical content, on which the contents of a person's beliefs are determined in part by the nature of his extrabodily environmental embedding, with a plausible account of self-knowledge, in particular, of a person's knowledge of the contents of his own beliefs. A difficulty for this combination is thought to be that it leads to the availability of a kind of non-empirical, a priori knowledge about the mind-independent physical world which is intuitively intolerable.[7] Abstracting a little further from the details of Burge's own example above, the inference which is held to create this difficulty can be put like this:

(E1) I believe that *p*.

(E2) If *x* believes that *p*, then *x*'s environmental embedding is thus and so.

∴ (E3) My environmental embedding is thus and so.

---

[6] The particular formulation of this issue which I address here is due to Martin Davies (1997). Indeed, my discussion draws upon the reply which I gave to an earlier version of his paper at a meeting of the European Society for Philosophy and Psychology in Barcelona during the summer of 1996. Paul Boghossian also presses the issue as a challenge to content externalism of the kind defined in the text below (1989, 1997). What follows is a summary of an extended discussion of these matters elsewhere (Brewer, forthcoming).

[7] Note that this content externalism is perfectly compatible with the epistemic internalism which I introduced in discussing classical foundationalism above (4.2, see esp. 4.2.3).

An example of this purportedly problematic inference might be the following:

(w1)   I believe that water is wet.

(w2)   If x believes that water is wet, then x's environment contains (or did contain) water.

∴ (w3)   My environment contains (or did contain) water.

Note that the truth of the consequent of (w2) requires that x's environment contains (or did contain) *water*, rather than any kind of 'twin water', which is like water in all superficial respects but happens to have a different chemical composition—that is, it requires that x's environment contains (or did contain) *this stuff* (H_2O) as opposed to *that stuff* (XYZ) (Putnam, 1975). This is precisely the force of the relevant form of content externalism. So the conclusion states that my environment contains *water*, as opposed to twin water. This is a contingent matter of empirical fact, though. Hence the prospect of my knowing it a priori, or without any kind of empirical investigation, certainly raises a prima facie problem.

The proponent of this line of objection to combining an adequate account of self-knowledge with content externalism argues as follows. First, any adequate account of a person's knowledge of the contents of his own beliefs entails that his knowledge of instances of (E1) is *non-empirical*: it does not necessarily involve any empirical investigation whatsoever. Second, content externalism entails that instances of (E2) can be derived from non-empirical philosophical reflection upon the necessary conditions upon determinate empirical belief possession. Third, therefore, the truth of content externalism—in the presence of an adequate account of self-knowledge—enables a person knowledgeably to derive instances of (E3), on the basis of the argument above, without any empirical investigation whatsoever. Fourth, such non-empirical knowledge of empirical facts is intuitively intolerable. Therefore, fifth, content externalism is incompatible with any adequate account of a person's knowledge of the contents of his own beliefs.

The reaction which is implicitly recommended by advocates of this argument, of course, is to reject content externalism. Yet I have explicitly endorsed a version of this very view, on which a person's possession of certain demonstrative beliefs about par-

ticular mind-independent things and their properties essentially
depends upon his standing in certain perceptual-attentional relations with those very things; and since I regard such perceptual
demonstrative beliefs as the indispensable core of his system of
empirical belief as a whole, and as the foundations, in a certain
sense (see 7.1), of all of his empirical knowledge, my commitment to content externalism runs very deep. So what alternative
do I propose to this recommended reaction?

There are obviously a number of possibilities. The one which
I myself favour is to reject the very first move of the objection set
out above: I deny that a person's knowledge of the contents of
his own beliefs is non-empirical in any way in which it really
would follow that he could thereby acquire intolerably non-
empirical knowledge of the contingent facts about his own
environmental embedding. Before outlining this claim, though,
I want briefly to mention the alternatives.[8] First, it might be possible to argue that the content externalist is not committed to the
a priori knowability of *specific instances* of (E2). Although he is
committed by definition to the conceptual necessity of the claim
that concepts of certain types are externally individuated, in a
way which entails the possibility of establishing that claim by
non-empirical reflection upon the necessary conditions upon
determinate empirical belief possession, he may nevertheless
deny that the question of which particular concepts instantiate
these types can be settled without empirical investigation.[9]
Second, it might also be possible to deny the third move above,
according to which the truth of content externalism—in the
presence of an adequate account of self-knowledge—enables a
person *knowledgeably* to derive instances of (E3) without any
empirical investigation.[10] There are two further possibilities,
which are in my view extremely unpromising from the start. The
first of these would be to insist, in extreme rationalist spirit, that
there is no difficulty whatsoever in the idea of wholly non-
empirical knowledge of empirical matters of fact. The second
would be to claim that a person's self-ascriptions of beliefs are

[8] See Brewer, forthcoming, for further clarification and critical discussion
of these alternatives to my own account.
[9] Christopher Peacocke urged me to take account of this possibility.
[10] This is Martin Davies's response (1997).

266 The Rational Role of Perceptual Experience

not, contrary to appearances, genuinely truth-evaluable statements, but rather non-truth-evaluable avowals of some kind
(Wittgenstein, 1958, pp. 190–2, 1980, §§ 470–504; Malcolm,
1991). Thus, they are incapable of constituting the premises of
an argument, as they are supposed to do in (E1) above, the first
premise of the argument which is in turn supposed to cause
trouble for content externalism.

The key to my own account of how content externalism is
satisfactorily to be combined with a plausible account of self-
knowledge lies in the idea that true content-externalist requirements are consequences of a generalized version of Russell's
Principle of Acquaintance in the sense in which I defended this
principle (8.2). What makes it the case—for those Ideas and concepts for which it is indeed the case—that a person's possession
of beliefs in whose contents certain Ideas and concepts occur
depends upon his being embedded in an environment actually
containing the objects and kinds which are their semantic values,
is that his reference to such items in belief depends upon his
being in a position to express non-inferential knowledge about
them. The relevant externalist conditions follow immediately
from this Russellian requirement. For a person cannot possibly
be in a position to express non-inferential knowledge about particular mind-independent objects or kinds unless his environment *actually contains* such things, or perhaps did so at some
earlier time at which he acquired the relevant Ideas or concepts
with such objects or kinds as their semantic values. What
remains to be shown, then, is exactly how this basis for content
externalism, in the Russellian thesis (A), undermines its purported incompatibility with any adequate account of self-
knowledge.

Suppose that a person's belief that p comprises an externalist
concept C. The putatively problematic inference would then be
this:

(e1) I believe that p.

(e2) If x believes that p, then x's environment contains (or
did contain) C.

∴ (e3) My environment contains (or did contain) C.

On my view, as I say, the externalist requirement upon possession of the concept C derives from the fact that its semantic value is necessarily a natural kind, say, about which any person who has the concept is in a position to express non-inferential knowledge, where what this amounts to is either that he currently has a non-inferential reason of some kind to believe something about that kind, or that he has retained knowledge based upon such a reason in memory. Now, if the inference set out above is to be an unwarrantedly non-empirical source of knowledge, then its premises must at least be true. The truth of (e1) depends upon the subject's grasp of the content p, though, which in turn depends upon his possession of the concept C. From (A), or its generalization, it follows that he is therefore in a position to express non-inferential knowledge about C. Hence he is already in a position to arrive at the knowledge that there is (or was) C in his environment if only he turns his mind to the matter. Therefore this argument cannot possibly constitute a problematic non-empirical *source* of new empirical knowledge: if its premises are simply true, then the subject already has the wherewithal to arrive at knowledge of its conclusion.[11]

Put slightly differently, the proponent of this line of objection to externalism wrongly neglects the empirical-epistemic constraints upon concept possession which essentially enter into a person's knowledge of (e1), through their application simply to its truth. This already presupposes his standing in an *epistemic* relation—Russell's *acquaintance*, as it were—with samples of C. It is the first move in the objector's reasoning above, then, that any adequate account of a person's knowledge of the contents of his own beliefs entails that this is *wholly non-empirical*, which is to be rejected. For this self-knowledge requires his grasp of the contents of the beliefs in question, his possession of whose component concepts in turn depends upon his empirical-epistemic relations with their semantic values. Thus, content externalism of this kind is perfectly compatible with an adequate account of a person's knowledge of the contents of his own beliefs.

All the materials for this response are really implicit in my discussion of the thesis (R), that perceptual experiences provide

---

[11] Similar considerations in my view undercut this threat as it might be thought to be posed by other arguments exploiting related externalist conditions. See Brewer, forthcoming, for the details.

reasons for empirical beliefs, in Part I above. The key idea is that determinate concept possession is an *epistemic* skill. It is a matter of a person's being in relations with the relevant worldly semantic values which enable his acquisition and retention in memory of non-inferential knowledge about such things. This is the source of the externalist requirements upon concept possession. That is to say, the world-involving perceptual and testimonial relations between a person and certain things in the world around him which are essential to his possession of Ideas and concepts with those things as their determinate semantic values are precisely the reason-giving content-determining relations which that earlier discussion aims to establish. Keeping such reason-giving relations firmly in focus, is, I contend, essential to getting a clear view of the philosophical logic and epistemology of empirical thought.

Bibliography

ALSTON, W. P. 1988. 'An Internalist Externalism.' *Synthese*, 74, 265–83.
—— 1993. *The Reliability of Sense Perception*. Ithaca, N.Y.: Cornell University Press.
AYERS, M. 1970. 'Perception and Action.' In G. N. A. Vesey (ed.), *Knowledge and Necessity: Royal Institue of Philosophy Lectures*, 3, 91–106.
—— 1991. *Locke*, vol. i. London: Routledge.
BELL, D. 1990. *Husserl*. London: Routledge.
BENNETT, J. 1971. *Locke, Berkeley, Hume*. Oxford: Oxford University Press.
BERMÚDEZ, J., MARCEL, A., and EILAN, N. (eds.). 1995. *The Body and the Self*. Cambridge, Mass.: MIT Press.
BOGHOSSIAN, P. 1989. 'Content and Self-Knowledge.' *Philosophical Topics*, 17, 5–26.
—— 1997. 'What the Externalist Can Know A Priori.' *Proceedings of the Aristotelian Society*, 97, 161–75.
BONJOUR, L. 1985. *The Structure of Empirical Knowledge*. Cambridge, Mass.: Harvard University Press.
BOWER, T. G. R. 1966. 'The Visual World of Infants.' *Scientific American*, 215, 80–92.
BREWER, B. 1992. 'Self-Location and Agency.' *Mind*, 101, 17–34.
—— 1993. 'The Integration of Spatial Vision and Action.' In N. Eilan, R. McCarthy, and B. Brewer (eds.), *Spatial Representation*. Oxford: Blackwell.
—— 1995a. 'Bodily Awareness and the Self.' In J. L. Bermúdez, A. Marcel, and N. Eilan (eds.), *The Body and the Self*. Cambridge, Mass: MIT Press.
—— 1995b. 'Mental Causation: Compulsion by Reason.' *Proceedings of the Aristotelian Society, Supplementary Volume*, 69, 237–53.
—— 1996. 'Internalism and Perceptual knowledge.' *European Journal of Philosophy*, 4, 259–75.
—— Forthcoming. 'Externalism and A Priori Knowledge of Empirical Facts.' In a collection of essays on the A Priori ed. P. Boghossian and C. Peacocke.
BURGE, T. 1991. 'Vision and Intentional Content.' In E. LePore and R. Van Gulick (eds.), *John Searle and His Critics*. Oxford: Blackwell.
—— 1993. 'The Sources and Resources of Reason.' John Locke Lectures at the University of Oxford.

BURGE, T. 1996. 'Our Entitlement to Self-Knowledge.' *Proceedings of the Aristotelian Society*, 96, 91-116.

CAMPBELL, J. 1984–5. 'Possession of Concepts.' *Proceedings of the Aristotelian Society*, 85, 149–70.

—— 1993a. 'A Simple View of Colour.' In J. Haldane and C. Wright (eds.), *Reality, Representation, and Projection*. Oxford: Oxford University Press.

—— 1993b. 'The Role of Physical Objects in Spatial Thinking.' In N. Eilan, R. McCarthy, and B. Brewer (eds.), *Spatial Representation*. Oxford: Blackwell.

—— 1994. *Past, Space and Self*. Cambridge, Mass.: MIT Press.

—— 1997. 'Sense, Reference and Selective Attention.' *Proceedings of the Aristotelian Society, Supplementary Volume*, 71, 55–74.

—— 1998. 'Joint Attention and the First Person.' In Anthony O'Hear (ed.), *Current Issues in Philosophy of Mind: Royal Institute of Philosophy Annual Supplement*, 43 (Cambridge: Cambridge University Press, 1998), 123–36.

—— 1999. 'Sense and Consciousness.' In Peter Sullivan and Johannes Brandl (eds.), *Festschrift for Michael Dummett, Grazer Philosophische Studien* (1999), 195–211.

—— Forthcoming. 'Wittgenstein on Attention.'

CASSAM, Q. 1989. 'Kant and Reductionism.' *Review of Metaphysics*, 43, 72–106.

—— 1992. 'Reductionism and First Person Thinking.' In D. Charles and K. Lennon (eds.), *Reduction, Explanation, and Realism*. Oxford: Oxford University Press.

—— 1993. 'Inner Sense, Body Sense, and Kant's "Refutation of Idealism".' *European Journal of Philosophy*, 1, 111–27.

—— 1997. *Self and World*. Oxford: Oxford University Press.

CHILD, W. 1993. 'Anomalism, Uncodifiability and Psychophysical Relations.' *Philosophical Review*, 102, 215–45.

—— 1994. *Causality, Interpretation and the Mind*. Oxford: Oxford University Press.

CHISHOLM, R. M. 1989. *Theory of Knowledge*. 3rd edn. Englewood Cliffs, N.J.: Prentice Hall.

COADY, C. A. J. 1992. *Testimony*. Oxford: Oxford University Press.

COHEN, S. 1988. 'How to Be a Fallibilist.' *Philosophical Perspectives*, 2, 91–123.

CRAIG, E. 1987. *The Mind of God and the Works of Man*. Oxford: Oxford University Press.

—— 1989. 'Nozick and the Sceptic: The Thumbnail Version.' *Analysis*, 49, 161–2.

CUSSINS, A. 1990. 'The Connectionist Construction of Concepts.' In

M. A. Boden (ed.), *The Philosophy of Artificial Intelligence*. Oxford: Oxford University Press.

DANCY, J. (ed.). 1988. *Perceptual Knowledge*. Oxford: Oxford University Press.

—— and SOSA, E. (eds.). 1993. *A Companion to Epistemology*. Oxford: Blackwell.

DAVIDSON, D. 1984. *Inquiries into Truth and Interpretation*. Oxford: Oxford University Press.

DAVIES, M. 1981. *Meaning, Quantification, Necessity*. London: Routledge.

—— 1997. 'Externalism, Architecturalism and Epistemic Warrant.' In C. MacDonald, B. Smith, and C. Wright (eds.), *Knowing Our Own Minds: Essays on Self-Knowledge*. Oxford: Oxford University Press.

DESCARTES, R. 1986. *Meditations on First Philosophy*, trans. J. Cottingham. Cambridge: Cambridge University Press.

DONNELLAN, K. 1966. 'Reference and Definite Descriptions.' *Philosophical Review*, 75, 281–304.

DRETSKE, F. 1969. *Seeing and Knowing*. London: Routledge.

—— 1970. 'Epistemic Operators.' *Journal of Philosophy*, 69, 1007–23.

—— 1981. 'The Pragmatic Dimension of Knowledge.' *Philosophical Studies*, 40, 363–78.

DRIVER, J. 1994. 'Spatial Synergies between Auditory and Visual Attention', with C. J. Spence. In C. Umilta and M. Moscovich (eds.), *Attention and Performance*, vol. xv. Amsterdam: North-Holland.

—— 1996. 'Multimodal Spatial Constraints on Tactile Selective Attention', with P. Grossenbacher. In T. Inui and J. L. McClelland (eds.), *Attention and Performance*, vol. xvi. Amsterdam: North-Holland.

DUMMETT, M. 1978. 'The Justification of Deduction.' In his *Truth and Other Enigmas*. London: Duckworth.

—— 1981. *The Interpretation of Frege's Philosophy*. London: Duckworth.

—— 1991*a*. *Frege: Philosophy of Mathematics*. London: Duckworth.

—— 1991*b*. *The Logical Basis of Metaphysics*. London: Duckworth.

EILAN, N. 1988. 'Self-Consciousness and Experience.' Oxford University D.Phil. thesis.

—— 1993. 'Molyneux's Question and the Idea of an External World.' In N. Eilan, R. McCarthy, and B. Brewer (eds.), *Spatial Representation*. Oxford: Blackwell.

—— 1995. 'Consciousness and the Self.' In J. L. Bermúdez, A. Marcel, and N. Eilan (eds.), *The Body and the Self*. Cambridge, Mass.: MIT Press.

EILAN, N. 1997*a*. 'Objectivity and the Perspective of Consciousness.' *European Journal of Philosophy*, 5, 235–50.

—— 1997*b*. 'Perceptual Intentionality, Attention and Consciousness.' In A. O'Hear (ed.), *Contemporary Issues in the Philosophy of Mind*. Cambridge: Cambridge University Press.

—— Forthcoming. *The Conscious Point of View*. Oxford: Oxford University Press.

EVANS, G. 1980. 'Things Without the Mind.' In Z. Van Straaten (ed.), *Philosophical Subjects*. Oxford: Oxford University Press.

—— 1982. *The Varieties of Reference*. Oxford: Oxford University Press.

—— 1985*a*. 'The Causal Theory of Names.' In his *Collected Papers*. Oxford: Oxford University Press.

—— 1985*b*. 'Molyneux's Question.' In his *Collected Papers*. Oxford: Oxford University Press.

—— 1985*c*. 'Understanding Demonstratives.' In his *Collected Papers*. Oxford: Oxford University Press.

—— and McDOWELL, J. (eds.). 1976. *Truth and Meaning*. Oxford: Oxford University Press.

FODOR, J. 1987. *Psychosemantics*. Cambridge, Mass.: MIT Press.

FOSTER, J. 1982. *The Case for Idealism*. London: Routledge.

FREGE, G. 1993. 'On Sense and Reference.' In A. Moore (ed.), *Meaning and Reference*. Oxford: Oxford University Press.

FRICKER, E. 1987. 'The Epistemology of Testimony.' *Proceedings of the Aristotelian Society, Supplementary Volume*, 61, 57–83.

GALLISTEL, C. R. 1990. *The Organization of Learning*. Cambridge, Mass: MIT Press.

GEACH, P. 1992. *Mental Acts*. Bristol: Thoemmes Press.

GETTIER, E. L. 1963. 'Is Justified True Belief Knowledge?' *Analysis*, 23, 121–3.

GIBSON, J. 1960. *Locke's Theory of Knowledge and Its Historical Relations*. Cambridge: Cambridge University Press.

GIBSON, J. J. 1979. *The Ecological Approach to Visual Perception*. Boston, Mass.: Houghton Mifflin.

GOLDMAN, A. I. 1976. 'Discrimination and Perceptual Knowledge.' *Journal of Philosophy*, 73, 771–91.

GORDON, R. 1995. 'Simulation without Introspection or Inference from Me to You.' In M. Davies and T. Stone (eds.), *Mental Simulation*. Oxford: Blackwell.

HEAL, J. Forthcoming. 'First Person Authority.'

HINTON, J. M. 1973. *Experiences*. Oxford: Oxford University Press.

HOLLIS, M. 1987. *The Cunning of Reason*. Cambridge: Cambridge University Press.

HUME, D. 1975. *Enquiries Concerning Human Understanding and*

Concerning the Principles of Morals, ed. L. A. Selby-Bigge, revised by P. H. Nidditch. Oxford: Oxford University Press.

—— 1978. *A Treatise of Human Nature*, ed. L. A. Selby-Bigge, revised by P. H. Nidditch. Oxford: Oxford University Press.

JACKSON, F. C. 1998. *From Metaphysics to Ethics: A Defence of Conceptual Analysis*. Oxford: Oxford University Press.

KANT, I. 1929. *Critique of Pure Reason*, trans. N. Kemp Smith. London: Macmillan.

KAPLAN, D. 1989. 'Demonstratives.' In J. Almog, J. Perry, and H. Wettstein (eds.), *Themes from Kaplan*. New York: Oxford University Press.

KRIPKE, S. 1980. *Naming and Necessity*. Oxford: Blackwell.

—— 1982. *Wittgenstein on Rules and Private Language*. Oxford: Blackwell.

LOCKE, J. 1975. *An Essay Concerning Human Understanding*, ed. P. H. Nidditch. Oxford: Oxford University Press.

McDOWELL, J. 1977. 'On the Sense and Reference of a Proper Name.' *Mind*, 86, 159–85.

—— 1978a. 'Are Moral Requirements Hypothetical Imperatives?' *Proceedings of the Aristotelian Society, Supplementary Volume*, 52, 13–29.

—— 1978b. 'Physicalism and Primitive Denotation: Field on Tarski.' *Erkenntnis*, 13, 131–52.

—— 1979. 'Virtue and Reason.' *The Monist*, 62, 331–50.

—— 1982. 'Criteria, Defeasibility and Knowledge.' *Proceedings of the British Academy*, 68, 455–79.

—— 1984. '*De Re* Senses.' In C. Wright (ed.), *Frege: Tradition and Influence*. Oxford: Blackwell.

—— 1985. 'Functionalism and Anomalous Monism.' In E. LePore and B. McLaughlin (eds.), *Actions and Events*. Oxford: Blackwell.

—— 1986. 'Singular Thought and the Extent of Inner Space.' In P. Pettit and J. McDowell (eds.), *Subject Thought, and Context*. Oxford: Oxford University Press.

—— 1990. 'Peacocke and Evans on Demonstrative Content.' *Mind*, 99, 255–66.

—— 1991. 'Intentionality *De Re*.' In. E. LePore and R. Van Gulick (eds.), *John Searle and His Critics*. Oxford: Blackwell.

—— 1994a. 'Knowledge by Hearsay.' In B. K. Matilal and A. Chakrabarti (eds.), *Knowing from Words*. Amsterdam: Kluwer.

—— 1994b. *Mind and World*. Cambridge, Mass.: Harvard University Press.

—— 1995. 'Might there be External Reasons?' In J. E. J. Altham and R. Harrison (eds.), *World, Mind and Ethics*. Cambridge: Cambridge University Press.

McGinn, C. 1983. *The Subjective View: Secondary Qualities and Indexical Thoughts*. Oxford: Oxford University Press.

Malcolm, N. 1991. '"I Believe That *P*".' In E. LePore and R. Van Gulick (eds.), *John Searle and His Critics*. Oxford: Blackwell.

Martin, M. G. F. 1992. 'Perception, Concepts and Memory.' *Philosophical Review*, 101, 745–63.

——— 1997. 'Sense, Reference and Selective Attention: The Shallows of the Mind.' *Proceedings of the Aristotelian Society, Supplementary Volume*, 71, 75–98.

Merleau-Ponty, M. 1962. *Phenomenology of Perception*, trans. C. Smith. London: Routledge.

Nozick, R. 1981. *Philosophical Explanations*. Oxford: Oxford University Press.

O'Shaughnessy, B. 1980. *The Will*, vol. i. Cambridge. Cambridge University Press.

Peacocke, C. 1983. *Sense and Content*. Oxford: Oxford University Press.

——— 1986a. 'Analogue Content.' *Proceedings of the Aristotelian Society, Supplementary Volume*, 60, 1–17.

——— 1986b. *Thoughts*. Oxford: Blackwell.

——— 1988. 'The Limits of Intelligibility: A Post-Verificationist Proposal.' *Philosophical Review*, 97, 463–96.

——— 1989a. 'Perceptual Content.' In J. Almog, J. Perry, and H. Wettstein (eds.), *Themes from Kaplan*. New York: Oxford University Press.

——— 1989b. *Transcendental Arguments in the Theory of Content*. Oxford: Oxford University Press.

——— 1991. 'Demonstrative Content: A Reply to John McDowell.' *Mind*, 100, 123–33.

——— 1992. *A Study of Concepts*. Cambridge, Mass: MIT Press.

——— 1996. 'Entitlement, Self-Knowledge and Conceptual Redeployment.' *Proceedings of the Aristotelian Society*, 96, 117–58.

——— 1998a. 'Conscious Attitudes, Attention and Self-Knowledge.' In C. Macdonald, B. Smith, and C. Wright (eds.), *Knowing Our Own Minds: Essays on Self-Knowledge*. Oxford: Oxford University Press.

——— 1998b. 'Implicit Conceptions, Understanding and Rationality.' In E. Villanueva (ed.), *Philosophical Issues*, vol. viii: *Concepts*. Atascadero, Calif.: Ridgeview.

Pettit, P., and McDowell, J. (eds.). 1986. *Subject, Thought, and Context*. Oxford: Oxford University Press.

Putnam, H. 1975. 'The Meaning of "Meaning".' In his *Mind, Language and Reality*. Cambridge: Cambridge University Press.

REID, T. 1983. *Inquiry and Essays*, ed. R. E. Beanblossom and K. Lehrer. Indianapolis, Ind.: Hackett.

ROESSLER, J. 1996. 'Self-Knowledge and Belief.' Oxford University D. Phil. thesis.

RUSSELL, B. 1905. 'On Denoting.' *Mind*, 14, 479-93.

—— 1917. 'Knowledge by Acquaintance and Knowledge by Description.' In his *Mysticism and Logic*. London: Allen & Unwin.

—— 1993. *Introduction to Mathematical Philosophy*. London: Routledge.

SEARLE, J. 1983. *Intentionality: An Essay in the Philosophy of Mind*. Cambridge: Cambridge University Press.

SELLARS, W. 1963. 'Empiricism and the Philosophy of Mind.' In his *Science, Perception and Reality*. Atascadero, Calif.: Ridgeview.

SLATER, A. 1989. 'Visual Memory and Perception in Early Infancy.' In A. Slater and G. Bremner (eds.), *Infant Development*. Hove: Lawrence Erlbaum Associates.

—— and MORRISON, V. 1985. 'Shape Constancy and Slant Perception at Birth.' *Perception*, 14, 337–44.

SMITH, M. 1993. 'Colour, Transparency, Mind-Independence.' In J. Haldane and C. Wright (eds.), *Reality, Representation, and Projection*. Oxford: Oxford University Press.

SNOWDON, P. 1980–1. 'Experience, Vision and Causation.' *Proceedings of the Aristotelian Society*, 81, 175–92.

—— 1990. 'The Objects of Perceptual Experience.' *Proceedings of the Aristotelian Society, Supplementary Volume*, 64, 121–50.

—— 1992. 'How to Interpret "Direct Perception".' In T. Crane (ed.), *The Contents of Experience*. Cambridge: Cambridge University Press.

SOSA, E. 1988. 'Knowledge in Context, Scepticism in Doubt.' In J. Tomberlin (ed.), *Philosophical Perspectives*, vol. ii: Epistemology. Atascadero, Calif.: Ridgeview.

—— 1991. *Knowledge in Perspective*. Cambridge: Cambridge University Press.

—— 1994. 'Philosophical Scepticism and Epistemic Circularity.' *Proceedings of the Aristotelian Society, Supplementary Volume*, 68, 263–90.

—— 1997a. 'How to Resolve the Pyrrhonian Problematic: A Lesson from Descartes.' *Philosophical Studies*, 85, 229–49.

—— 1997b. 'Reflective Knowledge in the Best Circles.' *Journal of Philosophy*, 94, 410–30.

STOUT, R. 1996. *Things That Happen Because They Should: A Teleological Approach to Action*. Oxford: Oxford University Press.

STRAWSON, P. F. 1959. *Individuals*. London: Methuen.

—— 1966. *The Bounds of Sense*. London: Methuen.

STRAWSON 1974a. 'Imagination and Perception.' In his *Freedom and Resentment and Other Essays*. London: Methuen.

—— 1974b. 'Self, Mind and Body.' In his *Freedom and Resentment and Other Essays*. London: Methuen.

STROUD, B. 1977. *Hume*. London: Routledge.

VAN CLEVE, J. 1979. 'Foundationalism, Epistemic Principles and the Cartesian Circle.' *Philosophical Review*, 88, 55–91.

WEISKRANTZ, L. 1986. *Blind Sight: A Case Study and Implications*. Oxford: Oxford University Press.

WIGGINS, D. 1963. 'The Individuation of Things and Places (I).' *Proceedings of the Aristotelian Society, Supplementary Volume*, 37, 177–202.

WILLIAMS, B. 1978. *Descartes: The Project of Pure Enquiry*. London: Penguin.

—— 1980. 'Internal and External Reasons.' In R. Harrison (ed.), *Rational Action*. Cambridge: Cambridge University Press.

—— 1995. 'Replies.' In J. E. J. Altham and R. Harrison (eds.), *World, Mind and Ethics*. Cambridge: Cambridge University Press.

WILLIAMSON, T. 1994. *Vagueness*. London: Routledge.

WITTGENSTEIN, L. 1958. *Philosophical Investigations*, trans. G. E. M. Anscombe. Oxford: Blackwell.

—— 1975. *On Certainty*, ed. G. E. M. Anscombe and G. H. von Wright, trans. D. Paul and G. E. M. Anscombe. Oxford: Blackwell.

—— 1980. *Remarks on the Philosophy of Psychology*, vol. i, ed. G. E. M. Anscombe and G. H. von Wright, trans. G. E. M. Anscombe.

WOODFIELD, A. 1982. *Thought and Object*. Oxford: Oxford University Press.

WOODS, M. 1963. 'The Individuation of Things and Places (II).' *Proceedings of the Aristotelian Society, Supplementary Volume*, 37, 203–16.

WRIGHT, C. 1989. 'Wittgenstein's Later Philosophy of Mind: Sensation, Privacy and Intention.' *Journal of Philosophy*, 86, 622–34.

WRIGHT, J. P. 1983. *The Sceptical Realism of David Hume*. Manchester: Manchester University Press.

Index